Section 2: Materials

1. Density — 122
2. Hooke's Law — 123
3. Stress and Strain — 127
4. The Young Modulus — 130
5. Interpreting Stress-Strain Curves — 132
6. Brittle Materials — 134
Exam-style Questions — **136**

Section 3: Waves

1. The Nature of Waves — 138
2. Transverse and Longitudinal Waves — 143
3. Refractive Index — 148
4. Critical Angle and TIR — 151
5. Superposition and Interference — 154
6. Stationary Waves — 157
7. Diffraction — 160
8. Interference — 162
9. Diffraction Gratings — 167
Exam-style Questions — **172**

Investigative and Practical Skills

HOW SCIENCE WORKS

1. Variables and Data — 174
2. Graphs and Charts — 176
3. Error Analysis — 179
4. Conclusions and Safety — 183

Exam Help

EXAM HELP

1. Exam Structure and Technique — 184

Reference

Answers — 188
Glossary — 205
Acknowledgements — 210
Index — 211
Data Tables — 214

How to use this book

Learning Objectives

- These tell you exactly what you need to learn, or be able to do, for the exam.
- There's a specification reference at the bottom that links to the AQA specification.

Tips

These are here to help you understand the theory.

Exam Tips

There are tips throughout the book to help with all sorts of things to do with answering exam questions.

Learning Objectives:
- Know that electric current is the rate of flow of charge.
- Understand and be able to use the equation: $I = \frac{\Delta Q}{\Delta t}$
- Know that potential difference is the work done per unit charge.
- Understand and be able to use the equation: $V = \frac{W}{Q}$

Specification Reference 3.1.3

Tip: Remember that conventional current flows from + to –, the opposite way from electron flow.

Exam Tip
When you're doing calculation questions in the exam, don't forget to check your units are correct. Sometimes you'll get an extra mark for using the right units.

2. Current and Potential Difference

After all that stuff in GCSE Physics about electricity, you wouldn't think there was much left to learn. Well, unfortunately you'd be wrong — there's a whole load more that you've got to learn about electricity for AS and it starts here...

What is current?

The current in a wire is like water flowing in a pipe. The amount of water that flows depends on the flow rate and the time. It's the same with electricity — current is the rate of flow of charge. In an electrical circuit, the charge is carried through the wires by electrons.

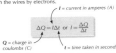

I = current in amperes (A)

$$\Delta Q = I\Delta t \text{ or } I = \frac{\Delta Q}{\Delta t}$$

Q = charge in coulombs (C) t = time taken in seconds (s)

The **coulomb** is the unit of charge. One coulomb (C) is defined as the amount of charge that passes in 1 second when the current is 1 ampere. You can work out the amount of charge passing through a circuit using the equation above.

┌─ **Example** ─
A component has a current of 0.430 A passing through it. Calculate the charge passing through the component in 3 minutes.

First convert the time taken from minutes to seconds:

3 minutes × 60 seconds per minute = 180 seconds.

Then substitute the values for current and time taken into the charge formula given above:

$\Delta Q = I \times \Delta t$
$= 0.430 \times 180$
$= 77.4$ C

You can measure the current flowing through a part of a circuit using an **ammeter**. You always need to attach an ammeter in series (so that the current through the ammeter is the same as the current through the component — see page 66).

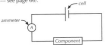

Figure 2: An ammeter connected in series with a power pack and a light bulb.

Figure 1: An ammeter connected in series with a component.

Tip: There's more on work done on page 111.

What is potential difference?

To make electric charge flow through a circuit, you need to transfer energy to the charge — this energy is supplied by the power source, e.g. a battery. When a charge flows through the power source it is 'raised' through a potential and energy is transferred to the charge as electrical potential energy.

┌─ **Example** ─
Calculate the energy of a photon with a wavelength of 3.9×10^{-9} m.
Substitute $\lambda = 3.9 \times 10^{-9}$ m, $h = 6.63 \times 10^{-34}$ Js and $c = 3.00 \times 10^{8}$ ms^{-1} into the equation $E = \frac{hc}{\lambda}$ to find the energy, E, of the photon.

$$E = \frac{hc}{\lambda} = \frac{(6.63 \times 10^{-34}) \times (3.00 \times 10^{8})}{3.9 \times 10^{-9}} = 5.1 \times 10^{-17} \text{ J}$$

Examples

These are here to help you understand the theory.

Antiparticles

In 1928, a physicist called Paul Dirac predicted the existence of a particle like the electron but with an opposite electric charge. The **positron** turned up later in a cosmic ray experiment — just as Dirac predicted. Positrons have identical mass and rest energy to electrons, but they carry a positive charge.

Each particle type has a corresponding **antiparticle** with the same mass and rest energy but with opposite charge (if charged). For instance, an antiproton is a negatively-charged particle with the same mass as the proton. The antineutrino released in β⁻ decay (p.10) is the antiparticle of the **neutrino**. All particles are known as **matter** and antiparticles are known as **antimatter**.

Figure 3 shows the relative charges of the proton, neutron, electron, electron neutrino (or just neutrino) and their antiparticles.

Figure 2: This is how positrons were discovered shortly after Dirac predicted them. The tracks in this picture are made by positrons and electrons moving through a liquid. Their tracks bend in opposite directions because of their opposite charges (you don't need to know why until A2).

Particle	Symbol	Relative charge	Antiparticle	Symbol	Relative charge
proton	p	+1	antiproton	p̄	–1
neutron	n	0	antineutron	n̄	0
electron	e⁻	–1	positron	e⁺	+1
electron neutrino	νₑ	0	electron antineutrino	ν̄ₑ	0

Figure 3: Relative charges of particles and their corresponding antiparticles.

Particle/ Antiparticle	Rest Energy (MeV)	Mass (kg)
Proton/ Antiproton	938.257	1.67 × 10⁻²⁷
Neutron/ Antineutron	939.551	1.67 × 10⁻²⁷
Electron/ Positron	0.510999	9.11 × 10⁻³¹

Figure 4: Masses and rest energies of particles and their antiparticles.

You need to know the masses in kg and rest energies in MeV of each of these particles and their antiparticles. Luckily, in the exam you'll be given them for the particles in your data and formulae booklet. You just need to remember that they are the same for a particle and its antiparticle. Neutrinos and antineutrinos are incredibly tiny — you can assume they have zero mass and zero rest energy.

Tip: You'll see later that there are different types of neutrinos and antineutrinos. The electron antineutrino is the one given out in β⁻ decay.

How Science Works

- For AS Physics you need to know about How Science Works. There's a section on it at the front of the book.
- How Science Works is also covered throughout the book wherever you see this symbol.

Exam Help

There's a section at the back of the book stuffed full of things to help with your exams.

AS-Level
Physics
for AQA A

The Complete Course for AQA A

Contents

Introduction

How to use this book   i

How Science Works

The Scientific Process   1

Unit 1

Section 1: Particles and Radiation

1. Atomic Structure   5
2. Stable and Unstable Nuclei   9
3. Antiparticles and Photons   12
4. Classification of Particles   16
5. Quarks and Antiquarks   20
6. Particle Interactions   25
Exam-style Questions   **31**

Section 2: Electromagnetic Radiation and Quantum Phenomena

1. The Photoelectric Effect   33
2. Energy Levels in Atoms   37
3. Wave-Particle Duality   41
Exam-style Questions   **45**

Section 3: Current Electricity

1. Circuit Diagrams   47
2. Current and Potential Difference   48
3. Resistance   50
4. *I-V* Characteristics   52
5. Resistivity & Superconductors   56
6. Power and Electrical Energy   58
7. E.m.f. and Internal Resistance   61
8. Conservation of Energy and Charge in Circuits   65
9. The Potential Divider   70
10. Alternating Current   73
Exam-style Questions   **78**

Unit 2

Section 1: Mechanics

1. Scalars and Vectors   80
2. Forces in Equilibrium   84
3. Moments   87
4. Centre of Mass and Stability   90
5. Uniform Acceleration   92
6. Displacement-Time Graphs   94
7. Velocity-Time Graphs   98
8. Newton's Laws of Motion   102
9. Free Fall and Projectile Motion   104
10. Drag and Terminal Speed   108
11. Work and Power   111
12. Conservation of Energy   114
Exam-style Questions   **119**

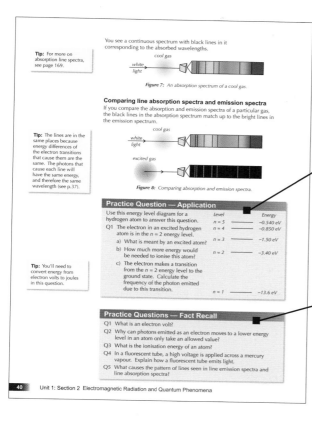
Practice Questions — Application

- Annoyingly, the examiners expect you to be able to apply your knowledge to new situations — these questions are here to give you plenty of practice at doing this.
- All the answers are in the back of the book (including any calculation workings).

Practice Questions — Fact Recall

- There are a lot of facts to learn for AS Physics — these questions are here to test that you know them.
- All the answers are in the back of the book.

Glossary

There's a glossary at the back of the book full of all the definitions you need to know for the exam, plus loads of other useful words.

Exam-style Questions

- Practising exam-style questions is really important — you'll find some at the end of each section.
- They're the same style as the ones you'll get in the real exams — some will test your knowledge and understanding and some will test that you can apply your knowledge.
- All the answers are in the back of the book, along with a mark scheme to show you how you get the marks.

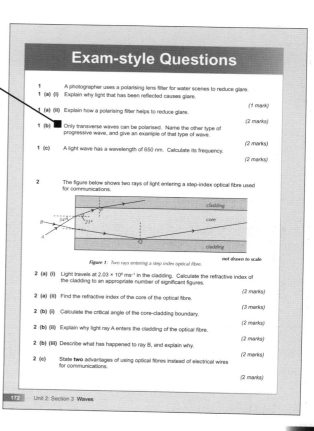
Investigative and Practical Skills

- For AS Physics you'll have to complete Unit 3 — Investigative and Practical Skills.
- There's a section at the back of the book with loads of stuff to help you plan, analyse and evaluate experiments.

Published by CGP

Editors:
Jane Ellingham, Helena Hayes, Matteo Orsini Jones, Helen Ronan, Charlotte Whiteley, Sarah Williams.

Contributors:
Tony Alldridge, Jane Cartwright, Peter Cecil, Mark Edwards, Barbara Mascetti, John Myers,
Zoe Nye, Andy Williams.

ISBN: 978 1 84762 904 3

With thanks to Mark Edwards, Ian Francis, Glenn Rogers and Karen Wells for the proofreading.
With thanks to Anna Lupton for the copyright research.

Groovy website: www.cgpbooks.co.uk

Printed by Elanders Ltd, Newcastle upon Tyne.
Jolly bits of clipart from CorelDRAW®

The Scientific Process

Science tries to explain how and why things happen. It's all about seeking and gaining knowledge about the world around us. Scientists do this by asking questions and suggesting answers and then testing them, to see if they're correct — this is the scientific process.

Developing and testing theories

A **theory** is a possible explanation for something. Theories usually come about when scientists observe something and wonder why or how it happens. (Scientists also sometimes form a **model** too — a simplified picture or representation of a real physical situation.) Scientific theories and models are developed and tested in the following way:

Tip: A theory is only scientific if it can be tested.

- Ask a question — make an observation and ask why or how whatever you've observed happens.

- Suggest an answer, or part of an answer, by forming a theory or a model (a possible explanation of the observations or a description of what you think is happening).

- Make a prediction or **hypothesis** — a specific testable statement, based on the theory, about what will happen in a test situation.

- Carry out tests — to provide evidence that will support the prediction or refute it.

Examples

Question: What is the nature of light?

Theory: Light is a wave.

Hypothesis: If light is a wave, then it should diffract through narrow gaps and interfere.

Test: Shine a laser light through a narrow slit and observe what happens to the light by placing a screen behind the slit. If the light has spread out (it's no longer a narrow beam), and if there are light and dark fringes of light on the screen (a diffraction pattern caused by the interference of light), the evidence supports the hypothesis.

Question: Why does pushing against a sharp object hurt even though you're the one doing the pushing?

Theory: If an object A exerts a force on object B, then object B exerts an opposite force on object A.

Hypothesis: Applying a force to an object will cause it to apply the same force back in the opposite direction. Increasing the applied force will increase the force applied back, and vice versa.

Test: Take two newton meters and hook them together, then attach the top end of one of them to the floor (or wall, etc.). Pull against the other meter and record the force shown on each, then repeat by pulling with differing strength. If the force shown on one meter always matches the force shown on the other meter, the evidence supports the hypothesis.

Figure 1: *The diffraction pattern created by green light from a laser shone through a single slit.*

Tip: The results of one test can't prove that a theory is true — they can only suggest that it's true. They can however disprove a theory — show that it's wrong.

PHILOSOPHICAL
TRANSACTIONS:
GIVING SOME
ACCOMP1
OF THE PRESENT
Undertakings, Studies, and Labours
OF THE
INGENIOUS
IN MANY
CONSIDERABLE PARTS
OF THE
WORLD.

Vol I.
For *Anno* 1665, and 1666.

In the *SAVOY*,
Printed by *T. N.* for *John Martyn* at the Bell, a little with-
out *Temple-Bar*, and *James Allestry* in *Duck-Lane*,
Printers to the Royal Society.

Figure 2: *The first scientific journal, 'Philosophical Transactions of the Royal Society', published in the 17th century.*

Tip: Scientific research is often funded by companies who have a vested interest in its outcomes. Scientists are ethically obliged to make sure that this does not bias their results.

Tip: Once an experimental method is found to give good evidence it becomes a protocol — an accepted method to test that particular thing that all scientists can use.

Communicating results

The results of testing a scientific theory are published — scientists need to let others know about their work. Scientists publish their results in scientific journals. These are just like normal magazines, only they contain scientific reports (called papers) instead of the latest celebrity gossip.

Scientists use standard terminology when writing their reports. This way they know that other scientists will understand them. For instance, there are internationally agreed units for measuring certain **variables**, so that scientists across the world will know exactly what the results of an experiment show.

Scientific reports are similar to the lab write-ups you do in school. And just as a lab write-up is reviewed (marked) by your teacher, reports in scientific journals undergo **peer review** before they're published. The report is sent out to peers — other scientists who are experts in the same area. They go through it bit by bit, examining the methods and data, and checking it's all clear and logical, and the conclusion is reasonable. Thorough evaluation allows decisions to be made about what makes a good methodology or experimental technique. Individual scientists may have their own ethical codes (based on their humanistic, moral and religious beliefs), but having their work scrutinised by other scientists helps to reduce the effect of personal bias on the conclusions drawn from the results.

When the report is approved, it's published. This makes sure that work published in scientific journals is of a good standard. But peer review can't guarantee the science is correct — other scientists still need to reproduce it. Sometimes mistakes are made and bad work is published. Peer review isn't perfect but it's probably the best way for scientists to self-regulate their work and to publish quality reports.

Validating theories

Other scientists read the published theories and results, and try to test the theory themselves. This involves repeating the exact same experiments, as well as using the theory to make new predictions, and then testing them with new experiments. This is known as **validation**. If all the experiments in the world provide evidence to back it up, the theory is thought of as scientific 'fact' (for now). If new evidence comes to light that conflicts with the current evidence the theory is questioned all over again. More rounds of testing will be carried out to try to find out where the theory falls down. This is how the scientific process works — evidence supports a theory, loads of other scientists read it and test it for themselves, eventually all the scientists in the world agree with it and then bingo, you get to learn it.

> **Example**
>
> **The structure of the atom**
>
> It took years and years for the current model of the atom to be developed and accepted — this is often the case with the scientific process.
>
> Dalton's theory in the early 1800s, that atoms were solid spheres, was disputed by the results of Thomson's experiments at the end of that century. As a result, Thomson developed the 'plum pudding' model of the atom, which was proven wrong by Rutherford's alpha scattering experiments in 1909. Rutherford's 'nuclear model' has since been developed and modified further to create the currently accepted model of the atom we use today — but scientists are still searching for more accurate models.

How do theories evolve?

Our currently accepted theories have survived this 'trial by evidence'. They've been tested over and over again and each time the results have backed them up. But they never become totally indisputable fact. Scientific breakthroughs or advances could provide new ways to question and test the theory, which could lead to changes and challenges to it. Then the testing starts all over again. This is the tentative nature of scientific knowledge — it's always changing and evolving.

Tip: Sometimes data from one experiment can be the starting point for developing a new theory.

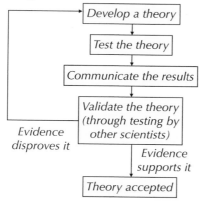

Figure 3: *Flow diagram summarising the scientific process.*

Develop a theory → Test the theory → Communicate the results → Validate the theory (through testing by other scientists). Evidence disproves it → Develop a theory. Evidence supports it → Theory accepted.

Example

Gravity and the speed of falling objects

For over a thousand years, the generally accepted theory was that heavier objects accelerated to the ground quicker than lighter objects — and why not? There was no evidence to say otherwise, and it seems like a fairly logical thing to think.

Then Galileo came on the scene and set up systematic and rigorous experiments to test this theory. He showed that, actually, all objects accelerate towards Earth at the same rate, regardless of their mass (page 104). Physicists around the world were able to reproduce his results and verify his conclusions, and Galileo's theory is still accepted today, over 400 years on.

Figure 4: *Italian physicist and astronomer Galileo Galilei.*

Collecting evidence

1. Evidence from lab experiments

Results from controlled experiments in laboratories are great. A lab is the easiest place to control variables so that they're all kept constant (except for the one you're investigating). This means you can draw meaningful conclusions. You always need to make your experiments as controlled as possible so you can be confident that any effects you see are linked to the variable you're changing. If you find a relationship, you need to be careful what you conclude. You need to decide whether the effect you're seeing is caused by changing a variable, or whether the two are just correlated.

Tip: There's more on controlling variables (p.174) and drawing conclusions from lab experiments (p.183) in the Practical and Investigative Skills section.

Example

Resistance of a piece of material

If you're investigating the resistance of a piece of material by altering a voltage across it and measuring the current flowing through it, you need to keep everything else constant. For example, you should make sure the dimensions of the piece of material are the same throughout.

2. Investigations outside the lab

There are things you can't study in a lab. And outside the lab controlling the variables is tricky, if not impossible.

> **Example**
>
> **Do the microwaves emitted by mobile phones increase the risk of developing certain types of cancer?**
>
> There are always differences between groups of people. The best you can do is to have a well-designed study using matched groups — choose two groups of people (those who use mobile phones and those who don't) which are as similar as possible (same mix of ages, same mix of diets etc.). But you still can't rule out every possibility. Taking newborn identical twins and treating them identically, except for making one use mobile phones regularly and not allowing the other near a mobile phone, might be a fairer test, but it would present huge ethical problems. It's also unlikely to be very practical, considering you'd need many sets of twins for any hope of a statistically significant result.

Figure 5: Some people think using mobile phones increases our risk of developing certain cancers.

Science and decision-making

Lots of scientific work eventually leads to important discoveries that could benefit humankind and improve everyone's quality of life. But there are often risks attached (and almost always financial costs). Society (that's you, me and everyone else) must weigh up the information in order to make decisions — about the way we live, what we eat, what we drive, and so on. Information can also be used by politicians to devise policies and laws. However, there is not always enough information available for society and politicians to be certain about the decisions made. The scientific evidence we do have can also be overshadowed by other influences such as personal bias and beliefs, public opinion, and the media. Decisions are also affected by social, ethical and economic factors.

Tip: Don't get mixed up — it's not the scientists who make the decisions, it's society. Scientists just produce evidence to help society make the decisions.

> **Examples**
>
> **Diagnosing illnesses**
>
> Sources of ionising radiation are used in hospitals to diagnose certain illnesses. Studies have provided fairly conclusive evidence that ionising radiation increases the risks of developing cancer. However, ionising radiation is often the best way to diagnose a patient. Without it, an illness could be diagnosed and treated wrongly, or take longer to diagnose correctly. So the benefits usually outweigh the risks.
>
> **Wind farms**
>
> Many scientists suggest that building wind farms would be a cheap and environmentally friendly way to generate electricity in the future. But some people think that because wind turbines can harm wildlife such as birds and bats, other methods of generating electricity should be used.
>
> **Investigating the atom**
>
> Large-scale experiments in particle physics, such as those at the Large Hadron Collider, cost billions of pounds. However, with the cooperation of scientists from countries all over the world, they could answer questions in science that we've been trying to solve for years.

Figure 6: Part of the 27 km loop of the Large Hadron Collider in its tunnel at CERN, Switzerland.

1. Atomic Structure

All elements are made of atoms, and atoms are made up of smaller particles — electrons, protons and neutrons. It's these particles that give different elements their characteristics.

Inside the atom

An **atom** is made up of three types of particle — **protons**, **neutrons** and **electrons**. At the centre of every atom there's a **nucleus** containing a combination of protons and neutrons. Protons and neutrons are both known as **nucleons**. Orbiting this core are the electrons..

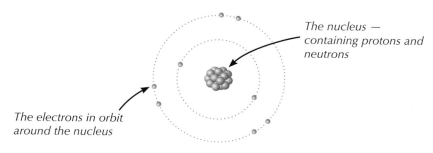

The nucleus —
containing protons and
neutrons

The electrons in orbit
around the nucleus

Figure 1: *An oxygen atom,
with eight protons and eight electrons.*

The particles in an atom have different charges and masses, shown in Figure 2. Charge is measured in coulombs (C) and mass is measured in kilograms (kg).

Particle	Charge (C)	Mass (kg)
Proton	$+1.60 \times 10^{-19}$	1.67×10^{-27}
Neutron	0	1.67×10^{-27}
Electron	-1.60×10^{-19}	9.11×10^{-31}

Figure 2: *Masses and charges of atomic particles.*

The charge and mass of atomic particles are so very tiny that it is often much easier and more useful to deal with them in relative units than in C and kg.

Particle	Relative Charge	Relative Mass
Proton	Positive, +1	1
Neutron	Neutral, 0	1
Electron	Negative, −1	0.0005

Figure 3: *Relative masses and charges of atomic particles.*

Learning Objectives:

- Understand that an atom is made up of protons, neutrons and electrons.
- Know the mass and charge of protons, neutrons and electrons.
- Know that the proton number, Z, is the number of protons.
- Know that the nucleon number, A, is the total number of protons and neutrons.
- Be able to use nuclide notation.
- Know how to calculate the specific charge of nuclei and ions.
- Know that isotopes have the same proton number but different nucleon numbers.

Specification Reference 3.1.1

Exam Tip
You'll be given the masses (in kg) of all three particles and the charge (in C) of an electron on a formula sheet in the exam. So all you need to remember is that a proton has the opposite charge to an electron, and a neutron has no charge.

You won't be given their relative masses or charges though — so learn the numbers in Figure 3.

Atomic size

Each atom is about a tenth of a nanometre (1×10^{-10} m) in diameter. To give you that in context, you'd need to line up around 4 million iron atoms side by side to give you a line 1 millimetre long.

And if you think that's small, try the nucleus. Although the proton and neutron are 2000 times more massive than the electron, the nucleus only takes up a tiny proportion of the atom. The electrons orbit at relatively vast distances. The nucleus is only one 10 000th the size of the whole atom — most of the atom is empty space.

As Figure 4 shows, if we were to shrink the Solar System (including Pluto) so that the Sun was the size of a gold nucleus, Pluto would only be half as far away as gold's furthest electron.

Tip: Positive protons in an atomic nucleus attract the negative electrons and keep them in orbit around the nucleus. This force is called the electromagnetic force (or sometimes the electrostatic force) — see page 9.

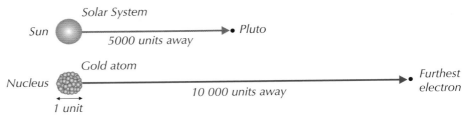

Figure 4: A comparison between the scale of the Solar System and a gold atom.

Proton number

The **proton number** is the number of protons in the nucleus. It is sometimes called the **atomic number**, and has the symbol Z. It's the proton number that defines the element — no two different elements will have the same number of protons.

In a neutral atom, the number of electrons equals the number of protons. The element's reactions and chemical behaviour depend on the number of electrons. So the proton number tells you a lot about its chemical properties.

Tip: A neutral atom must have the same number of protons and electrons so that the positive and negative charges cancel each other out.

Nucleon number

The **nucleon number** is also called the **mass number**, and has the symbol A. It tells you how many protons and neutrons are in the nucleus. Since each proton or neutron has an atomic mass of (approximately) 1 and the electrons have very little mass, the number of nucleons is the same as the atom's mass.

The **nuclide notation** of an element summarises all the information about its atomic structure. Figure 5 shows the nuclide notation for an element X, with nucleon number A and proton number Z:

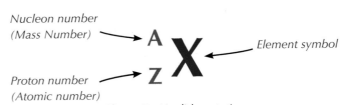

Figure 5: Nuclide notation.

Example

A carbon-12 atom has 6 protons and 6 neutrons.

The nucleon number —
there are a total of 12
protons and neutrons in a
carbon-12 atom.

$\rightarrow 12$

$\rightarrow 6$ C

The symbol for the
element carbon

The proton number —
there are six protons in a
carbon atom.

Figure 6: *Nuclide notation of carbon-12.*

Specific charge

The **specific charge** of a particle is the ratio of its charge to its mass, given
in coulombs per kilogram (C kg^{-1}). To calculate specific charge, you just
divide the charge in C by the mass in kg.

$$specific\ charge = \frac{charge}{mass}$$

You could be asked to find the specific charge of any particle, from a
fundamental particle like an electron, to the nucleus of an atom or an ion.

Example

Calculate the specific charge of a proton.

A proton has a charge of $+1.60 \times 10^{-19}$ C and a mass of 1.67×10^{-27} kg.

Divide the charge by the mass to find the specific charge:
$$(+1.60 \times 10^{-19}) \div (1.67 \times 10^{-27}) = 9.58 \times 10^7\ C\ kg^{-1}$$

Example

Calculate the specific charge of a nucleus of a carbon-12 atom.

- Carbon-12 has 12 nucleons and 6 protons
  (see example at the top of the page).
- The mass of a nucleon is 1.67×10^{-27} kg, so the mass of a carbon-12
  nucleus is:
  $$12 \times (1.67 \times 10^{-27}) = 2.004 \times 10^{-26}\ kg$$
- The charge of a proton is $+1.60 \times 10^{-19}$ C, so the charge of the
  carbon-12 nucleus is:
  $$6 \times (+1.60 \times 10^{-19}) = 9.6 \times 10^{-19}\ C$$
- So the specific charge $= (9.6 \times 10^{-19}) \div (2.004 \times 10^{-27})$
  $$= 4.79 \times 10^8\ C\ kg^{-1}$$

Tip: In physics,
'specific' usually means
'per unit mass'.

Tip: A fundamental
particle is a particle that
cannot be split up into
anything smaller.
An electron is one.

Exam Tip
You'll be given the mass
of a proton on a formula
sheet in the exam. The
charge of an <u>electron</u>
is given on the formula
sheet, and the charge
of a proton is equal and
opposite to the charge of
an electron.

Tip: When calculating
specific charge, make
sure you've got the
charge and mass in the
right units.

Isotopes

Atoms with the same number of protons but different numbers of neutrons are called **isotopes**. Changing the number of neutrons doesn't affect the atom's chemical properties. The number of neutrons affects the stability of the nucleus though. In general, the greater the number of neutrons compared with the number of protons, the more unstable the nucleus. Unstable nuclei may be radioactive and decay to make themselves more stable (see page 10).

Figure 7: *Isotopes have many important uses. For example, tritium is used to illuminate fire exit signs and watch faces without the need for electricity.*

Example

Hydrogen has three isotopes — protium, deuterium and tritium.

Protium has 1 proton and 0 neutrons.

Deuterium has 1 proton and 1 neutron.

Tritium has 1 proton and 2 neutrons.

Figure 8: *The three isotopes of hydrogen.*

Practice Questions — Application

Q1 An atom of oxygen has 8 protons and 8 neutrons.
   a) What is the proton number of this atom?
   b) What is the nucleon number of this atom?
   c) Write this information in nuclide notation.

Q2 Element X has 21 protons and 24 neutrons.
   a) Write this in nuclide notation.
   b) Suggest the nuclide notation for a different isotope of element X.

Q3 Helium is written in nuclide notation as: ^4_2He
   a) How many protons does an atom of helium have?

   An isotope of helium has a nucleon number of 3.
   b) How many protons does this isotope have?
   c) Calculate the specific charge of a nucleus of this isotope.

Exam Tip
This question asks for the specific charge of the nucleus, not the whole atom. Remember, the charge of a proton is the same as an electron but positive.

Practice Questions — Fact Recall

Q1 Describe the structure of the atom.
Q2 Give the relative charges of each of the particles in the atom.
Q3 Give the relative masses of each of the particles in the atom.
Q4 What is the proton number of an atom?
Q5 What is the nucleon number of an atom?
Q6 How can you work out the relative mass of an atom?
Q7 What is specific charge and what units is it measured in?
Q8 What are isotopes?

2. Stable and Unstable Nuclei

Learning Objectives:

- Understand the role of the strong nuclear force in keeping the nucleus stable.
- Know how the strong nuclear force varies with nucleon separation.
- Know the equations for alpha and beta-minus decay.

Specification Reference 3.1.1

Nuclei are positively charged, so keeping them stable requires a very strong force — otherwise they will decay by emitting particles.

Forces in the nucleus

There are several different forces acting on the nucleons in a nucleus. The **electromagnetic force** causes the positively charged protons in the nucleus to repel each other. The **gravitational force** causes all the nucleons in the nucleus to attract each other due to their mass.

However the repulsion from the electromagnetic force is much, much bigger than the gravitational attraction. If these were the only forces acting in the nucleus, the nucleons would fly apart. So there must be another attractive force that holds the nucleus together — called the **strong nuclear force**.

The strong nuclear force

To hold the nucleus together, the strong nuclear force must be an attractive force that's stronger than the electromagnetic force.

Experiments have shown that the strong nuclear force has a very short range. It can only hold nucleons together when they're separated by up to a few femtometres (1 fm = 1×10^{-15} m) — the size of a nucleus. The strength of the strong nuclear force quickly falls beyond this distance. At very small separations, the strong nuclear force must be repulsive — otherwise there would be nothing to stop it crushing the nucleus to a point.

Experiments also show that the strong nuclear force works equally between all nucleons. This means that the size of the force is the same whether it's proton-proton, neutron-neutron or proton-neutron.

Figure 2 shows how the strong nuclear force changes with the distance between nucleons. It also shows how the electromagnetic force changes so that you can see the relationship between these two forces (although only protons feel the electromagnetic force).

Tip: The gravitational attraction in the nucleus is so small compared to the other forces, you can just ignore it.

Tip: Interactions that use the strong nuclear force are sometimes called strong interactions — see p.26.

Figure 1: *The Large Hadron Collider at CERN collides lead ions to try to find out more about the strong nuclear force.*

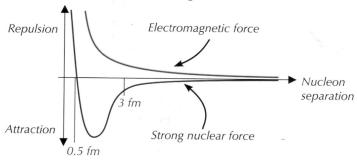

Figure 2: *A graph to show how the strong nuclear and electromagnetic forces vary with nucleon separation.*

Notice that:

- The strong nuclear force is repulsive for very small separations of nucleons (less than about 0.5 fm).

- As nucleon separation increases past about 0.5 fm, the strong nuclear force becomes attractive. It reaches a maximum attractive value and then falls rapidly towards zero after about 3 fm.

- The electromagnetic repulsive force extends over a much larger range (infinitely, actually).

Exam Tip
The strong nuclear force does very different things at different nucleon separations. Make sure you know how it changes.

Nuclear decay

Unstable nuclei will emit particles to become more stable —
this is known as **nuclear decay**.

Tip: The range of the
strong nuclear force is
only a few femtometres.
It struggles to hold
together very large
nuclei, which makes
them unstable.

Tip: An alpha particle is
the nucleus of a helium
atom, ^4_2He.

Alpha decay

Alpha (α) **decay** only happens in very big atoms (with more than 82
protons), like uranium and radium. The nuclei of these atoms are just too
big for the strong nuclear force to keep them stable. To make themselves
more stable, they emit an **alpha particle**, $^4_2\alpha$, from their nucleus. When
an alpha particle is emitted the proton number decreases by two and the
nucleon number decreases by four — see Figure 4.

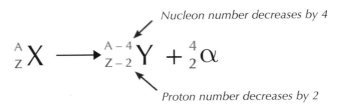

Nucleon number decreases by 4

$$^A_Z\text{X} \longrightarrow \, ^{A-4}_{Z-2}\text{Y} + \, ^4_2\alpha$$

Proton number decreases by 2

Figure 4: *An equation showing the alpha decay of an element X.*

Figure 3: *These yellow
tracks show the paths of
alpha particles emitted
from a piece of radioactive
radium.*

> **Example**
>
> Uranium decays to thorium by alpha emission.
> $$^{238}_{92}\text{U} \longrightarrow \, ^{234}_{90}\text{Th} + \, ^4_2\alpha$$

Beta-minus decay

Beta-minus (β^-) decay (usually just called beta decay) is the emission of an
electron from the nucleus along with an **antineutrino** particle. Beta decay
happens in isotopes that are "neutron rich" (i.e. have too many neutrons
compared to protons in their nucleus). When a nucleus ejects a beta
particle, one of the neutrons in the nucleus is changed into a proton.
The proton number increases by one, and the nucleon number stays the
same — see Figure 5. The antineutrino particle released carries away
some energy and momentum.

Tip: A β^- particle is
just another name for an
electron.

Tip: There's more
about neutrinos and
antineutrinos on p.18.

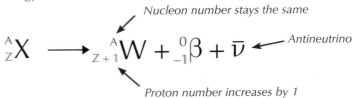

Nucleon number stays the same

$$^A_Z\text{X} \longrightarrow \, ^A_{Z+1}\text{W} + \, ^0_{-1}\beta + \bar{\nu}$$

Antineutrino

Proton number increases by 1

Figure 5: *An equation showing the beta-minus decay of an element X.*

Tip: Make sure
you don't forget the
antineutrino in
beta-minus decay
equations. It can be
easily missed because
it doesn't change the
nucleon or proton
numbers.

> **Example**
>
> Rhenium decays to osmium by beta emission.
> $$^{187}_{75}\text{Re} \longrightarrow \, ^{187}_{76}\text{Os} + \, ^0_{-1}\beta + \bar{\nu}$$

Practice Questions — Application

Q1 $^{228}_{88}$Ra decays to form $^{228}_{89}$Ac. What type of decay is this?

Q2 What type of decay would you expect in an unstable nucleus with 14 nucleons, 6 of which are protons — alpha decay or beta-minus decay? Explain your answer.

Q3 Explain how the strong nuclear force acts between nucleons that are:
    a) 0.4 fm apart.
    b) 1.5 fm apart.
    c) 4.2 fm apart.

Q4 Element X has 89 protons and 137 neutrons and decays into element Y. Write down the nuclide notation for element Y if X emits:
    a) an α particle.
    b) a β^- particle.

Q5 Complete the equation below to show what happens when plutonium decays into uranium by alpha decay.

$$^{238}_{94}\text{Pu} \rightarrow \,^{...}_{...}\text{U} + \,^{...}_{...}\alpha$$

Q6 Complete the equation below to show what happens when carbon-14 decays into nitrogen by beta-minus decay.

$$^{14}_{6}\text{C} \rightarrow \,^{...}_{...}\text{N} + \,^{...}_{...}\beta + ...$$

Practice Questions — Fact Recall

Q1 What are the two largest forces acting on the particles in a nucleus?

Q2 What is the range of repulsion of the strong nuclear force?

Q3 What is the range of attraction of the strong nuclear force?

Q4 Explain how we know there must be a strong nuclear force.

Q5 Sketch a graph to show how the strong nuclear force changes with nucleon separation, marking on any key separation distances.

Q6 What is a β^- particle also known as?

Q7 Why does a nucleus undergo nuclear decay?

Q8 How do the nucleon and proton numbers of an atom change in alpha decay?

Q9 a) What particles are emitted during beta-minus decay?
    b) What type of nuclei will decay by beta-minus decay?
    c) Describe the changes in the nucleus of an atom when it undergoes beta-minus decay.

3. Antiparticles and Photons

There's more than just particles to think about now — for every particle you learn about, there's a corresponding antiparticle. But don't worry, particles and antiparticles have got pretty similar properties.

Electromagnetic radiation

Visible light is just one type of electromagnetic (EM) radiation.
The **electromagnetic spectrum** is a continuous spectrum of all the possible frequencies of electromagnetic radiation.

- The frequency of a wave is the number of complete waves passing a point per second (see page 140).
- The wavelength of a wave is the distance between two adjacent crests of a wave.

Electromagnetic radiation is split up into seven different types based on the frequency of the radiation and its properties (see Figure 1).

RADIO WAVES	MICRO WAVES	INFRA RED	VISIBLE LIGHT	ULTRA VIOLET	X-RAYS	GAMMA RAYS

←———————————————— *Increasing wavelength*

Increasing frequency ————————————————→

Figure 1: *The electromagnetic spectrum.*

The higher the frequency of electromagnetic radiation, the greater its energy.

Photons

When Max Planck was investigating black body radiation, he suggested that EM waves can only be released in discrete packets, or quanta.

Einstein went further by suggesting that EM waves (and the energy they carry) can only exist in discrete packets. He called these wave-packets **photons**. The energy, E, carried by one of these photons had to be:

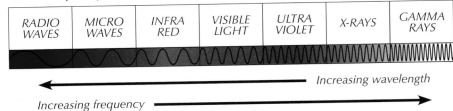

E = energy of one photon in J ———→ $E = hf$ ←——— f = frequency of light in Hz

h = Planck's constant = 6.63×10^{-34} Js

The frequency, wavelength, and speed of light are related by the equation:

f = frequency in Hz ———→ $f = \frac{c}{\lambda}$ ←——— c = speed of light in a vacuum = 3.00×10^8 ms^{-1}

λ = wavelength in m

You can substitute this equation into $E = hf$ to give another equation for the energy of one photon:

$$E = hf = \frac{hc}{\lambda}$$

Pair production

One of Einstein's most famous theories says that energy can turn into mass and mass can turn into energy. When energy is converted into mass you get equal amounts of matter and antimatter. This is called **pair production**. Pair production only happens if there is enough energy to produce the masses of the particles. It must always produce a particle and its corresponding antiparticle because certain quantities must be conserved (see p.23).

For example, fire two protons at each other at high speed and you'll end up with a lot of energy at the point of impact. This energy might be converted into more particles. If an extra proton is formed then there will always be an antiproton to go with it.

Figure 5: A proton-proton collision in the LHC at CERN. The collision has happened at the centre and the tracks show the different particles produced from this high energy collision.

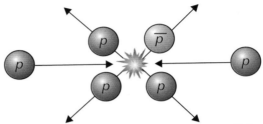

Figure 6: Pair production — two protons colliding and producing a proton-antiproton pair.

It's not just protons that can be produced in pair production. If a photon has enough energy, it can produce an electron-positron pair. It tends to happen when a photon passes near a nucleus. The particles produced in a detector curve away from each other in opposite directions because of the opposite charges on the electron and positron.

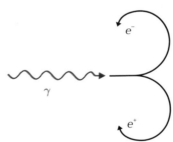

Figure 7: Pair production — an electron-positron pair produced from a gamma ray photon.

The minimum energy needed for pair production is the total rest energy of the particles that are produced. Pair production always produces a particle-antiparticle pair, which both have a rest energy, E_0. So the minimum energy needed is at least $2E_0$ for there to be enough energy to produce the particles (for energy to be conserved).

E_{min} = minimum energy needed $\longrightarrow$ $E_{min} = 2E_0$ $\longleftarrow$ E_0 = rest energy of particle type produced in MeV

Tip: Protons repel each other so it takes a lot of energy to make them collide. The energy supplied is released when they collide, so proton-proton collisions release a lot of energy.

Tip: Remember — photons are packets of EM radiation.

Tip: The particles follow a curved path because of an applied magnetic field — you see why this happens in A2 physics.

Tip: Only gamma ray photons (γ) have enough energy to produce an electron-positron pair — see page 34 for more on the photon model of electromagnetic radiation.

Tip: Energy is always conserved — it can't be created or destroyed, only turned into other forms.

--- Example ---
The minimum energy needed to produce an electron-positron pair is:

$$E_{min} = 2E_0 = 2 \times (0.510999) = 1.021998 \text{ MeV}$$

rest energy of e^+ and e^- in MeV

Annihilation

When a particle meets its antiparticle the result is **annihilation**. All the mass of the particle and antiparticle gets converted back to energy in the form of two gamma ray photons. Antiparticles can only exist for a fraction of a second before this happens, so you don't get them in ordinary matter.

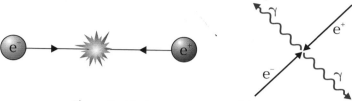

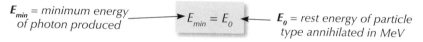

Figure 8: *Electron-positron annihilation.*

You can calculate the minimum energy of a photon produced by annihilation. The interaction is between a particle-antiparticle pair, which both have a rest energy, E_0. The two photons need to have a total energy of at least $2E_0$ for energy to be conserved in this interaction. So $2E_{min} = 2E_0$ and:

E_{min} = minimum energy of photon produced $\longrightarrow$

$$E_{min} = E_0$$

$\longleftarrow E_0$ = rest energy of particle type annihilated in MeV

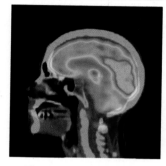

Figure 9: *PET (Positron Emission Tomography) scanners in hospitals work by putting a positron emitting isotope into the bloodstream, and detecting the gamma rays produced by the electron-positron annihilation that occurs.*

Practice Questions — Application

Q1 A photon has a frequency of 6.0×10^{13} Hz. Calculate its energy in J.

Q2 A photon has a wavelength of 2.4×10^{-9} km. Calculate its energy in J.

Q3 A proton collision can produce enough energy to create a proton-antiproton pair. What is the minimum energy in MeV required for this pair production to take place?

Q4 If a positron and an electron meet, they will annihilate each other. Calculate the minimum energy in MeV of a single photon produced by this interaction.

Practice Questions — Fact Recall

Q1 What is a photon?

Q2 What equation would you use to calculate the energy of a photon from its wavelength?

Q3 a) How does an antiparticle differ from its corresponding particle?

   b) How is it the same?

Q4 Name the electron's antiparticle.

Q5 Write down the relative charge of an:

   a) antiproton   b) antineutron   c) antineutrino

Q6 Describe the process of pair production.

Q7 What is produced in the annihilation of matter and antimatter?

- Know that there are two types of hadrons — baryons and mesons.

- Know that protons and neutrons are baryons and that antiprotons and antineutrons are antibaryons.

- Know that the proton is the only stable baryon and that other baryons (e.g. neutrons) decay into it.

- Know the baryon numbers of all hadrons.

- Know that pions and kaons are mesons.

- Know that electrons, muons and neutrinos are leptons.

- Know that hadrons feel the strong nuclear force and leptons feel the weak interaction.

- Know the lepton numbers of all leptons

- Know that baryon and lepton number must be conserved.

Specification Reference 3.1.1

Tip: You might wonder why there aren't equal numbers of baryons and antibaryons, since they are produced and annihilated in pairs (p.14-15). Well, that's a very good question. Scientists are pretty sure that there is more matter than antimatter in the universe, but no one is really sure why.

Exam Tip
You need to know the baryon numbers of all particles in the exam, so make sure you know these rules.

4. Classification of Particles

You've already seen four different particles and their antiparticles — but there are loads more. Some decay very quickly so they're difficult to get a handle on. Nonetheless, you need to learn about them and their properties. Luckily, they can be classified into useful groups, which makes them easier to remember.

Hadrons

The nucleus of an atom is made up of protons and neutrons. Since the protons are positively charged they need a strong force to hold them together — the strong nuclear force or the strong interaction (see page 9). Not all particles can feel the strong nuclear force. The ones that can are called **hadrons**.

Hadrons aren't fundamental particles (page 20). They're made up of smaller particles called quarks (see pages 20-23). There are two types of hadrons — **baryons** and **mesons**. They're classified according to the number of quarks that make them up, but don't worry about that until page 21.

Baryons

It's helpful to think of protons and neutrons as two versions of the same particle — the nucleon. They just have different electric charges. Protons and neutrons are both baryons. There are other baryons that you don't get in normal matter like sigmas (Σ) — but they're short-lived and you don't need to know their properties for AS.

All baryons except the proton are unstable. This means that all baryons apart from protons decay to become other particles. The particles a baryon ends up as depends on what it started as, but it always includes a proton. All baryons except protons decay to a proton.

Antibaryons

The antiparticles of protons and neutrons (antiprotons and antineutrons) are antibaryons. But, if you remember from the previous page, antiparticles are annihilated when they meet the corresponding particle — which means that you don't find antibaryons in ordinary matter.

Baryon number

The **baryon number** is just the number of baryons.
(A bit like nucleon number but including unusual baryons like Σ too.)

- The proton and the neutron (and all other baryons) each have a baryon number $B = +1$.

- Antibaryons have a baryon number $B = -1$.

- Other particles (i.e. things that aren't baryons) are given a baryon number $B = 0$.

When particles interact and produce or emit new particles (e.g. alpha decay), the total baryon number before and after is the same. You can use this fact to predict whether a particle interaction can happen — if the overall baryon number changes in the interaction, it can't.

The total baryon number in any particle interaction never changes.

Neutron decay

You saw on page 10 that beta-minus decay involves a neutron changing into a proton. This happens when there are many more neutrons than protons in a nucleus. Beta decay is caused by the **weak interaction** (see page 22).

When a neutron decays, it forms a proton, an electron and an antineutrino:

$$n \rightarrow p + e^- + \overline{\nu}_e$$

Electrons and antineutrinos aren't baryons (they're leptons, as you'll see on the next page), so they have a baryon number $B = 0$. Neutrons and protons are baryons, so have a baryon number $B = +1$. This means that the total baryon number before and after the interaction are equal (to +1), so the interaction can happen.

Tip: The weak force is one of the four fundamental forces along with the strong nuclear force, the electromagnetic force and the gravitational force (see p.26). The weak interaction just means that particles exert the weak force on each other.

Tip: The baryon number is only one of the properties that has to be conserved in particle interactions (see pages 23-24).

Tip: This is just the same as β^- decay — a neutron decaying into a proton, electron and electron antineutrino.

Example

The baryon number is +1 before and after the interaction.

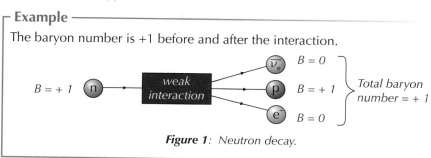

Figure 1: Neutron decay.

Mesons

The second type of hadron you need to know about is the **meson**. Mesons interact with baryons via the strong force. All mesons are unstable and have baryon number $B = 0$ (because they're not baryons).

Pions

Pions (π-mesons) are the lightest mesons. There are three versions, each with different electric charges — π^+, π^0 and π^-. Pions were discovered in high energy charged particles coming from outer space called cosmic rays. You get loads of them in high-energy particle collisions like those studied at the CERN particle accelerator.

Pion interactions swap protons with neutrons and neutrons with protons, but leave the overall baryon number unchanged.

Figure 2: A pion interaction turning a proton into a neutron.

The π^- meson is just the antiparticle of the π^+ meson, and the antiparticle of a π^0 meson is itself.

Kaons

Kaons (K-mesons) are heavier and more unstable than pions. You get different ones like K^+ and K^0.

Figure 3: Particle tracks of a pion-proton collision recorded by CERN.

Hadron properties summary

Tip: Don't panic if you don't understand all this yet. For now, just learn these properties. You'll need to work through to the end of page 24 to see how it all fits together.

There's a lot to know about all the hadrons, but the main properties that you need to know are summarised in Figure 4.

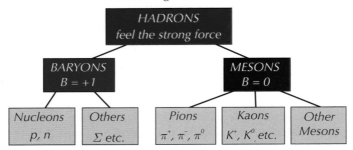

Figure 4: Classification of hadrons.

Leptons

Leptons are fundamental particles and they don't feel the strong nuclear force. They only really interact with other particles via the weak interaction (along with a bit of gravitational force and the electromagnetic force as well if they're charged).

Electrons (e^-) are stable leptons. But there are other leptons too. Muons (μ^-) are just like heavy electrons but they are unstable, and decay eventually into ordinary electrons or positrons.

The electron and muon leptons each come with their own neutrino, ν_e and ν_μ. Neutrinos have zero (or almost zero) mass, and zero electric charge — so they don't do much. Neutrinos only take part in weak interactions (see p.22). In fact, a neutrino can pass right through the Earth without anything happening to it.

Tip: Remember... antineutrinos are realeased in β⁻ decay (page 10).

As always, each of these four lepton particles has an antiparticle with opposite charge — the positron e^+, the antimuon μ^+, and the two different antineutrinos, $\overline{\nu_e}$ and $\overline{\nu_\mu}$.

Lepton numbers

Like the baryon number, the **lepton number** is just the number of leptons. Each lepton is given a lepton number of +1, but the electron and muon types of lepton have to be counted separately.

Tip: You'll be given these lepton numbers in the data and formulae book in the exam.

You get two different lepton numbers, L_e and L_μ. e^- and ν_e have a L_e number of +1. μ^- and ν_μ have a L_μ number of +1 (see Figure 5). The antiparticles of leptons have opposite lepton numbers (see Figure 6).

Symbol	Relative charge	L_e	L_μ
e^+	+1	−1	0
$\overline{\nu_e}$	0	−1	0
μ^+	+1	0	−1
$\overline{\nu_\mu}$	0	0	−1

Figure 6: The charges and lepton numbers of the lepton antiparticles.

Name	Symbol	Relative charge	L_e	L_μ
electron	e^-	−1	+1	0
electron neutrino	ν_e	0	+1	0
muon	μ^-	−1	0	+1
muon neutrino	ν_μ	0	0	+1

Figure 5: The charges and lepton numbers of leptons.

Conservation of lepton and baryon numbers

Both baryon number and the two separate types of lepton number must be conserved in all particle interactions. To check that a particle interaction can happen all you need to do is work out the baryon and lepton numbers of each side of the interaction equation.

┌─ **Example** ─────────────────────────────

The following equation shows the decay of a K^- kaon:

$$K^- \longrightarrow \mu^- + \overline{\nu}_\mu$$

Baryon number (B):	0	=	0 +	0
Electron lepton number (L_e):	0	=	0 +	0
Muon lepton number (L_μ):	0	=	+1 +	−1

The baryon number and both lepton numbers are conserved in this interaction.

Tip: If any of these properties are not conserved on each side of an equation, the equation does not represent a possible interaction.

Practice Questions — Application

Q1 State the baryon number of a helium nucleus with nuclide notation: ^4_2He

Q2 A neutron decays into a proton.
  a) Show that L_e is conserved in this interaction.
  b) Show that charge is conserved in this interaction.

Q3 Give one reason why the following interaction cannot occur:

$$K^- \rightarrow \mu^- + \nu_\mu$$

Practice Questions — Fact Recall

Q1 What type of particle feels the strong nuclear force?

Q2 What particle is believed to be the only stable baryon?

Q3 Write down the baryon number of:
  a) an electron   b) an antineutron   c) a kaon (K-meson)

Q4 What particles are produced when a neutron decays into a proton?

Q5 What is the antiparticle of π^0?

Q6 What is a lepton?

Q7 Write down the relative charge of an antimuon.

Q8 What three numbers must be conserved in any particle interaction?

Learning Objectives:

- Knowledge of the up, down and strange quarks and their antiquarks.
- Understand the properties of quarks: charge, baryon number and strangeness.
- Know the quark composition of protons, neutrons, antiprotons, antineutrons, pions and kaons.
- Understand the change of quark character in β⁺ and β⁻ decay.
- Know that strangeness and charge must be conserved in particle interactions (as well as baryon number and lepton number).

Specification Reference 3.1.1

Tip: Particle physicists have found six different quarks altogether, but you only need to know about three of them.

Figure 2: Murray Gell-Mann won the 1969 Nobel Prize in Physics for predicting the existence of quarks.

5. Quarks and Antiquarks

Quarks are fundamental particles — they are the building blocks for hadrons (baryons and mesons). They also sound pretty cool...

Quarks

To make protons and neutrons you only need two types of quark — the up quark (u) and the down quark (d). There is also another quark called the strange quark (s) which gives particles a property called strangeness.

Figure 1 shows the properties of each type of quark — don't worry, you'll be given these in the data and formulae booklet in the exam.

Name	Symbol	Charge	Baryon number	Strangeness
up	u	+ 2/3	+ 1/3	0
down	d	− 1/3	+ 1/3	0
strange	s	− 1/3	+ 1/3	−1

Figure 1: Properties of up, down and strange quarks.

The properties of a particle depend on the properties of the quarks that make it up. A proton has a charge of +1 because the quarks that make it up have an overall charge of +1. Kaons have 'strangeness' because they contain strange quarks. So hopefully learning about quarks will help to make everything you've learnt so far about particles make sense.

Quarks are a fundamental part of the Standard Model of particle physics that we use. But before the 1960s, we didn't even know they existed, and the last quark to be discovered was only found in 1995. Evidence for quarks came from hitting protons with high-energy electrons. The way the electrons scattered showed that there were three concentrations of charge (quarks) inside the proton.

Antiquarks

The antiquarks have opposite properties to the quarks — as you'd expect. Antiparticles of hadrons can be made with antiquarks.

Name	Symbol	Charge	Baryon number	Strangeness
anti-up	$\overline{u}$	− 2/3	− 1/3	0
anti-down	$\overline{d}$	+ 1/3	− 1/3	0
anti-strange	$\overline{s}$	+ 1/3	− 1/3	+1

Figure 3: Properties of antiquarks.

Quark composition of baryons

All baryons are made up of three quarks. Antibaryons are made up of three antiquarks. The charge and baryon number of a baryon is the total charge and baryon number of its quarks.

Figure 4: *The nucleus of an atom can be broken right down into quarks, but no further, since they're fundamental particles.*

Examples

Protons are made of two up quarks and one down quark (uud) — giving the properties you'd expect.

- The total charge of a proton is $2/3 + 2/3 - 1/3 = +1$.
- The total baryon number of a proton is $1/3 + 1/3 + 1/3 = +1$.

Neutrons are made up of one up quark and two down quarks (udd).

- The total charge of a neutron is $2/3 + (-1/3) + (-1/3) = 0$.
- The total baryon number of a neutron is $1/3 + 1/3 + 1/3 = +1$.

Proton   *Neutron*

Figure 5: *The quark composition of nucleons.*

Antiprotons are $\bar{u}\bar{u}\bar{d}$ and antineutrons are $\bar{u}\bar{d}\bar{d}$ — so no surprises there then.

Quark composition of mesons

All mesons are made from one quark and one antiquark. Pions are just made from combinations of up, down, anti-up and anti-down quarks. Kaons have strangeness so you need to put in s quarks as well (remember, the s quark has a strangeness of $S = -1$). You can work out the quark composition of mesons if you know their properties.

Example

The pion π^+ has:

- a charge of +1,
- a strangeness of 0 (only kaons have strangeness) and
- a baryon number of 0 (it isn't a baryon).

The only way you can get a charge of +1 with two quarks is $u\bar{d}$ or $u\bar{s}$, but pions don't have strangeness so it must be $u\bar{d}$.

Tip: You can do the same for baryons too (see the top of this page) — you might be asked to work out the quark composition of any baryon in the exam.

The nine possible quark-antiquark combinations give seven different mesons (π^0 can have any of three quark combinations). They can be arranged in a pattern like this.

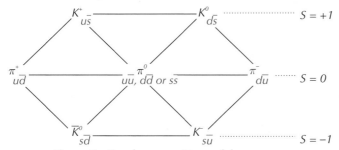

Figure 6: *Quark compositions of the mesons.*

Tip: Patterns like this helped Murray Gell-Mann to predict the existence of the 'omega-minus' particle two years before it was observed.

In the exam, you might be given a particle that you've not seen before and be asked to write down its quark composition. All the information you need will be in the question or in the formula book, you might just need to look carefully.

- You'll be told whether the particle is a baryon, antibaryon or meson so you'll know how many quarks and antiquarks to use.
- You'll be told the strangeness so you'll know if strange quarks are needed.
- You'll either be told the charge, or you will have to look at its symbol.

Example

Find the quark composition of the baryon Σ^-, which has a strangeness of –1.

- It must be made up of 3 quarks (not antiquarks) as it is a baryon.
- It must have a strange quark (s) because it has a strangeness of –1, and two other quarks.
- The symbol has a minus sign in it which means it has a charge of –1. So the other two quarks must make the total charge –1.
- The only option is dds.

Quark confinement

What if you blasted a proton with enough energy — could you remove a quark? Nope. The energy that you supply to remove a quark just gets changed into matter — more quarks and antiquarks. It's pair production again (page 14) and you just make mesons (quark-antiquark pairs). It's not possible to get a quark by itself — this is called **quark confinement**.

| A proton. | Energy supplied to remove u quark. | When enough energy is supplied, a u and $\overline{u}$ pair is produced and the u quark stays in the proton. |

Figure 7: *Quark confinement — the energy used trying to remove a u quark only creates a u and $\overline{u}$ pair in a pair production.*

Weak interaction
Beta-minus decay

In β^- decay a neutron is changed into a proton — in other words udd changes into uud. It means turning a d quark into a u quark. Only the weak interaction can do this. A quark changing into another quark is known as changing a quark's character.

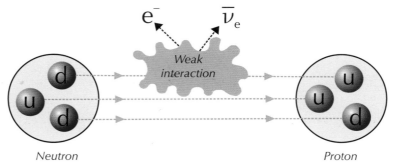

Neutron   *Proton*

Figure 8: *A quark changing character in β^- decay.*

Beta-plus decay

Some unstable isotopes like carbon-11 decay by beta-plus (β^+) emission. β^+ decay just means a positron (a β^+ particle) is emitted. In this case a proton changes to a neutron, so a u quark changes to a d quark and we get:

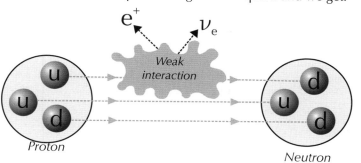

Figure 9: A quark changing character in β^+ decay.

The equation for β^+ decay is:

$$p \rightarrow n + e^+ + \nu_e$$

Conservation of properties

So you've got four properties to think about in particle interactions — baryon number, lepton number, charge and strangeness. Some are conserved in all particle reactions, while others are only conserved sometimes.

Charge

In any particle interaction, and in all of physics, the total charge after the interaction must equal the total charge before the interaction.

┌─ **Examples** ───────────────

- In pair production (page 14), a photon with enough energy can produce an electron-positron pair. It could not produce just one or the other, because the total charge before the interaction is 0, so the charges of the particles produced must cancel out.

- When a neutral neutron decays into a proton (page 22), a particle with a negative charge (e^-) must also be produced to cancel the proton's positive charge.

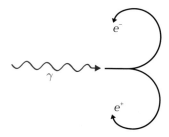

Figure 10: Pair production.

Baryon number

Just like with charge, in any particle interaction, the baryon number after the interaction must equal the baryon number before the interaction.

┌─ **Example** ───────────────

When a proton is produced in pair-production, the overall baryon number would be +1. You need an antiproton to be produced as well to conserve the baryon number of 0.

Lepton numbers

The electron and muon lepton numbers, L_e and L_μ, have to be conserved separately — think of them as completely different properties.

Examples

- $\pi^- \rightarrow \mu^- + \nu_\mu$ has $L_\mu = 0$ at the start and $L_\mu = 1 + (-1) = 0$ at the end, so it's OK.
- On the other hand, the interaction $\nu_\mu + \mu^- \rightarrow e^- + \nu_e$ can't happen. At the start $L_\mu = 2$ and $L_e = 0$ but at the end $L_\mu = 0$ and $L_e = 2$.

Strangeness

Tip: Remember, only particles that have a strange quark have strangeness.

Strangeness is only conserved for strong interactions. The only way to change the type of quark is with the weak interaction, so in strong interactions there has to be the same number of strange quarks at the beginning as at the end.

Even though strangeness is conserved in the beta-decay examples on p.22-23, it isn't always conserved when the weak interaction is involved.

Example

The strong interaction between hadrons $K^- + p \rightarrow n + \pi^0$ is fine for charge and baryon number but not for strangeness — so it won't happen. The negative kaon has an s quark in it, but neither n, p or π^0 has any strangeness.

Practice Questions — Application

Q1 A lambda particle Λ^0 is a baryon with strangeness −1. Write down its quark composition.

Q2 Which of the following interactions can happen? How do you know?

   a) $\mu^- \rightarrow e^- + \overline{\nu}_e + \nu_\mu$

   b) $K^- \rightarrow \pi^0 + e^- + \overline{\nu}_e$

   c) $K^+ \rightarrow \mu^+ + \overline{\nu}_\mu$

Q3 Show that strangeness is conserved in the interaction
$$\pi^- + p \rightarrow \Lambda^0 + K^0$$
using the information given in Q1.

Practice Questions — Fact Recall

Q1 Name three quarks.

Q2 What is the baryon number of a quark?

Q3 What is the strangeness of a strange quark?

Q4 Write down the quark composition of a:

   a) proton   b) neutron   c) antineutron

Q5 What is the quark composition of a meson?

Q6 Why can you not have a quark on its own?

Q7 What sort of interaction can change a quark character? Name and describe an interaction in which this happens.

Q8 What properties are always conserved in particle interactions?

6. Particle Interactions

Particle interactions are just what happens when two particles interact. You've seen a few already (beta decay, neutron decay, etc.)... but you need to know a bit more about how they happen.

Particle exchange

All forces are caused by particle exchange. You can't have instantaneous action at a distance (according to Einstein, anyway). So, when two particles interact and exert a force on one another, something must happen to let one particle know that the other one's there. That's the idea behind exchange particles. It helps to have an analogy to imagine this bit — consider two ice skaters standing on an ice rink.

Repulsion

Imagine the skaters are standing facing each other and throwing a ball between them. Each time the ball is thrown or caught the people get pushed apart. It happens because the ball carries momentum, which is mass multiplied by velocity.

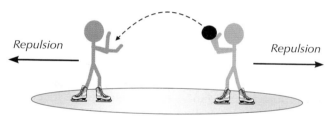

Figure 1: *A ball thrown between two people on ice skates will cause both people to move away from each other.*

The people represent particles that are interacting with each other, and the ball is an '**exchange particle**' that causes a repulsive force.

Attraction

Particle exchange also explains attraction, but you need a bit more imagination. Imagine this time that the skaters are facing away from each other and throwing a boomerang between them. Each time the boomerang is thrown or caught the people get pushed together.

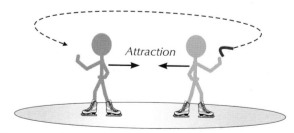

Figure 3: *A boomerang thrown between two people on ice skates will cause both people to move towards each other.*

Again, the people represent particles that are interacting with each other, and the boomerang is an 'exchange particle'.

Learning Objectives:

- Understand the concept of exchange particles to explain forces between elementary particles.
- Know that virtual photons are the exchange particles for the electromagnetic force.
- Know that W bosons are the exchange particles for the weak interaction.
- Understand the following weak interactions and the exchange particles involved: β^- and β^+ decay, electron capture and electron-proton collisions.
- Be able to construct Feynman diagrams to represent the above reactions or interactions in terms of particles going in and out and exchange particles.

Specification Reference 3.1.1

Figure 2: *In 1983, the Super Proton Synchrotron (SPS) particle accelerator at CERN was used to observe the first exchange particle, a discovery which was rewarded with the 1984 Nobel Prize in Physics.*

Tip: The virtual photon passed between the particles causes them to repel, just like the ball on the previous page.

Exchange particles are how forces act between two particles. They are **virtual particles**. Virtual particles only exist for a very short time — long enough to transfer energy, momentum and other properties between particles in the interaction... and then they're gone. The repulsion between two protons is caused by the exchange of virtual photons, which are the exchange particles of the electromagnetic force.

All forces in nature are caused by four fundamental forces. Each one has its own exchange particle:

Tip: Particle physicists never bother about gravity because it's so incredibly feeble compared with the other types of interaction. Gravity only really matters when you've got big masses like stars and planets. The graviton may exist but there's no evidence for it.

Type of Interaction	Exchange Particle	Particles Affected
strong	gluon	hadrons only
electromagnetic	virtual photon (symbol, γ)	charged particles only
weak	W^+, W^- bosons	all types
gravity	graviton?	all types

Figure 4: Exchange particles of the four fundamental forces.

The size of the exchange particle determines the range of the force. Heavier exchange particles have a shorter range. This explains why the force itself has a shorter range. W bosons have a mass of about 100 times that of a proton, which gives the weak force a very short range. Creating a virtual W boson uses so much energy that it can only exist for a very short time and it can't travel far. On the other hand, the photon has zero mass, which gives the electromagnetic force an infinite range.

Feynman diagrams

Richard Feynman was a brilliant physicist who was famous for explaining complicated ideas in a fun way that actually made sense. He worked out a really neat way of solving particle problems by drawing pictures rather than doing calculations. These are called **Feynman diagrams**.

Figure 5: *Richard Feynman, an American physicist.*

Feynman diagrams are used by physicists to represent particle interactions:

- Exchange particles are represented by wiggly lines (technical term).
- Other particles are represented by straight lines.

The Feynman diagram on the right shows the repulsion between two protons via the virtual photon γ.

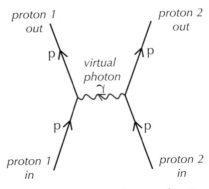

Figure 6: *A Feynman diagram showing two protons repelling each other.*

Feynman diagrams turn tricky physics into squiggly lines. There are a few rules you need to stick to when drawing them, but as long as you follow them, it should be easy. You'll only have to draw them for the weak interaction and the electromagnetic force.

- Incoming particles start at the bottom of the diagram and move upwards.
- The baryons stay on one side of the diagram, and the leptons stay on the other side.
- The W bosons carry charge from one side of the diagram to the other — make sure charges balance.
- A W⁻ particle going to the left has the same effect as a W⁺ particle going to the right.

There are a few types of particle interactions caused by the weak interaction and the electromagnetic force you'll need to be able to draw Feynman diagrams for.

Beta-minus and beta-plus decay

Beta-minus decay is where a neutron decays into a proton, an electron and an antineutrino:

$$n \rightarrow p + e^- + \overline{\nu}_e$$

There is one particle going in and three coming out. This means you need a neutron coming in at the bottom of the diagram and moving upwards. The proton will leave the diagram on the same side as the neutron. The two leptons will leave the diagram on the other side.

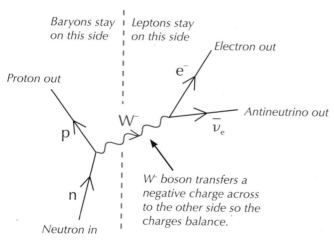

Baryons stay on this side | Leptons stay on this side

Proton out

Electron out

e^-

W^-

Antineutrino out

$\overline{\nu}_e$

p

n

W⁻ boson transfers a negative charge across to the other side so the charges balance.

Neutron in

Figure 7: A Feynman diagram for β⁻ decay.

The Feynman diagram for β⁺ decay is similar. The equation is:

$$p \rightarrow n + e^+ + \nu_e$$

e^+

n

W^+

ν_e

p

Figure 8: A Feynman diagram for β⁺ decay.

Tip: Some easy things to check when you've drawn a Feynman diagram:

- The whole diagram is connected by lines — there are no lines stuck on their own.
- There are two arrows connected to every single wiggly line end.

- There's only one wiggly line in your diagram.

Tip: You've seen beta-plus and beta-minus decay before — see pages 10, 22, 23.

Tip: For a reminder on the difference between baryons and leptons, see pages 16-18.

Tip: You can draw Feynman diagrams to show an interaction in terms of quarks too:

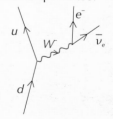

u

e^-

W^-

$\overline{\nu}_e$

d

Tip: You get an antineutrino in β⁻ decay and a neutrino in β⁺ decay so that lepton number is conserved.

Electron capture

You've seen that neutron-rich nuclei can emit an electron to turn a neutron into a proton (β⁻ decay), but it can work the other way round too. It's called **electron capture**. Proton-rich nuclei can 'capture' an electron from inside the atom and change into a neutron.

$$p + e^- \rightarrow n + \nu_e$$

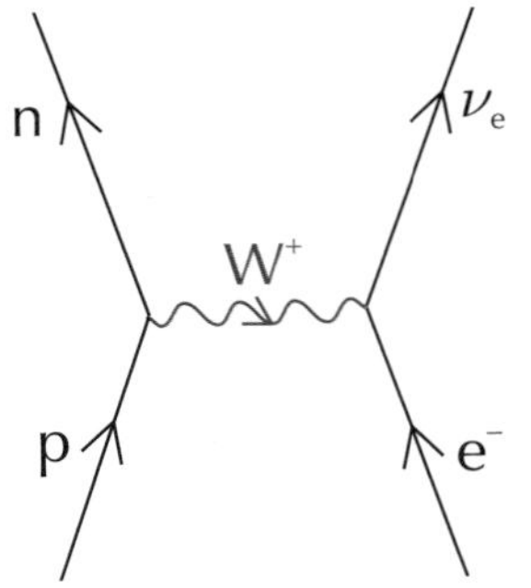

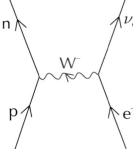

Figure 9: A Feynman diagram for electron capture.

The proton is 'acting' on the electron as it captures the electron, so the W boson comes from the proton. Like with β⁻ decay, an electron neutrino is emitted to conserve electron lepton number.

Tip: Electron capture by a proton and electron-proton collisions are confusingly similar. They have different Feynman diagrams and use different W bosons because the boson comes from the particle that is 'acting'.

Electron-proton collisions

Electron capture is where a proton captures an electron from the atom. An **electron-proton collision** is where an electron collides (at high speed) with a proton. They have almost the same Feynman diagram, and exactly the same equation, but there is a difference.

In an electron-proton collision, the electron is the particle that's acting because it is being fired at the proton, so the W boson comes from the electron. It must be a W⁻ boson to conserve charge.

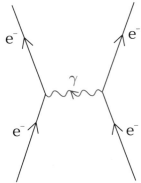

Figure 10: A Feynman diagram for an electron-proton collision.

Electromagnetic repulsion

This is the easiest interaction of the lot. When two particles with equal charge get close to each other, they repel. The exchange particle is a virtual photon.

Tip: Any two non-neutral particles with the same charge will do this. The Feynman diagram for two protons repelling is shown on page 26 in Figure 6.

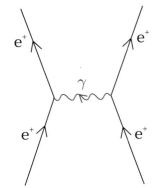

Figure 11: A Feynman diagram for two electrons repelling each other.

Figure 12: A Feynman diagram for two positrons repelling each other.

Practice Questions — Application

Q1 Sodium-22 decays into neon as shown below:

$$^{22}_{11}Na \rightarrow {}^{22}_{10}Ne + e^+ + \nu_e$$

a) What is the name of this interaction?

b) Draw a Feynman diagram of this interaction.

Q2 In electron capture, an up quark changes into a down quark. Complete the Feynman diagram for this reaction:

Q3 When two positrons collide, there is repulsion force between them.

a) Name the force and exchange particle.

b) Draw a Feynman diagram for this interaction.

Practice Questions — Fact Recall

Q1 What is an exchange particle?

Q2 Name the electromagnetic force exchange particle.

Q3 Name two exchange particles of the weak interaction.

Q4 What do the straight lines on Feynman diagrams represent?

Q5 Draw a Feynman diagram to show beta-minus decay.

Q6 Why would a nucleus undergo electron capture?

Q7 What is the difference between electron capture and electron-proton collisions?

Q8 Name the interaction in the following Feynman diagram.

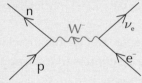

Q9 What is the exchange particle for electron capture, and what particles are produced?

Section Summary

Make sure you know...

- The structure of the atom — the three particles that make it up and their location within the atom.
- The charges and masses of protons, neutrons and electrons in relative units.
- What proton number (Z) and nucleon number (A) mean.
- How to represent elements in nuclide notation.
- How to calculate the specific charge of a particle in $C\ kg^{-1}$.
- What isotopes are and be able to give examples of isotopes of elements.
- The role of the strong nuclear force in keeping nuclei stable.
- The effect of the strong nuclear force for the following ranges of nucleon separation: less than 0.5 fm, between 0.5 fm and 3 fm, more than 3 fm.
- That unstable particles will decay to make themselves more stable.
- The equation for alpha decay and how it affects the nucleon and proton numbers of an element.
- The equation for beta-minus decay and how it affects the nucleon and proton numbers of an element.
- That photons are 'wave packets' of electromagnetic radiation.
- How to calculate the energy of a photon.
- That every particle has a corresponding antiparticle with equal mass and energy, and an equal but opposite charge.
- What is meant by pair production.
- How to calculate the minimum energy needed for pair production.
- That a particle and an antiparticle will annihilate to produce two gamma ray photons.
- How to calculate the minimum energy of a photon produced in an annihilation.
- Which particles are hadrons and which are leptons.
- That hadrons feel the strong nuclear force and leptons do not.
- Which hadrons are baryons and which are mesons based on their quark structure.
- That the proton is the only stable baryon and all other baryons eventually decay into protons.
- The quark compositions of protons, neutrons, antiprotons, antineutrons, pions and kaons.
- How to work out the quark composition of any hadron when given its charge, strangeness, and whether it is a baryon or a meson.
- How the weak interaction can change a quark's character, and its role in beta-decay.
- That charge, baryon number and lepton number must be conserved in all particle reactions.
- That strangeness is not conserved by the weak interaction.
- How exchange particles allow forces to act between particles.
- The exchange particles for the electromagnetic force and the weak interaction.
- How to draw Feynman diagrams of β^- and β^+ decay, electron capture and electron-proton collisions.

Exam-style Questions

1   The Ξ^0 particle is a baryon with a strangeness of -2.

1 (a) (i)   State how many quarks the Ξ^0 particle contains.

(1 mark)

1 (a) (ii) How many of the quarks in Ξ^0 are strange?

(1 mark)

1 (a) (iii) The Ξ^0 is a neutral particle. Write down its full quark composition.

(1 mark)

1 (b)   The Ξ^0 particle decays into the Λ^0 particle in the following way:
$$\Xi^0 \rightarrow \Lambda^0 + \pi^0$$
Λ^0 has a strangeness of -1.

1 (b) (i)   Other than energy and momentum, name two quantities that are conserved in this decay.

(2 marks)

1 (b) (ii) State a quantity that is **not** conserved in this reaction.

(1 mark)

1 (b) (iii) Give a reason for why the quantity in **1 (b) (ii)** is not conserved.

(1 mark)

1 (c)   The Λ^0 particle formed in the decay of Ξ^0 will decay in the following reaction.
$$\Lambda^0 \rightarrow \pi^0 + n$$

1 (c) (i)   What baryon will the neutron eventually decay into?

(1 mark)

1 (c) (ii) Complete the following Feynman diagram for the neutron's decay.

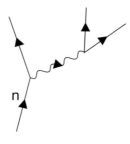

(4 marks)

1 (c) (iii) What is the name of this type of decay?

(1 mark)

1 (c) (iv) State the type of interaction involved in this decay and the exchange particle.

(2 marks)

2 (a) A neutral atom of a plutonium isotope can be represented by $^{240}_{94}$Pu.

2 (a) (i) State how many neutrons and protons are in the nucleus of an atom of $^{240}_{94}$Pu.

(2 marks)

2 (a) (ii) Calculate the specific charge of $^{240}_{94}$Pu.

(3 marks)

2 (a) (iii) What force stabilises an atomic nucleus?

(1 mark)

2 (a) (iv) $^{240}_{94}$Pu decays by α decay to form an element with symbol, U.
Write an equation for this decay using nuclide notation.

(3 marks)

2 (b) Another isotope of plutonium, with nucleon number 241, decays by emitting α and β^- particles in stages, eventually forming $^{205}_{81}$Tl.

2 (b) (i) Represent the plutonium isotope in nuclide notation.

(2 marks)

2 (b) (ii) There are nine α decays in the decay chain from the plutonium isotope to $^{205}_{81}$Tl.
How many β^- decays are there?

(3 marks)

3 (a) (i) State the type of interaction involved and the exchange particle when two positively charged protons repel each other.

(2 marks)

3 (a) (ii) Draw a Feynman diagram for the interaction in **3 (a) (i)**.

(3 marks)

3 (b) A proton and an antiproton are produced by a proton-proton collision.

3 (b) (i) Name this process.

(1 mark)

3 (b) (ii) Explain why a proton cannot be produced on its own.

(1 mark)

3 (b) (iii) What is the minimum energy, in MeV, needed to produce a proton-antiproton pair?

(2 marks)

3 (b) (iv) The antiproton produced interacts with a proton. What is the name of this process and what is produced?

(2 marks)

1. The Photoelectric Effect

Most of the time we think of light as a wave, but there are some situations where it acts as a particle too. The most famous of these cases is the photoelectric effect. Read on to find out more...

What is the photoelectric effect?

If you shine radiation of a high enough frequency onto the surface of a metal, it will instantly emit electrons (see Figure 1). For most metals, this frequency falls in the ultraviolet range.

Because of the way atoms are bonded together in metals, metals contain 'free electrons' that are able to move about the metal. The free electrons on or near the surface of the metal absorb energy from the radiation, making them vibrate.

If an electron absorbs enough energy, the bonds holding it to the metal break and the electron is released. This is called the **photoelectric effect** and the electrons emitted are called photoelectrons.

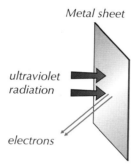

Metal sheet

ultraviolet radiation

electrons

Figure 1: *The photoelectric effect.*

You don't need to know the details of any experiments on this, you just need to learn the main conclusions:

Conclusion 1 For a given metal, no photoelectrons are emitted if the radiation has a frequency below a certain value — called the **threshold frequency**.

Conclusion 2 The photoelectrons are emitted with a variety of kinetic energies ranging from zero to some maximum value. This value of maximum kinetic energy increases with the frequency of the radiation.

Conclusion 3 The intensity of radiation is the amount of energy per second hitting an area of the metal. The maximum kinetic energy of the photoelectrons is unaffected by varying the intensity of the radiation.

Conclusion 4 The number of photoelectrons emitted per second is proportional to the intensity of the radiation.

Learning Objectives:

- Explain how the photoelectric effect provides evidence for the particle nature of light.
- Be able to define the threshold frequency of a metal, f_o.
- Be able to define and use the work function of a metal, ϕ.
- Be able to understand and use the photoelectric equation:
  $hf = \phi + E_k$.

Specification Reference 3.1.2

Exam Tip
You might have to explain how changing the intensity and frequency of the light affects the photoelectrons emitted — so make sure you learn it.

Tip: Remember — photoelectrons are just the electrons released from a metal's surface.

The photoelectric effect and wave theory

You can't explain all the observations and conclusions of the photoelectric effect experiment if EM radiation only acts as a wave...

Threshold frequency

Tip: The key thing about the photoelectric effect is that it shows that light <u>can't just act as a wave</u>. Certain observations of the photoelectric effect can't be explained by classic wave theory.

Wave theory says that for a particular frequency of EM wave, the energy carried should be proportional to the intensity of the beam. The energy carried by the EM wave would also be spread evenly over the wave-front.

This means that if an EM wave were shone on a metal, each free electron on the surface of the metal would gain a bit of energy from each incoming wave. Gradually, each electron would gain enough energy to leave the metal. If the EM wave had a lower frequency (i.e. was carrying less energy) it would take longer for the electrons to gain enough energy, but it would happen eventually. However, electrons are never emitted unless the wave is above a threshold frequency — so wave theory can't explain the threshold frequency.

Kinetic energy of photoelectrons

The higher the intensity of the wave, the more energy it should transfer to each electron — the kinetic energy should increase with intensity.

Wave theory can't explain the fact that the kinetic energy depends only on the frequency in the photoelectric effect.

The photon model of light

Max Planck's wave-packets

Max Planck was the first to suggest that EM waves can only be released in discrete packets, or quanta. As you saw on page 12, the energy, E, carried by one of these wave-packets is:

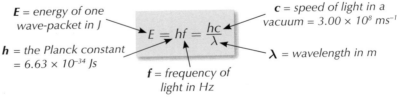

E = energy of one wave-packet in J

h = the Planck constant = 6.63×10^{-34} Js

$$E = hf = \frac{hc}{\lambda}$$

f = frequency of light in Hz

c = speed of light in a vacuum = 3.00×10^{8} ms^{-1}

λ = wavelength in m

Exam Tip
Remember that for calculations like this you'll be given Planck's constant, h, and the speed of light, c — hurrah.

Example

Calculate the wavelength of a wave-packet with an energy of 3.06 × 10⁻¹⁹ J.

Rearrange $E = \frac{hc}{\lambda}$ into $\lambda = \frac{hc}{E}$ and substitute in the values for E, h and c to calculate the wavelength.

$$\lambda = \frac{hc}{E} = \frac{(6.63 \times 10^{-34}) \times (3.00 \times 10^{8})}{3.06 \times 10^{-19}} = 6.50 \times 10^{-7} \text{m}$$

Figure 2: *Albert Einstein, the physicist who explained the photoelectric effect using photons.*

Einstein's photons

Einstein went further by suggesting that EM waves (and the energy they carry) can only exist in discrete packets. He called these wave-packets **photons**.

He saw these photons of light as having a one-on-one, particle-like interaction with an electron in a metal surface. Each photon would transfer all its energy to one specific electron. The photon model could be used explain the photoelectric effect.

Explaining the photoelectric effect

The photon model of light can explain the observations and conclusions for the photoelectric effect that the wave model of light can't...

Work function and threshold frequency

When EM radiation hits a metal, the metal's surface is bombarded by photons. If one of these photons collides with a free electron, the electron will gain energy equal to hf (as $E = hf$).

Before an electron can leave the surface of the metal, it needs enough energy to break the bonds holding it there. This energy is called the **work function** energy (symbol ϕ) and its value depends on the metal.

If the energy gained from the photon is greater than the work function energy, the electron is emitted. If it isn't, the electron will just shake about a bit, then release the energy as another photon. The metal will heat up, but no electrons will be emitted. Since, for electrons to be released $hf \geq \phi$, the threshold frequency, f_o, must be:

$$f_o = \frac{\phi}{h}$$

Example

For a metal with a work function of 7.2×10^{-19} J, the minimum frequency of EM radiation needed for a photoelectron to be released would be:

$$f_o = \frac{\phi}{h} = \frac{7.2 \times 10^{-19}}{6.63 \times 10^{-34}} = 1.1 \times 10^{15}\,\text{Hz} \quad \text{(to 2 s.f.)}$$

Maximum kinetic energy

The energy transferred from EM radiation to an electron is the energy it absorbs from one photon, hf. The kinetic energy it will be carrying when it leaves the metal is hf minus any other energy losses. These energy losses are the reason the electrons emitted from a metal have a range of kinetic energies.

The minimum amount of energy an electron can lose is the work function energy, so the maximum kinetic energy, E_k, is given by the equation $E_k = hf - \phi$. Rearranging this equation gives you the photoelectric equation:

$$hf = \phi + E_k$$

Kinetic energy = ½ mass × velocity², so the maximum kinetic energy a photoelectron can have is:

E_k = maximum kinetic energy of a photoelectron ⟶ $E_k = \frac{1}{2}mv_{max}^2$ ⟵ v_{max} = maximum velocity of an emitted electron

m = mass of an electron = 9.11×10^{-31} kg

You can use this to write the photoelectric equation as:

$$hf = \phi + \frac{1}{2}mv_{max}^2$$

The kinetic energy of the electrons is independent of the intensity, because they can only absorb one photon at a time.

Figure 3: Solar cells use the photoelectric effect to convert light energy into electricity.

Exam Tip
You won't get this equation in the exam data booklet, but you will get $E = hf$. As long as you remember that the work function is the energy of a photon with the threshold frequency, you don't have to learn this equation — just replace E for ϕ and f for f_o then rearrange.

Tip: There are loads of ways electrons leaving the metal can lose energy, e.g. they might have to do work to get to the surface of the metal.

Exam Tip
You'll be given the equations $hf = \phi + E_k$ and $E_k = \frac{1}{2}mv_{max}^2$ in the exam data booklet, so you don't need to learn them as long as you know what each part shows and how to use them.

┌─ Example ─────────────────────────────

The threshold frequency of light needed to cause the photoelectric effect in aluminium is 1.03×10^{15} Hz. Light with a frequency of 3.45×10^{15} Hz is shone on an aluminium sheet. Calculate the maximum kinetic energy of a photoelectron emitted from the surface of this sheet.

To work out the maximum kinetic energy you need to rearrange and use the photoelectric equation.

First, use the threshold frequency to calculate the work function, ϕ.

$\phi = hf_o = (6.63 \times 10^{-34}) \times (1.03 \times 10^{15}) = 6.83 \times 10^{-19}$ J (to 3 s.f.)

Then substitute this, Planck's constant and the frequency of the light being shone on the metal into the photoelectric equation. $hf = \phi + E_k$, so

$E_k = hf - \phi$

$\quad = (6.63 \times 10^{-34} \times 3.45 \times 10^{15}) - 6.83 \times 10^{-19}$

$\quad = 1.60 \times 10^{-18}$ J (to 3 s.f.)

└───────────────────────────────────

Practice Questions — Application

Q1 Each photon in a beam of light carries an energy of 4.3×10^{-20} J. Calculate the frequency of the light.

Q2 Photons each with an energy 6.0×10^{-18} J strike the surface of a sheet of zinc. The work function of zinc is 5.82×10^{-19} J. Will any photoelectrons be emitted from the surface of the zinc sheet? Explain your answer.

Q3 Electrons are emitted from a metal's surface when it is irradiated with light with a frequency of 1.20×10^{16} Hz.

a) What effect would increasing the frequency of the incident light have on the electrons emitted by the metal? Explain your answer.

b) Calculate the energy of a single photon of incident light.

c) The maximum kinetic energy of an electron emitted from the metal's surface is 7.26×10^{-18} J. Calculate the work function of the metal.

Practice Questions — Fact Recall

Q1 Describe what is meant by the 'photoelectric effect'.

Q2 Describe what will happen to the electrons emitted by a metal if the intensity of the light shining on it is increased.

Q3 a) What is a photon?

b) What equation would you use to calculate the energy of a photon when given the frequency of the light?

Q4 Explain why there is a threshold frequency below which no electrons will be emitted by a metal.

Q5 Explain why electrons emitted due to the photoelectric effect have a maximum possible kinetic energy.

Q6 Write down the photoelectric equation, define all the symbols you use.

2. Energy Levels in Atoms

Learning Objectives:
- To be able to use and define the electron volt.
- Be able to understand and explain the terms ionisation and excitation in atoms.
- Be able to understand ionisation and excitation in a fluorescent tube.
- Explain why line spectra are evidence of transitions between discrete energy levels in atoms: $hf = E_1 - E_2$.

Specification Reference 3.1.2

The electrons in atoms exist in different energy levels. They jump up and down between energy levels by absorbing or emitting a photon.

The electron volt

The energies of electrons in an atom are usually so tiny that it makes sense to use a more appropriate unit than the joule. The **electron volt** (eV) is defined as the kinetic energy carried by an electron after it has been accelerated through a potential difference of 1 volt. The energy gained by an electron (eV) is equal to the accelerating voltage (V).

You can convert between eV and J with this formula:

$$1 \text{ eV} = 1.6 \times 10^{-19} \text{ J}$$

Discrete energy levels in atoms

Electrons in an atom can only exist in certain well-defined energy levels. Each level is given a number, with n = 1 representing the lowest energy level an electron can be in — the **ground state**. We say that an atom is excited when one or more of its electrons is in an energy level higher than the ground state.

Electrons can move down an energy level by emitting a photon. Since these transitions are between definite energy levels, the energy of each photon emitted can only take a certain allowed value. Figure 1 shows the energy levels for atomic hydrogen.

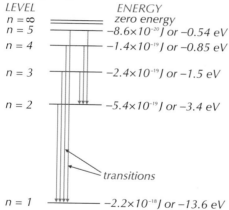

Figure 1: The energy levels in atomic hydrogen.

LEVEL   ENERGY
- n = ∞   zero energy
- n = 5 -8.6×10^{-20} J or -0.54 eV
- n = 4 -1.4×10^{-19} J or -0.85 eV
- n = 3 -2.4×10^{-19} J or -1.5 eV
- n = 2 -5.4×10^{-19} J or -3.4 eV
- transitions
- n = 1 -2.2×10^{-18} J or -13.6 eV

Tip: To convert energy in electron volts to joules, just multiply it by 1.60×10^{-19}.

Tip: The energies are only negative because of how "zero energy" is defined. It's just one of those silly convention things — don't worry about it.

Electron transitions

The energy carried by a photon emitted after a transition is equal to the difference in energies between the two levels of the transition. Electrons can also move up energy levels if they absorb a photon with the exact energy difference between the two levels. The movement of an electron to a higher energy level is called **excitation**.

The equation below shows a transition between levels n = 2 and n = 1.

ΔE = change in energy in J

$$\Delta E = E_1 - E_2 = hf$$

hf = photon energy (see p.12)

E_1 = energy of level n = 1 in J

E_2 = energy of level n = 2 in J

Exam Tip
The equation $hf = E_2 - E_1$ will be in the data booklet you'll get in the exam — you don't need to learn it but you do need to be able to use it.

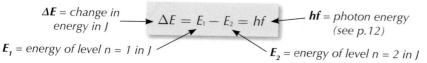

You can substitute in $f = \frac{c}{\lambda}$ (see p.12) to give the equation:

$$\Delta E = E_1 - E_2 = hf = \frac{hc}{\lambda}$$

(see p.12)

Example

Figure 2 shows some of the energy levels in a hydrogen atom.

Calculate the wavelength of the photon produced by an electron transition from n = 3 to n = 2.

First find the difference in energy between the two energy levels. This will be the photon energy.

$\Delta E = E_2 - E_3 = 3.40 - 1.50 = 1.90$ eV.

To find the frequency or wavelength of the photon, you need to convert this photon energy into joules.

1 eV = 1.60×10^{-19} J, so 1.90 eV is $1.90 \times 1.60 \times 10^{-19} = 3.04 \times 10^{-19}$ J

LEVEL		ENERGY
n = 5	———	−0.540 eV
n = 4	———	−0.850 eV
n = 3	———	−1.50 eV
n = 2	———	−3.40 eV
n = 1	———	−13.6 eV

Figure 2: *Energy levels in atomic hydrogen.*

Substitute this energy, the speed of light and the Planck constant into the equation $E = \frac{hc}{\lambda}$ to find the wavelength of the photon.

$3.04 \times 10^{-19} = \frac{(6.63 \times 10^{-34}) \times (3.00 \times 10^{8})}{\lambda}$

$\lambda = \frac{(6.63 \times 10^{-34}) \times (3.00 \times 10^{8})}{3.04 \times 10^{-19}} = 6.54 \times 10^{-7}$ m (to 3 s.f.)

Tip: As all the energies are negative, you can just subtract the magnitude of one from the other and ignore the minuses — it'll be quicker to do the calculation.

Tip: Electrons are excited whenever energy is transferred to them — this can happen when they collide with other particles or when they absorb a photon (see page 37).

(see page 37)

Ionisation

When an electron has been removed from an atom, the atom is ionised. The energy of each energy level within an atom shows the amount of energy needed to remove an electron from that level. The **ionisation energy** of an atom is the amount of energy needed to remove an electron from the ground state atom.

Example

The ionisation energy of an unexcited hydrogen atom is 13.6 eV — this is the energy you need to remove an electron from the n = 1 energy level.

Photon emission — fluorescent tubes

Fluorescent tubes use the excitation of electrons and photon emission to produce visible light. They contain mercury vapour, across which a high voltage is applied. When the fast-moving free electrons (emitted by electrodes in the tube and accelerated by the high voltage) collide with the electrons in the mercury atoms, the atomic mercury electrons are excited to a higher energy level.

When these excited electrons return to their ground states, they lose energy by emitting high energy photons in the UV range. The photons emitted have a range of energies and wavelengths that correspond to the different transitions of the electrons.

Figure 3: *Low energy light bulbs are made up of fluorescent tubes.*

A phosphorus coating on the inside of the tube absorbs these photons, exciting its electrons to much higher energy levels. These electrons then cascade down the energy levels and lose energy by emitting many lower energy photons of visible light.

Exam Tip
You might get asked to describe how a fluorescent bulb works in the exam — so make sure you know all the juicy details.

Line emission spectra

If you split the light from a fluorescent tube with a prism or a diffraction grating, you get a **line spectrum**. A line emission spectrum is seen as a series of bright lines against a black background. Each line corresponds to a particular wavelength of light emitted by the source.

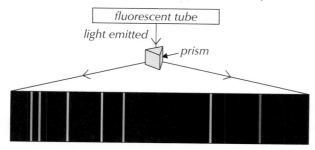

Figure 4: *Line emission spectrum for light emitted by a fluorescent tube.*

Line spectra provide evidence that the electrons in atoms exist in discrete energy levels. Atoms can only emit photons with energies equal to the difference between the two energy levels. Since only certain photon energies are allowed, you only see the corresponding wavelengths in the line spectrum.

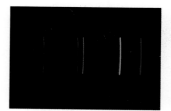

Figure 5: *The emission spectrum for helium.*

Line absorption spectra

Continuous spectra

The spectrum of white light is continuous. If you split the light up with a prism, the colours all merge into each other — there aren't any gaps in the spectrum. Hot things emit a continuous spectrum in the visible and infrared.

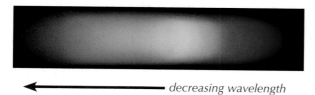

← *decreasing wavelength*

Figure 6: *The continuous spectrum of white light.*

What are line absorption spectra?

You get a line absorption spectrum when light with a continuous spectrum of energy (white light) passes through a cool gas. At low temperatures, most of the electrons in the gas atoms will be in their ground states. Photons of the correct wavelength are absorbed by the electrons to excite them to higher energy levels. These wavelengths are then missing from the continuous spectrum when it comes out the other side of the gas.

Tip: All atoms and molecules have their own emission and absorption spectra. Scientists use these spectra to identify elements, e.g. in the Earth's atmosphere.

You see a continuous spectrum with black lines in it corresponding to the absorbed wavelengths.

Tip: For more on absorption line spectra, see page 169.

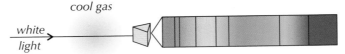

Figure 7: *An absorption spectrum of a cool gas.*

Comparing line absorption spectra and emission spectra

If you compare the absorption and emission spectra of a particular gas, the black lines in the absorption spectrum match up to the bright lines in the emission spectrum.

Tip: The lines are in the same places because energy differences of the electron transitions that cause them are the same. The photons that cause each line will have the same energy, and therefore the same wavelength (see p.37).

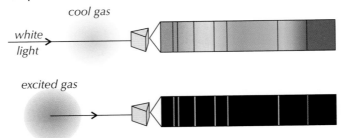

Figure 8: *Comparing absorption and emission spectra.*

Practice Question — Application

Use this energy level diagram for a hydrogen atom to answer this question.

Q1 The electron in an excited hydrogen atom is in the $n = 2$ energy level.

a) What is meant by an excited atom?

b) How much more energy would be needed to ionise this atom?

c) The electron makes a transition from the $n = 2$ energy level to the ground state. Calculate the frequency of the photon emitted due to this transition.

Level		Energy
$n = 5$	——————	−0.540 eV
$n = 4$	——————	−0.850 eV
$n = 3$	——————	−1.50 eV
$n = 2$	——————	−3.40 eV
$n = 1$	——————	−13.6 eV

Tip: You'll need to convert energy from electron volts to joules in this question.

Practice Questions — Fact Recall

Q1 What is an electron volt?

Q2 Why can photons emitted as an electron moves to a lower energy level in an atom only take an allowed value?

Q3 What is the ionisation energy of an atom?

Q4 In a fluorescent tube, a high voltage is applied across a mercury vapour. Explain how a fluorescent tube emits light.

Q5 What causes the pattern of lines seen in line emission spectra and line absorption spectra?

3. Wave-Particle Duality

The photoelectric effect (see page 33) shows that light can act as a particle, but there's plenty of evidence that it acts as a wave too. It turns out that not only can waves act like particles, but particles can also act like waves.

Is light a particle or a wave?

Diffraction

When a beam of light passes through a narrow gap, it spreads out. This is called **diffraction** (see p.160). Diffraction can only be explained using waves. If the light was acting as a particle, the light particles in the beam would either not get through the gap (if they were too big), or just pass straight through and the beam would be unchanged.

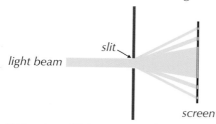

light beam

slit

screen

Figure 1: *Diffraction of light waves as they pass through a narrow slit.*

The photoelectric effect

The results of photoelectric effect experiments (see p.33) can only be explained by thinking of light as a series of particle-like photons. If a photon of light is a discrete bundle of energy, then it can interact with an electron in a one-to-one way. All the energy in the photon is given to one electron.

The photoelectric effect and diffraction show that light behaves as both a particle and a wave — this is known as **wave-particle duality**.

Wave-particle duality theory

Louis de Broglie made a bold suggestion in his PhD thesis. He said if 'wave-like' light showed particle properties (photons), 'particles' like electrons should be expected to show wave-like properties.

The de Broglie equation relates a wave property (wavelength, λ) to a moving particle property (momentum, mv).

λ = de Broglie wavelength in m

$$\lambda = \frac{h}{mv}$$

h = the Planck constant = 6.63×10^{-34} Js.

m = mass in kg   **v** = velocity in ms^{-1}

The de Broglie wave of a particle can be interpreted as a 'probability wave'. Many physicists at the time weren't very impressed — his ideas were just speculation. But later experiments confirmed the wave nature of electrons and other particles.

HOW SCIENCE WORKS

Learning Objectives:

- Understand that electron diffraction suggests the wave nature of particles.

- Understand that the photoelectric effect suggests the particle nature of electromagnetic waves.

- Be able to understand and calculate the de Broglie wavelength of a particle, given by $\lambda = \frac{h}{mv}$, where mv is the momentum.

Specification Reference 3.1.2

Exam Tip
Make sure you know these two examples that show light acts as both a wave and a particle — they might just come up in the exam.

Figure 2: *Louis de Broglie, the physicist who first suggested the idea of wave-particle duality.*

Tip: Remember that momentum is the mass multiplied by the velocity of an object.

Electron diffraction

Diffraction patterns are observed when accelerated electrons in a vacuum tube interact with the spaces in a graphite crystal. As they pass through the spaces, they diffract just like waves passing through a narrow slit and produce a pattern of rings. This provides evidence that electrons have wave properties.

Tip: There's more coming up on diffraction on page 160.

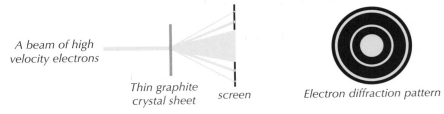

A beam of high velocity electrons

Thin graphite crystal sheet

screen

Electron diffraction pattern

Figure 3: *Electron diffraction — an experiment that shows electrons have wave properties.*

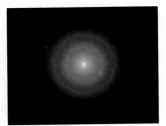

Figure 4: *An electron diffraction pattern.*

According to wave theory, the spread of the lines in the diffraction pattern increases if the wavelength of the wave is greater. In electron diffraction experiments, a smaller accelerating voltage, i.e. slower electrons, gives widely spaced rings. Increase the electron speed and the diffraction pattern circles squash together towards the middle. This fits in with the de Broglie equation — if the velocity is higher, the wavelength is shorter and the spread of lines is smaller.

In general, λ for electrons accelerated in a vacuum tube is about the same size as electromagnetic waves in the X-ray part of the spectrum. You only get diffraction if a particle interacts with an object of about the same size as its de Broglie wavelength.

Exam Tip
You don't need to know all the detail of this experiment for the exam — just make sure you know that electron diffraction shows that electrons have wave-like properties.

Tip: Electrons can be used to investigate the spacing between atoms in a crystal — an electron beam will diffract when the de Broglie wavelength of the electrons is roughly the same size as the spaces between the atoms.

Tip: Be careful when you're dealing with numbers in standard form — make sure you punch everything into your calculator correctly. Always check that the magnitude of your answer seems about right.

Example

A tennis ball, with a mass of 0.058 kg and speed 100 ms^{-1} has a de Broglie wavelength of 10^{-34} m. That's 10^{19} times smaller than the nucleus of an atom. There's nothing that small for it to interact with, and so it only acts as a particle.

Example

An electron of mass 9.11 × 10^{-31} kg is fired from an electron gun at 7.0 × 10^6 ms^{-1}. What size object will the electron need to interact with in order to diffract?

An electron will diffract when the size of the object is roughly the same size as its de Broglie wavelength, so you need to find λ.

Momentum of electron $= mv$
$= 9.11 \times 10^{-31} \times 7.0 \times 10^6$
$= 6.377 \times 10^{-24}$ kg ms^{-1}

Substitute this into de Broglie's equation:

$\lambda = \dfrac{h}{mv} = \dfrac{6.63 \times 10^{-34}}{6.377 \times 10^{-24}} = 1.0 \times 10^{-10}$ m (to 2 s.f.)

So, only crystals with atom layer spacing around this size are likely to cause the diffraction of this electron.

Electrons with a wavelength of 1.70×10^{-10} m are diffracted as they pass between atoms in a crystal lattice. Calculate the velocity of the electrons.

Substitute $\lambda = 1.7 \times 10^{-10}$ m, $h = 6.63 \times 10^{-34}$ Js, and $m = 9.11 \times 10^{-31}$ kg into the de Broglie equation.

$\lambda = \dfrac{h}{mv}$, so $1.7 \times 10^{-10} = \dfrac{6.63 \times 10^{-34}}{9.11 \times 10^{-31} \times v}$

Rearrange and solve for v:

$v = \dfrac{6.63 \times 10^{-34}}{9.11 \times 10^{-31} \times 1.7 \times 10^{-10}} = 4\,280\,000$ ms^{-1} (to 3 s.f.)

Tip: You could write the answer to this calculation in standard form as 4.28×10^6 ms^{-1}.

Electron microscopes

A shorter wavelength gives less diffraction effects. This fact is used in the electron microscope. Diffraction effects blur detail on an image. If you want to resolve tiny detail in an image, you need a shorter wavelength. Light blurs out detail more than 'electron-waves' do, so an electron microscope can resolve finer detail than a light microscope. They can let you look at things as tiny as a single strand of DNA.

Figure 5: A laboratory technician using an electron microscope.

Practice Questions — Application

Q1 Electrons fired from an electron gun have a de Broglie wavelength of 2.4×10^{-10} m. How will increasing the velocity of the electrons affect their de Broglie wavelength?

Q2 An electron has a de Broglie wavelength of 1.62×10^{-10} m. The mass of an electron is 9.11×10^{-31} kg.

a) Calculate the momentum of the electron.

b) Calculate the kinetic energy of the electron.

Q3 An alpha particle has a mass of 6.64×10^{-27} kg.

a) Calculate the de Broglie wavelength of an alpha particle travelling at a velocity of 60 ms^{-1}.

b) Calculate the speed of an electron that has the same de Broglie wavelength as the alpha particle in part a). (The mass of an electron is 9.11×10^{-31} kg.)

Tip: Remember kinetic energy $E_k = \frac{1}{2}mv^2$.

Practice Questions — Fact Recall

Q1 Describe what is meant by wave-particle duality.

Q2 Name two effects that show electromagnetic waves have both wave and particle properties.

Q3 What phenomenon shows that electrons have wave-like properties?

Section Summary

Make sure you know...

- What the photoelectric effect is.
- That light with a frequency equal to or above the threshold frequency, f_0, will cause electrons to be released from a metal.
- How the photoelectrons emitted by the photoelectric effect are affected by increasing the frequency and intensity of the incident light.
- That a photon is a discrete wave-packet of energy.
- How to calculate the energy of a photon given the frequency or the wavelength of the light.
- How the threshold frequency and kinetic energy of the photoelectrons observed in the photoelectric effect provide evidence that light acts as a particle.
- How to calculate the threshold frequency, f_0, for a metal.
- How to calculate the work function, ϕ, of a metal.
- How to use the photoelectric equation to calculate the maximum kinetic energy, E_k, of photoelectrons, the work function of a metal and the energy of an incident photon.
- What an electron volt is.
- How to convert the units of energy between electron volts and joules.
- That electrons in an atom can only exist in certain energy levels.
- What is meant by the ground state of an atom.
- That atoms are 'excited' when one or more of its electrons is in an energy level higher than the ground state.
- How to calculate the frequency, energy or wavelength of a photon emitted by an atom.
- That an atom is ionised when an electron is removed, and the ionisation energy of an atom is the energy required to remove an electron from the atom.
- How fluorescent tubes work.
- What line emission spectra and line absorption spectra are.
- Why line spectra show electrons exist in set energy levels.
- That diffraction and the photoelectric effect show that light has both particle and wave properties.
- That particles can show wave-like properties, and this is known as wave-particle duality.
- How to calculate the de Broglie wavelength of a particle.
- That electron diffraction shows electrons have wave-like properties.

Exam-style Questions

1   A metal surface emits electrons when a certain frequency of light is shone onto it. This effect is called the photoelectric effect.

1 (a) (i)   State what is meant by the work function of a metal.

(1 mark)

1 (a) (ii)   Explain why there is a threshold frequency for the light being shone onto the metal, below which no electrons are emitted.

(2 marks)

1 (a) (iii)   The photoelectric effect supports the theory that light acts as a particle. Explain how the threshold frequency provides evidence against the wave theory of light.

(2 marks)

1 (b)   The threshold frequency of lead is 1.03×10^{15} Hz.

1 (b) (i)   Calculate the work function of lead.

(2 marks)

1 (b) (ii)   A beam of light is shone onto a sheet of lead. Each photon has an energy of 3.0×10^{-18} J. Calculate the maximum kinetic energy of an electron emitted from this surface.

(2 marks)

2   A fluorescent tube emits visible light when a voltage is applied across it. Atoms of mercury vapour inside the tube are excited by free electrons flowing through the tube and emit photons of ultraviolet radiation.

2 (a)   Describe what is meant by an 'excited atom'.

(1 mark)

2 (b)   Describe the rest of the process by which fluorescent tubes emit visible light.

(2 marks)

2 (c)   A free electron with an energy of 8.0 eV collides with an electron of a mercury atom. After the collision, the free electron has an energy of 1.80 eV and the electron in the mercury atom emits a photon.

2 (c) (i)   Calculate the energy, in joules, that is transferred to the electron in the atom.

(2 marks)

2 (c) (ii)   Calculate the smallest possible wavelength of the emitted photon.

(2 marks)

2 (d)   Some of the mercury atoms in the fluorescent tube are excited such that they become ionised. The ground state energy of a mercury atom is −10.4 eV. State the ionisation energy of a mercury atom.

(1 mark)

3   Louis de Broglie was the first scientist to propose wave-particle duality.

3 (a)   Describe what is meant by the term 'wave-particle duality'.

(1 mark)

3 (b)   Name one phenomenon that provides evidence that
particles have wave-like properties.

(1 mark)

3 (c)   Electrons fired from an electron gun each have a kinetic energy of 1.02×10^{-26} J.

3 (c) (i)   Calculate the velocity of one electron.
Give your answer to an appropriate number of significant figures.

(3 marks)

3 (c) (ii) Calculate the de Broglie wavelength of each electron.

(2 marks)

4   The wavelengths of the emission spectrum lines for atomic hydrogen in the
visible spectrum are shown in the diagram below.

wavelength (nm)

4 (a)   Explain how line spectra provide evidence for the
existence of discrete energy levels in atoms.

(3 marks)

4 (b)   The diagram below shows some of the energy levels in a hydrogen atom.

Level		Energy
$n = 5$	————	–0.54 eV
$n = 4$	————	–0.85 eV
$n = 3$	————	–1.50 eV
$n = 2$	————	–3.40 eV
$n = 1$	————	–13.6 eV

4 (b) (i)   Show that the photons that produce the spectral line with a wavelength of 434 nm
are produced by an electron transition between the levels $n = 5$ and $n = 2$.

(5 marks)

4 (b) (ii) Write down an energy level transition that would cause a photon with a larger energy
to be emitted by the atom.

(1 mark)

1. Circuit Diagrams

Unit 1 Section 3 is all about electricity. Before we start going into all the detail, it's important that you can understand the circuit diagrams that are used throughout the section. That's what this page is for — a brief intro to circuits...

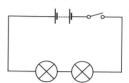

Figure 1: A simple circuit diagram.

Circuit symbols

In physics, we use circuit symbols to represent different electrical components. Here are some of the basic ones you should recognise...

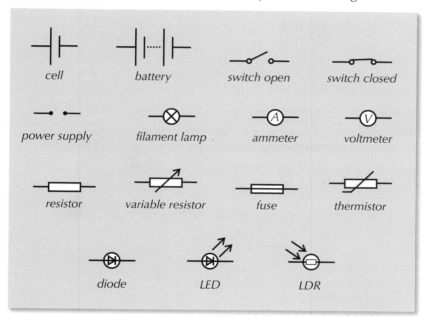

cell   battery   switch open   switch closed

power supply   filament lamp   ammeter   voltmeter

resistor   variable resistor   fuse   thermistor

diode   LED   LDR

Tip: Some of these components will be covered in more detail later on in the section...

Figure 2: An electronic circuit. The red dome-shaped components to the right of the picture are LEDs.

Drawing circuits

The lines between components in a circuit diagram represent wires and show how the components are connected together. You can connect components in series...

Here the filament lamp and the fuse are connected in series.

or in parallel...

Here the filament lamp and the fuse are connected in parallel.

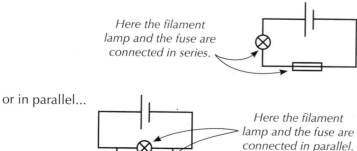

Exam Tip
You could be asked to draw a circuit diagram in the exam — so make sure you get loads of practice at it before then.

Tip: A circuit needs to be complete for a current to flow through it.

2. Current and Potential Difference

After all that stuff in GCSE Physics about electricity, you wouldn't think there was much left to learn. Well, unfortunately you'd be wrong — there's a whole load more that you've got to learn about electricity for AS and it starts here...

Learning Objectives:

- Know that electric current is the rate of flow of charge.
- Understand and be able to use the equation: $I = \dfrac{\Delta Q}{\Delta t}$
- Know that potential difference is the work done per unit charge.
- Understand and be able to use the equation: $V = \dfrac{W}{Q}$

Specification Reference 3.1.3

Tip: Remember that conventional current flows from + to −, the opposite way from electron flow.

Exam Tip
When you're doing calculation questions in the exam, don't forget to check your <u>units</u> are correct. Sometimes you'll get an extra mark for using the right units.

What is current?

The current in a wire is like water flowing in a pipe. The amount of water that flows depends on the flow rate and the time. It's the same with electricity — **current** is the rate of flow of charge. In an electrical circuit, the charge is carried through the wires by electrons.

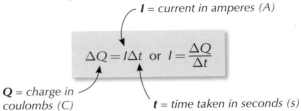

I = current in amperes (A)

$$\Delta Q = I\Delta t \ \text{ or } \ I = \frac{\Delta Q}{\Delta t}$$

Q = charge in coulombs (C)

t = time taken in seconds (s)

The **coulomb** is the unit of charge. One coulomb (C) is defined as the amount of charge that passes in 1 second when the current is 1 ampere. You can work out the amount of charge passing through a circuit using the equation above.

> ### Example
>
> **A component has a current of 0.430 A passing through it. Calculate the charge passing through the component in 3 minutes.**
>
> First convert the time taken from minutes to seconds:
>
> 3 minutes × 60 seconds per minute = 180 seconds.
>
> Then substitute the values for current and time taken into the charge formula given above:
>
> $\Delta Q = I \times \Delta t$
> $\quad\quad = 0.430 \times 180$
> $\quad\quad = 77.4$ C

You can measure the current flowing through a part of a circuit using an **ammeter**. You always need to attach an ammeter in series (so that the current through the ammeter is the same as the current through the component — see page 66).

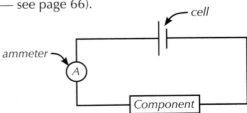

Figure 1: *An ammeter connected in series with a component.*

Figure 2: *An ammeter connected in series with a power pack and a light bulb.*

Tip: There's more on work done on page 111.

What is potential difference?

To make electric charge flow through a circuit, you need to transfer energy to the charge — this energy is supplied by the power source, e.g. a battery. When a charge flows through the power source it is 'raised' through a potential and energy is transferred to the charge as electrical potential energy.

When energy is transferred, we say that work is done — so the power source does work to move the charge around the circuit. The **potential difference** (p.d.), or voltage, between two points is defined as the work done in moving a unit charge between the points.

$V = \text{potential difference in volts (V)}$ $V = \dfrac{W}{Q}$ $W = \text{work done in joules (J)}$ $Q = \text{charge in coulombs (C)}$

The potential difference across a component is 1 volt when you convert 1 joule of energy moving 1 coulomb of charge through the component.

$$1\,V = 1\,JC^{-1}$$

Tip: When a charge flows through a component, it transfers energy to the component (it does work).

Example

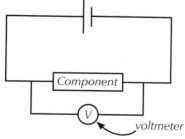

Resistor

6 V

Here you do 6 J of work moving each coulomb of charge through the resistor, so the p.d. across it is 6 V.

$$V = \frac{W}{Q} = \frac{6}{1} = 6\,V$$

The energy gets converted to heat.

Tip: Back to the 'water analogy' again... the p.d. is like the pressure that's forcing water along the pipe.

You can measure the potential difference across an electrical component by using a **voltmeter**. You always need to attach a voltmeter in parallel (see Figure 4).

Component

V

voltmeter

Figure 4: A voltmeter connected in parallel with a component.

Figure 3: A voltmeter connected in parallel with a light bulb.

Practice Questions — Application

Q1 A cell has a charge of 91 C passing through it every 30 seconds. Calculate the current passing through the cell.

Q2 In a circuit, it takes 114 J to move 56.0 C of charge through a filament lamp. Calculate the potential difference across the lamp.

Q3 A resistor has a current of 1.30 A passing through it.

a) Calculate the charge passing through it every five minutes.

b) The potential difference across the resistor is 24.0 V. Calculate the total work done to move the charge through the resistor over five minutes.

Practice Questions — Fact Recall

Q1 Define the term current.

Q2 Are ammeters attached to a component in series or in parallel?

Q3 Define the term potential difference.

3. Resistance

This topic covers everything you need to know about resistance. It's Georg Simon Ohm you've got to blame for these pages — this German physicist developed Ohm's law and got the unit for resistance named after him.

What is resistance?

If you put a potential difference (p.d.) across an electrical component, a current will flow. How much current you get for a particular potential difference depends on the **resistance** of the component.

You can think of a component's resistance as a measure of how difficult it is to get a current to flow through it. Resistance is measured in ohms (Ω). A component has a resistance of 1 Ω if a potential difference of 1 V makes a current of 1 A flow through it. This equation defines resistance:

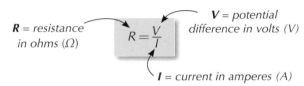

$$R = \frac{V}{I}$$

R = resistance in ohms (Ω)

V = potential difference in volts (V)

I = current in amperes (A)

Examples

The potential difference across a component is 230 V. The current flowing through the component is 12.4 A. Calculate the resistance of the component.

All you need to do to answer this question is to plug the numbers into the equation for resistance, so...

$R = V \div I$

$\quad = 230 \div 12.4$

$\quad = 18.5 \ \Omega$ (to 3 s.f.)

A fixed resistor has a resistance of 4.43 Ω and the potential difference across it is 12.0 V. Calculate the current flowing through the fixed resistor.

You just need to rearrange the resistance equation and plug the numbers in.

$I = V \div R$

$\quad = 12.0 \div 4.43$

$\quad = 2.71 \ \text{A}$ (to 3 s.f.)

Ohmic conductors

A chap called Georg Simon Ohm (see Figure 1) did most of the early work on resistance. He developed a rule to predict how the current would change as the applied potential difference increased for certain types of conductor. The rule is now called **Ohm's law** and the conductors that obey it (mostly metals) are called **ohmic conductors**.

Provided the temperature is constant, the current through an ohmic conductor is directly proportional to the potential difference across it.

Figure 1: Georg Simon Ohm — the physicist who developed Ohm's law.

I = current in amperes (A)

$I \propto V$

V = potential difference in volts (V)

Figure 2 shows what happens if you plot current against potential difference for an ohmic conductor.

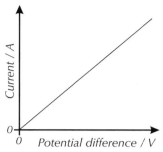

Figure 2: *I-V graph for an ohmic conductor.*

Tip: Some typical ohmic conductors are... aluminium, titanium, iron, copper, silver, gold, platinum. Basically anything that's a metallic conductor.

Tip: The gradient of an *I-V* graph (like the one shown in Figure 2) is $\frac{1}{R}$.

Tip: There's more on why light and temperature affect the resistance of a material on page 53.

As you can see it's a straight-line graph — doubling the p.d. doubles the current. What this means is that the resistance is constant — the gradient is always a fixed value.

Often factors such as light level or temperature will have a significant effect on resistance, so you need to remember that Ohm's law is only true for ohmic conductors at constant temperature.

Ohm's law is a special case — lots of components aren't ohmic conductors and have characteristic current-voltage (*I–V*) graphs of their very own (see pages 53-55).

Practice Questions — Application

Q1 A thermistor has a resistance of 8.62 Ω. Calculate the potential difference across the thermistor when there is a current of 2.10 A flowing through it.

Q2 A fuse has a current of 1.21 A flowing through it. Calculate the resistance of the fuse when the potential difference across it is 13.4 V.

Q3 A student is testing a component in a circuit by varying the current in the circuit and measuring the voltage across the component. As the current increases, the voltage stays the same. What is happening to the resistance of the component?

Q4 A section of copper wire acts as an ohmic conductor. When the current flowing through the wire is 3.20 A, the potential difference across the wire is 15.6 V. Calculate the potential difference across the wire when the current is increased to 4.10 A.

Practice Questions — Fact Recall

Q1 What is meant by resistance?

Q2 What quantity must remain constant for Ohm's law to be true?

Q3 What happens to the resistance of an ohmic conductor if you double the potential difference across it? Give a reason for your answer.

Learning Objectives:

- Recognise and understand *I-V* curves for semiconductor diodes and filament lamps.
- Be able to describe the qualitative effect of temperature on the resistance of metal conductors and thermistors.
- Know that semiconductors can be used as sensors (e.g. temperature sensors).

Specification Reference 3.1.3

4. *I-V* Characteristics

You've had a glimpse of the characteristic I-V graph for an ohmic conductor — now it's time to meet a few more...

What are *I-V* characteristics?

The term '*I-V* characteristic' is just a fancy way of saying an *I-V* graph. The shallower the gradient of a characteristic *I-V* graph, the greater the resistance of the component.

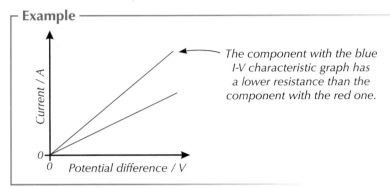

— Example —

The component with the blue I-V characteristic graph has a lower resistance than the component with the red one.

A curve shows that the resistance is changing (see next page).

Finding the *I-V* characteristic of a component

You can use the circuit in Figure 1 to find the characteristic *I-V* graph for a component.

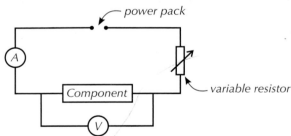

Figure 1: *A circuit that could be used to find the I-V characteristic for a component.*

Exam Tip
I-V curves crop up a lot in exams, so make sure that you really get to grips with the stuff on the next few pages.

Figure 2: *A variable resistor.*

Tip: When you're collecting data, you need to make sure that you keep all the variables (except the resistance) constant to make it a fair test — more on this on page 174.

Tip: Repeating your measurements improves the reliability of the data.

The circuit can be used to collect the data needed to plot an *I-V* graph for the component. Here is the method:

1. Use the variable resistor to decrease (or increase) the resistance of the circuit in small, equal steps. Changing the resistance changes the amount of current flowing through the circuit.

2. For each change in resistance, take a reading from the ammeter to find the current through the component, and a reading from the voltmeter to find the voltage across it. Take a sensible number of measurements — enough so you can plot a graph (see below) and be able to spot a pattern.

3. Reverse the direction of electricity flow by switching the wires connected to the power pack. Then repeat steps 1 and 2, to collect data for negative values of V and I.

Once you've collected all your data, plot it on a pair of axes and voilá — you've got yourself the *I-V* characteristic for the component.

Metallic conductors

Metallic conductors are ohmic (see page 50) at a constant temperature — the current through a metallic conductor is directly proportional to the voltage. So their characteristic graph is a straight line as their resistance doesn't change (see Figure 3).

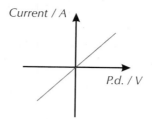

Current / A

P.d. / V

Figure 3: *The I-V graph for a metallic conductor.*

Tip: All *I-V* graphs go through (0, 0) — without a potential difference no current will flow.

Tip: There's more about ohmic conductors on pages 50-51.

Filament lamps

The characteristic *I-V* graph for a filament lamp is a curve that starts steep but gets shallower as the voltage rises (see Figure 5).

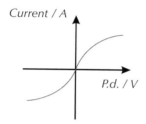

Current / A

P.d. / V

Figure 5: *The characteristic I-V graph for a filament lamp.*

Figure 4: *Filament lamp circuit symbol.*

The filament is a thin coil of metal wire, so you might think it should have the same characteristic graph as a metallic conductor. It doesn't because the current flowing through the lamp increases its temperature, which increases the resistance of the lamp (see below).

When a current flows through a metal conductor (like the filament in a filament lamp), some of the electrical energy is transferred into heat energy and causes the metal to heat up. This extra heat energy causes the particles in the metal to vibrate more. These vibrations make it more difficult for the charge-carrying electrons to get through the resistor — the current can't flow as easily and the resistance increases.

For most resistors there is a limit to the amount of current that can flow through them. More current means an increase in temperature, which means an increase in resistance, which means the current decreases again. This is why the *I-V* graph for the filament lamp levels off at high currents.

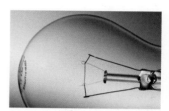

Figure 6: *A filament lamp contains a thin coil of metal wire inside it.*

Tip: This is true for most materials.

Why filament lamps blow

Filament bulbs are more likely to blow (the filament breaks) when you first switch them on...

- When you first switch a bulb on, the filament has a lower resistance because it's cold. This means that the initial current flowing through the filament will be larger than the normal current, so the filament is more likely to burn out at this time.

- The filament also heats up very quickly from cold to its operating temperature when it's switched on. This rapid temperature change could cause the filament wire to blow too.

Semiconductors

Semiconductors are a group of materials that aren't as good at conducting electricity as metals, because they have far fewer charge carriers (i.e. electrons) available. However, if energy is supplied to a semiconductor, e.g. by an increase in temperature, more charge carriers can be released and the resistance decreases. This means that they can make excellent sensors for detecting changes in their environment. You need to know about three semiconductor components — thermistors, diodes and LDRs.

Thermistors

A **thermistor** is a component with a resistance that depends on its temperature. You only need to know about NTC thermistors — NTC stands for 'Negative Temperature Coefficient'. This means that the resistance decreases as the temperature goes up.

To collect the data to produce an *I-V* curve for a thermistor, you need to measure its resistance (or voltage and current) at different temperatures. You can easily control the temperature of a thermistor by using a water bath and a digital thermometer. Then just follow the method shown on page 52.

The characteristic *I-V* graph for an NTC thermistor curves upwards.

Figure 7: Thermistor circuit symbol.

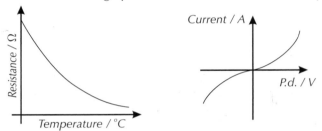

Figure 8: A resistance vs temperature graph (left) and a characteristic I-V graph (right) for an NTC thermistor.

Figure 9: A thermistor.

Increasing the current through the thermistor increases its temperature. The increasing gradient of its characteristic *I-V* graph (Figure 8) tells you that the resistance is decreasing. Warming the thermistor gives more electrons enough energy to escape from their atoms. This means that there are more charge carriers available, so the resistance is lower. This sensitivity to temperature makes them really good temperature sensors.

Diodes

Diodes (including light-emitting diodes (LEDs)) are designed to let current flow in one direction only. You don't need to be able to explain how they work, just what they do. Forward bias is the direction in which the current is allowed to flow. Most diodes require a voltage of about 0.6 V in the forward direction before they will conduct — this is called the threshold voltage. In reverse bias, the resistance of the diode is very high and the current that flows is very tiny.

Figure 10: Diode circuit symbol.

Figure 11: LED circuit symbol.

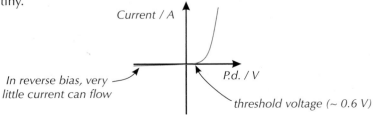

In reverse bias, very little current can flow

threshold voltage (~ 0.6 V)

Figure 12: The characteristic I-V graph for a diode.

LDRs

LDR stands for light-dependent resistor. The greater the intensity of light shining on an LDR, the lower its resistance (see Figure 14). The explanation for this is similar to that for the thermistor. In this case, light rather than heat provides the energy that releases more electrons and lowers the component's resistance.

Figure 13: *LDR circuit symbol.*

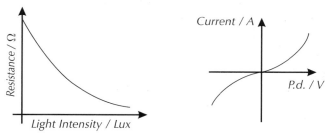

Figure 14: *A resistance vs light intensity graph (left) and a characteristic I-V graph (right) for an LDR.*

Tip: You don't need to know the characteristic *I-V* graph for an LDR, but you do for a thermistor and a diode (see previous page).

Practice Questions — Application

Q1 A student wants to plot the *I-V* graph for an LDR.

a) Draw a diagram of a suitable circuit the student could use to collect the data they need to do this.

b) Describe how the student could use the circuit drawn in part a) to collect their data, giving an example of one variable that needs to be kept constant during this experiment and explaining why.

Q2 The graph below shows the characteristic *I-V* curve for a component.

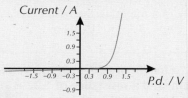

a) What type of component has this *I-V* characteristic graph?

b) Describe how the current and voltage vary in the forward bias direction.

c) Describe the resistance of the component in the reverse direction.

Exam Tip
Questions like Q1 pop up all over the place in physics exams. Make sure you're really comfortable with drawing circuit diagrams and describing experiments.

Practice Questions — Fact Recall

Q1 Sketch the characteristic *I-V* graph of:
a) a metal conductor at a constant temperature,
b) a filament lamp.

Q2 Is a filament lamp an ohmic conductor? How can you tell from its characteristic *I-V* graph?

Q3 Does the resistance of a metal conductor increase or decrease with temperature? Explain your answer.

Q4 Why does a thermistor's resistance decrease with temperature?

Q5 Give one application of a thermistor.

- Know that the resistivity (ρ) of a material is defined as:
$\rho = \dfrac{RA}{L}$
- Know that superconductivity is a property of certain materials which have zero resistivity at and below a critical temperature which depends on the material.
- Know some applications of superconductors (e.g. very strong electromagnets and power cables).

Specification Reference 3.1.3

Tip: Don't confuse resistance and resistivity. <u>Resistance</u> is a property of an <u>object</u> and it depends on the material and dimensions of the object. <u>Resistivity</u> is a property of a <u>material</u>.

Exam Tip
For resistivity calculations, don't forget that you need to have the length in m and the cross-sectional area in m^2 — you'll lose marks if you don't use the correct units.

Exam Tip
Give your answers to the lowest number of significant figures given in the question, or one more. E.g. the data in the first example is given to a mixture of s.f. but 1 s.f. is the lowest — so the answer could be given as 2×10^{-8} (to 1 s.f.) or 2.4×10^{-8} (to 2 s.f.).

5. Resistivity & Superconductors

Now here's a topic you might not have seen before. The resistivity of a material tells you how difficult it is for current to flow through it. This may seem suspiciously similar to the resistance... make sure you get them both clear in your head.

What is Resistivity?

If you think about a nice, simple electrical component, like a length of wire, its resistance depends on:

- **Length (L).** The longer the wire, the more difficult it is to make a current flow through it. The resistance is proportional to the length of the wire.

- **Area (A).** The wider the wire, the easier it will be for the electrons to pass along it.

- **Resistivity (ρ).** This is a measure of how much a particular material resists current flow. It depends on the structure of the material as well as on environmental factors such as temperature and light intensity. It is a property of the material.

The resistivity of a material is defined as the resistance of a 1 m length with a $1~m^2$ cross-sectional area. It is measured in ohm-metres (Ωm).

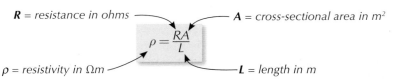

R = resistance in ohms ⟶ ⟵ A = cross-sectional area in m^2

$$\rho = \dfrac{RA}{L}$$

ρ = resistivity in Ωm ⟶ ⟵ L = length in m

The lower the resistivity of a material, the better it is at conducting electricity, e.g. for copper (at 25 °C) $\rho = 1.72 \times 10^{-8}~\Omega m$.

Examples

A piece of metal has a length of 0.5 cm, a square cross-sectional area with a width of 10 cm, and a resistance of $1.22 \times 10^{-8}~\Omega$. Find the resistivity of the metal.

Convert all lengths into metres.

The cross-sectional area (A) of the metal = 0.1 m × 0.1 m = 0.01 m^2

Length = L = 0.005 m

The resistivity of the metal:

$$\rho = \dfrac{RA}{L} = \dfrac{1.22 \times 10^{-8} \times 0.01}{0.005} = 2.4 \times 10^{-8}~\Omega m \text{ (to 2 s.f.)}$$

The heating element in a toaster is a bare nichrome wire with a radius of 0.2 mm and a length of 0.8 m. Find the resistance of the wire. (Resistivity of nichrome = $1.10 \times 10^{-6}~\Omega m$.)

First of all, you need to find the cross-sectional area of the wire (A) in m^2. Assuming the wire to be cylindrical, its cross-sectional area will be the area of the circle, πr^2.

Wire radius = 0.2 mm = 2×10^{-4} m, so $A = \pi(2 \times 10^{-4})^2 = 1.256... \times 10^{-7}~m^2$

Rearrange the resistivity equation to get $R = \dfrac{\rho L}{A}$, and plug in the numbers...

$$R = (1.10 \times 10^{-6} \times 0.8) \div 1.256... \times 10^{-7} = 7.0~\Omega \text{ (to 2 s.f.)}$$

Superconductors

Normally, all materials have some resistivity — even really good conductors like silver and copper. That resistance means that whenever electricity flows through them, they heat up, and some of the electrical energy is wasted as heat.

You can lower the resistivity of many materials like metals by cooling them down. If you cool some materials down to below a 'transition temperature', their resistivity disappears entirely and they become a **superconductor**. Without any resistance, none of the electrical energy is turned into heat, so none of it's wasted.

There's a catch, though. Most 'normal' conductors, e.g. metals, have transition temperatures below 10 kelvin (–263 °C). Getting things that cold is tricky, and really expensive. Solid-state physicists all over the world are trying to develop room-temperature superconductors. So far, they've managed to get some weird metal oxide things to superconduct at about 140 K (–133 °C), which is a much easier temperature to get down to. They've still got a long way to go though.

Uses of Superconductors

Superconducting wires can be used to make:

- Power cables that transmit electricity without any loss of power.
- Really strong electromagnets that have lots of applications, e.g. in medicine and Maglev trains.
- Electronic circuits that work really fast, because there's no resistance to slow the current down.

Figure 1: *A small magnet levitating above a cooled slab of superconducting ceramic.*

Practice Questions — Application

Q1 A piece of silicon has a length of 3.0 mm, a cross-sectional area of 6 mm² and a resistance of 200 Ω. Calculate the resistivity of this piece of silicon.

Q2 A tungsten wire has a length of 14.1 cm and a radius of 2.34 mm. Tungsten has a resistivity of 5.6×10^{-8} Ωm. Calculate the resistance of the tungsten wire.

Q3 A scientist is designing a circuit and needs a copper wire 1.00 cm long with a resistance of 0.000457 Ω. The resistivity of copper is 1.68×10^{-8} Ωm. Calculate the radius his copper wire needs to be.

Tip: The formula for the area of a circle is $A = \pi r^2$. Always assume wires have circular cross-sections, unless you're told otherwise.

Tip: Remember, the unit for resistivity is Ωm — so make sure all lengths are in m and areas in m².

Practice Questions — Fact Recall

Q1 State the three things that the resistance of a material depends on.

Q2 What is resistivity?

Q3 What is a superconductor?

Q4 Give one disadvantage of using superconducting wires.

Q5 Give two uses of superconducting wires.

6. Power and Electrical Energy

Learning Objectives:

- Be able to find the power of a component using: $P = VI$, $P = I^2R$ or $P = \dfrac{V^2}{R}$.
- Know how to find the energy transferred in a circuit: $E = VIt$.
- Understand the high current requirement for a starter motor in a motor car.

Specification Reference 3.1.3

You should remember all about energy and power from GCSE Physics. Well, here they are again because you need to know about them for AS-Level too. Remember — the faster a device transfers energy, the more powerful it is.

Power

Power (P) is defined as the rate of transfer of energy. It's measured in watts (W), where 1 watt is equivalent to 1 joule per second.

P = power in watts (W) $P = \dfrac{E}{t}$ **E** = energy in joules (J)

t = time in seconds (s)

There's a really simple formula for power in electrical circuits:

P = power in watts (W) $P = VI$ **I** = current in amperes (A)

V = potential difference in volts (V)

This makes sense, since:

- Potential difference (V) is defined as the energy transferred per coulomb.
- Current (I) is defined as the number of coulombs transferred per second.
- So p.d. × current is energy transferred per second, i.e. power.

Tip: If your mind needs refreshing about current and potential difference, flick back to page 48.

Equations for calculating power

As well as the two equations above, you can derive two more equations for calculating power in electrical circuits...

You know from the definition of resistance that:

Tip: There's more about resistance on page 50.

V = potential difference in volts (V) $V = IR$ **I** = current in amperes (A)

R = resistance in ohms (Ω)

You can rearrange the equation for power in electrical circuits to make **I** the subject:

$$I = \frac{P}{V}$$

And then substitute this into the definition of resistance to give:

$$P = \frac{V^2}{R}$$

Figure 1: *The label on an electrical appliance tells you its power rating — the rate at which it transfers energy.*

By rearranging the equation for power in electrical circuits to make **V** the subject...

$$V = \frac{P}{I}$$

...and then substituting into the definition of resistance you get:

$$P = I^2R$$

Exam Tip
The good news is you'll be given all of the boxed equations in the exam, so you don't have to memorise them — hurrah.

Obviously, which equation you should use depends on what quantities you know.

Phew... that's quite a few equations you've just met. And as if they're not exciting enough, here are some examples to get your teeth into...

Examples

A 24 W car headlamp is connected to a 12 V car battery. Assume the wires connecting the lamp to the battery have negligible resistance.

a) **How much energy will the lamp convert into light and heat energy in 2 hours?**

b) **Find the total resistance of the lamp.**

a) Number of seconds in 2 hours = $120 \times 60 = 7200$ s
Rearrange the equation $P = E \div t$:
$E = P \times t = 24 \times 7200 = 172\,800$ J $= 170$ kJ (to 2 s.f.)

b) Rearrange the equation $P = \dfrac{V^2}{R}$, $R = \dfrac{V^2}{P} = \dfrac{12^2}{24} = \dfrac{144}{24} = 6$ Ω

A machine converts 750 J of electrical energy into heat every second.

a) **What is the power rating of the machine?**

b) **All of the machine's components are connected in series, with a total resistance of 30 Ω. What current flows through the machine's wires?**

a) Power $= E \div t = 750 \div 1 = 750$ W

b) Rearrange the equation $P = I^2 R$, $I = \sqrt{\dfrac{P}{R}} = \sqrt{\dfrac{750}{30}} = \sqrt{25} = 5$ A

> **Exam Tip**
> Always double-check that you've rearranged equations correctly in the exam — it'd be sad to lose marks for making such an easy mistake.

Energy

Sometimes it's the total energy transferred that you're interested in. In this case, you just substitute $P = E \div t$ into the power equations on the previous page and tah dah — you get these equations for energy:

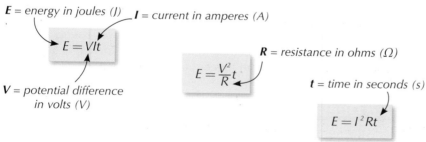

E = energy in joules (J) I = current in amperes (A)

$E = VIt$

V = potential difference in volts (V)

$E = \dfrac{V^2}{R}t$

R = resistance in ohms (Ω)

t = time in seconds (s)

$E = I^2 Rt$

Example

It takes 4.5 minutes for a kettle to boil the water inside it. A current of 4 A flows through the kettle's heating element once it is connected to the mains (230 V).

a) **What is the power rating of the kettle?**

b) **How much energy does the kettle's heating element transfer to the water in the time it takes to boil?**

a) Use $P = V \times I = 230 \times 4 = 920$ W

b) Time the kettle takes to boil in seconds $= 4.5 \times 60 = 270$ s.
Use the equation $E = P \times t$ and your answer to part a):
$E = 920 \times 270 = 248\,400$ J $= 250$ kJ (to 2 s.f.)

> **Exam Tip**
> When you're doing these questions, make sure the time you use is always in seconds — otherwise you could lose precious marks.

Figure 2: *The starter motor from a car.*

Starter motors in cars

A modern car has a starter motor which provides the energy needed to start the engine. The power produced by the starter motor needs to be very high, as it needs to provide a lot of energy in a very short time to "turn over" the engine (rotate the engine to set it off working). However, the potential difference across the starter motor, provided by the battery, is usually very small (~12 V). As $P = VI$, to provide a large power you need the current flowing through the motor to be very high.

Example

A starter motor requires a power of 1.3 kW to start the engine. The potential difference across the battery is 12 V. Calculate the current required to start the engine.

$$I = \frac{P}{V} = \frac{1300}{12} = 108 \text{ A (to 3 s.f.)}$$

The current flowing through the starter motor will need to be at least this high to start the engine.

Practice Questions — Application

Q1 A battery provides 3400 J of energy per second. What is the power of the battery?

Q2 A car starter motor requires 12.5 kJ of energy to flow through it in 2.00 seconds to start the engine.

  a) Calculate the power necessary to start the engine.

  b) The car battery supplies 8.00 V to the starter motor. Calculate the current required to start the engine.

Q3 A motor has a power rating of 5.2 kW. The potential difference across the motor is 230 V. Calculate the current flowing through the motor.

Q4 A lamp has a potential difference of 230 V across it and a current of 1.2 A flowing through it. Calculate the energy transferred to the lamp in 45 seconds.

Q5 A circuit in an electric car converts 1250 J of electrical energy into heat every second. The resistance in that circuit of the car is 54.2 Ω. Calculate the current through that circuit.

Practice Questions — Fact Recall

Q1 Define the term power.

Q2 Write down three equations you could use to calculate electrical power.

Q3 Why does a starter motor in a car need a high current?

7. E.m.f. and Internal Resistance

There's resistance in almost all wires and components — including inside batteries and cells. This makes some resistance calculations a little more tricky. But don't worry — the next few pages are here to help you conquer those questions.

What is internal resistance?

Resistance comes from electrons colliding with atoms and losing energy. In a battery, chemical energy is used to make electrons move. As they move, they collide with atoms inside the battery — so batteries must have resistance. This is called **internal resistance**. Internal resistance is what makes batteries and cells warm up when they're used.

Load resistance is the total resistance of all the components in the external circuit. You might see it called 'external resistance'.

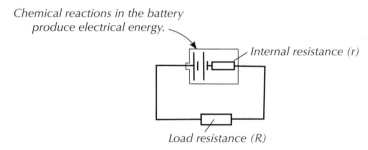

Chemical reactions in the battery produce electrical energy.

Internal resistance (r)

Load resistance (R)

Figure 1: *A circuit diagram showing the internal and external resistances in a circuit.*

What is e.m.f.?

The amount of electrical energy the battery produces and transfers to each coulomb of charge is called its **electromotive force** or **e.m.f.** (ε). Be careful — e.m.f. isn't actually a force. It's measured in volts.

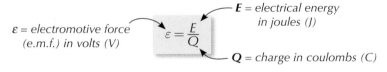

ε = electromotive force (e.m.f.) in volts (V)

$$\varepsilon = \frac{E}{Q}$$

E = electrical energy in joules (J)

Q = charge in coulombs (C)

The potential difference (p.d.) across the load resistance (R) is the energy transferred when one coulomb of charge flows through the load resistance. This potential difference is called the terminal p.d. (V). If there was no internal resistance, the terminal p.d. would be the same as the e.m.f. However, in real power supplies, there's always some energy lost overcoming the internal resistance. The energy wasted per coulomb overcoming the internal resistance is called the **lost volts** (v).

Conservation of energy tells us for any electrical circuit:

energy per coulomb supplied by the source	=	**energy per coulomb used in load resistance**	+	**energy per coulomb wasted in internal resistance**

Learning Objectives:

- Know what is meant by the internal resistance of a power source, *r*.
- Know what is meant by the electromotive force (e.m.f.), ε.
- Be able to use: $\varepsilon = \frac{E}{Q}$ and $\varepsilon = I(R + r)$
- Understand applications of e.m.f. and internal resistance, e.g. the low internal resistance of a car battery.

Specification Reference 3.1.3

Tip: In circuit diagrams, internal resistance is show as a tiny resistor inside the battery.

Tip: In general, you can assume the connecting wires in a circuit have no resistance — and it's no different for internal resistance problems. But in practice, they do have a small resistance.

Tip: Remember, V = IR (see page 50).

Tip: There's more on the conservation of energy on pages 114-117.

Calculations using e.m.f. & internal resistance

Examiners can ask you to do calculations with e.m.f. and internal resistance in lots of different ways. You've got to be ready for whatever they throw at you. Here are some of the equations you might need and how to derive them...

You'll get this equation for e.m.f. in a formulae and data booklet in the exam:

ε = electromotive force (e.m.f.) in volts (V)

R = load resistance in ohms (Ω)

$$\varepsilon = I(R + r)$$

I = current in amperes (A)

r = internal resistance in ohms (Ω)

Tip: $V = IR$ is just the definition of resistance, $R = \dfrac{V}{I}$, rearranged (see page 50).

Expanding the brackets of this equation gives: $\varepsilon = IR + Ir$

Then using the equation $V = IR$, you can substitute V and v for IR and Ir...

V = terminal p.d. in volts (V)

$$\varepsilon = V + v$$

v = lost volts in volts (V)

Exam Tip
You won't be given these three equations in the exam, so you're going to have to learn how to derive them from $R = \dfrac{V}{I}$ and $\varepsilon = I(R + r)$, which are given to you.

Rearranging the equation gives the equation for terminal p.d...

$$V = \varepsilon - v$$

And re-substituting v for Ir gives...

$$V = \varepsilon - Ir$$

These are all basically the same equation, just written differently. Which equation you should use depends on what information you've got, and what you need to calculate.

Example

A battery has an e.m.f. of 1.50 V and an internal resistance of 0.50 Ω. Calculate the terminal p.d. when the current flowing through the battery is 0.06 A.

The values for the e.m.f., the internal resistance and the current have been given in the question — so you can use the equation $V = \varepsilon - Ir$ to calculate the terminal p.d.

$V = \varepsilon - Ir = 1.50 - (0.06 \times 0.50) = 1.47$ V

Power Supplies

A car battery has to deliver a really high current to start the car (see page 60). Since the voltage supplied by the battery is constant and relatively low (and $V = IR$), the battery needs to have a low internal resistance to supply a large current. The cells used to power a torch or a personal stereo are the same — they need a low internal resistance. Generally, batteries have an internal resistance of less than 1 Ω.

As mentioned on the previous page, some power (or energy) is lost as heat when overcoming the internal resistance in a power supply. We can calculate the energy dissipated (lost) due to the internal resistance of a power supply using $P = I^2R$ (see page 58).

Figure 2: A car battery has a very low internal resistance.

Example

A cell has an internal resistance of 0.35 Ω and current flowing through it of 0.60 A. Calculate the energy dissipated due to the internal resistance of the cell every second.

$P = I^2R = (0.60)^2 \times 0.35 = 0.13$ W (to 2 s.f.)

So the energy dissipated every second is 0.13 J (to 2 s.f.)

Exam Tip
You'll be given $P = I^2R$ in your exam formulae and data booklet.

Since internal resistance causes energy loss, you'd think all power supplies should have a low internal resistance. High voltage power supplies are the exception — they have very high internal resistances. This means that if they're accidentally short-circuited only a very small current can flow (since $I = V \div R$), making them much safer. Uses of high voltage power supplies include cathode ray tubes, which are used in oscilloscopes (see page 73) and old-style televisions.

Measuring internal resistance and e.m.f.

You can measure the internal resistance and e.m.f. of a cell or battery using the circuit in Figure 4.

Figure 3: *The cathode ray tube in a TV has a high voltage power supply and a high internal resistance.*

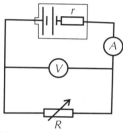

Figure 4: *The circuit needed to work out the internal resistance of a power source.*

Vary the value of R and take readings in the same way as in the experiment to find the resistance of a component (see page 52). Once you have data for the current and potential difference of a power supply for different resistances, plot a graph of V against I — the graph you get will be a straight-line graph (see Figure 5).

You can rearrange the equation $V = \varepsilon - Ir$ to get $V = -rI + \varepsilon$. The equation of a straight line is $y = mx + c$, where m = gradient and c = y-intercept. Since ε and r are constants, $V = -rI + \varepsilon$ is just the equation of a straight line (in the form $y = mx + c$). You can just read ε and r from the graph — the intercept on the vertical axis is ε and the gradient is $-r$. As the graph is a straight line, you can find the gradient of the graph by dividing the change in y (p.d.) by the change in x (current).

Tip: Remember that ammeters are always connected in series and voltmeters are always connected in parallel (see pages 48-49).

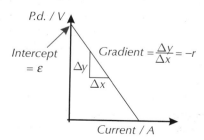

Figure 5: *Using a V-I graph to calculate internal resistance and e.m.f.*

Tip: The e.m.f. of a power source could also be measured by connecting a high-resistance voltmeter across its terminals. Note that a small current flows through the voltmeter, so there must be some lost volts — this means you measure a value very slightly less than the e.m.f.

Tip: For all these questions assume that the resistance due to the wires in the circuit is negligible.

Q1 A power source has an e.m.f. of 2.50 V. The terminal potential difference is 2.24 V. Calculate the lost volts (v) for this power source.

Q2 A battery has a terminal voltage of 4.68 V and an internal resistance of 0.89 Ω when 0.63 A of current is flowing through it. Calculate the e.m.f. of the battery.

Q3 The power source in a circuit has an e.m.f. of 15.0 V. The internal resistance of the power source is 8.28×10^{-3} Ω. Calculate the load resistance of the circuit when the current flowing through the power source is 26.1 A.

Q4 A power source has a current of 1.2 A flowing through it and an internal resistance of 0.50 Ω. Calculate the energy dissipated in the internal resistance of the power source each second.

Q5 A student varies the load resistance in a circuit to produce the V-I graph shown below.

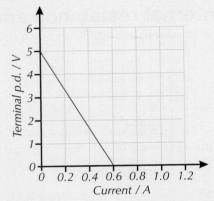

a) Use the graph to find the e.m.f. (ε) of the power supply.

b) Use the graph to find the internal resistance of the power supply.

c) Describe how the graph would be different if the student swapped the power supply for one with the same e.m.f. but half the internal resistance.

Exam Tip
In the exam, the examiners could write 'find the terminal voltage of a battery' or 'find the voltage across the terminals of a battery'. They mean exactly the same thing.

Tip: Remember, voltage and potential difference (p.d.) are the same thing.

Practice Questions — Fact Recall

Q1 Explain why batteries have an internal resistance.

Q2 What is the load resistance in a circuit?

Q3 What units is electromotive force measured in?

Q4 Explain what lost volts are.

Q5 Why are car batteries made so they have a low internal resistance?

Q6 What do the gradient and vertical intercept on a V-I graph for a power supply show?

8. Conservation of Energy and Charge in Circuits

Learning Objectives:

- Understand that energy and charge are conserved in circuits.

- Know the relationships between currents, voltages and resistances in series and parallel circuits, including cells in series and identical cells in parallel.

- Be able to use $R = R_1 + R_2 + R_3 + \ldots$ for resistors in series.

- Be able to use $\frac{1}{R} = \frac{1}{R_1} + \frac{1}{R_2} + \frac{1}{R_3} + \ldots$ for resistors in parallel.

Specification Reference 3.1.3

Conservation of energy is another topic you'll probably have met at GCSE. Questions on this stuff are almost guaranteed to be in the exam so I've put in a lot of time and effort to make sure this topic's as easy to grasp as possible...

Conservation of charge

As charge flows through a circuit, it doesn't get used up or lost. This means that whatever charge flows into a junction will flow out again. Since current is rate of flow of charge, it follows that whatever current flows into a junction is the same as the current flowing out of it.

Example

If a charge of 6 C flows into a junction...

$Q_1 = 6\ C \Rightarrow I_1 = 6\ A$

$Q_2 = 2\ C \Rightarrow I_2 = 2\ A$

$Q_3 = 4\ C \Rightarrow I_3 = 4\ A$

$I_1 = I_2 + I_3$

... a charge of 6 C must flow out of it as well.

Gustav Kirchhoff was a German scientist who developed a set of laws for the current and potential difference of different components in a circuit. Conservation of current is known as his first law.

Kirchhoff's first law

> The total current entering a junction = the total current leaving it.

Conservation of energy

Energy is conserved. You already know that. In electrical circuits, energy is transferred round the circuit. Energy transferred to a charge is e.m.f. (see page 61), and energy transferred from a charge is potential difference (p.d.). In a closed loop, these two quantities must be equal if energy is conserved (which it is).

Kirchhoff's second law:

> The total e.m.f. around a series circuit = the sum of the p.d.s across each component.

This is Kirchhoff's second law in symbols:

$$\varepsilon = \Sigma IR$$

— This symbol means 'sum of'.

Figure 1: *Gustav Kirchhoff, the German scientist that formulated Kirchhoff's laws.*

Tip: Remember... current is rate of flow of charge. If 6 C flows into a junction in 1 second, that's a current of 6 A.

Exam Tip
You won't get asked directly about Kirchhoff's laws in the exam, but you do need to know how to <u>use</u> them.

Applying Kirchhoff's Laws

A typical exam question will give you a circuit with bits of information missing, leaving you to fill in the gaps. Not the most fun... but on the plus side you get to ignore any internal resistance stuff (unless the question tells you otherwise)... hurrah. You need to remember the following rules:

Series circuits

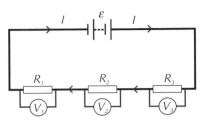

Figure 2: *Fairy lights are the classic example of a series circuit.*

- There will be the same current at all points of the circuit (since there are no junctions).
- The e.m.f. is split between the components (by Kirchhoff's 2nd law), so:

$$\varepsilon = V_1 + V_2 + V_3$$

- The voltage splits proportionally to the resistance, as $V = IR$.

Tip: Remember that even in series circuits, voltmeters are placed in parallel with components.

Example
If you had a 1 Ω resistor and a 3 Ω resistor, you'd get 1/4 of the p.d. across the 1 Ω resistor and 3/4 across the 3 Ω.

- $V = IR$, so if I is constant:

$$IR_{total} = IR_1 + IR_2 + IR_3$$

- Cancelling the Is gives:

$$R_{total} = R_1 + R_2 + R_3$$

Parallel circuits

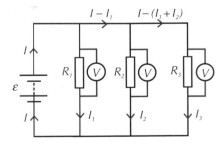

- The current is split at each junction, so:

$$I = I_1 + I_2 + I_3$$

Tip: Don't worry if you don't quite understand what's going on here... it'll all become clear when you have a look at the example on the next page.

- There is the same p.d. across all components — there are three separate loops and within each loop the e.m.f. equals the sum of the individual p.d.s. So:

$$\frac{V}{R_{total}} = \frac{V}{R_1} + \frac{V}{R_2} + \frac{V}{R_3}$$

- Cancelling the Vs gives:

$$\frac{1}{R_{total}} = \frac{1}{R_1} + \frac{1}{R_2} + \frac{1}{R_3}$$

A battery of e.m.f. 16 V and negligible internal resistance is connected in a circuit as shown:

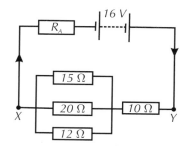

Exam Tip
If an exam question tells you that something's got a negligible internal resistance, you can completely ignore it in your calculations.

a)   Show that the group of resistors between X and Y could be replaced by a single resistor of resistance 15 Ω.

You can find the combined resistance of the 15 Ω, 20 Ω and 12 Ω resistors using:

$1/R = 1/R_1 + 1/R_2 + 1/R_3 = 1/15 + 1/20 + 1/12 = 1/5 \Rightarrow R = 5\ \Omega$

So overall resistance between X and Y can be found by:

$R = R_1 + R_2 = 5 + 10 = 15\ \Omega$

b)   If $R_A = 20\ \Omega$:

   i)   calculate the potential difference (p.d.) across R_A.

Careful — there are a few steps here. You need the p.d. across R_A, but you don't know the current through it. So start there:

Total resistance in circuit = 20 + 15 = 35 Ω, so the current through R_A can be found using $I = V_{total} \div R_{total} = \frac{16}{35}$ A

then you can use $V = IR_A$ to find the p.d. across R_A:

$V = \frac{16}{35} \times 20 = 9.1$ V (to 2 s.f.)

Exam Tip
If you get a question like this in the exam and you don't know where to start, write down all the information you do know and work out anything you can work out. You might spot how to do the question whilst you're playing around with the numbers.

   ii)   calculate the current in the 15 Ω resistor.

You know the current flowing into the group of three resistors and out of it, but not through the individual branches. But you know that their combined resistance is 5 Ω (from part a)) so you can work out the p.d. across the group:

$V = IR = \frac{16}{35} \times 5 = \frac{16}{7}$ V

The p.d. across the whole group is the same as the p.d. across each individual resistor, so you can use this to find the current through the 15 Ω resistor:

$I = V \div R = \frac{16}{7} \div 15 = 0.15$ A (to 2 s.f.)

Tip: Keeping numbers as fractions in your working can help avoid rounding errors creeping into your answers.

Cells in series and parallel

For cells in series in a circuit, you can calculate the total e.m.f. of their combination by adding their individual e.m.f.s. This makes sense if you think about it, because each charge goes through each of the cells and so gains e.m.f. (electrical energy) from each one.

$$\varepsilon_{total} = \varepsilon_1 + \varepsilon_2 + \varepsilon_3...$$

--- Example ---

Three cells of negligible internal resistance are connected in series, as shown below. Cells A, B and C have an e.m.f. of 1.5 V, 1 V and 3 V respectively. Find the total e.m.f. of the combination of cells.

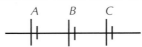

Total e.m.f. $= \varepsilon_A + \varepsilon_B + \varepsilon_C = 1.5\text{ V} + 1\text{ V} + 3\text{ V} = 5.5\text{ V}$

For identical cells in parallel in a circuit, the total e.m.f. of the combination of cells is the same size as the e.m.f. of each of the individual cells. This is because the amount of charge flowing in the circuit doesn't increase by adding cells in parallel, but the number of paths the charges can take does. The current will split equally between identical cells. The charge only gains e.m.f. from the cells it travels through — so the overall e.m.f. in the circuit doesn't increase.

--- Example ---

Three identical cells, A, B and C, are connected as shown to the right. Each cell has an e.m.f. of 2 V and negligible internal resistance. Find the total e.m.f. of the combination of cells.

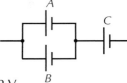

Total e.m.f. of the combination A and $B = \varepsilon_A = \varepsilon_B = 2\text{ V}$

So, total e.m.f. of cells = (total e.m.f. of A and B combined) + ε_C
$$= 2\text{ V} + 2\text{ V} = 4\text{ V}$$

In real life, power sources will usually have an internal resistance.

--- Example ---

Three identical cells with an e.m.f. of 2.0 V and an internal resistance of 0.20 Ω are connected in parallel in the circuit shown to the right. A current of 0.90 A is flowing through the circuit. Calculate the total p.d. across the cells.

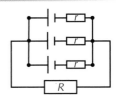

First calculate the lost volts, v, for 1 cell using $v = Ir$.

Since the current flowing through the circuit is split equally between each of the three cells, the current through one cell is $\frac{I}{3}$. So for 1 cell:

$$v = \frac{I}{3} \times r = \frac{0.90}{3} \times 0.20 = 0.30 \times 0.20 = 0.06\text{ V}$$

Then find the terminal p.d. across 1 cell using the equation:

$$V = \varepsilon - Ir = 2 - 0.06 = 1.94 = 1.9\text{ V} \text{ (to 2 s.f.)}$$

So the total p.d. across A, B and C combined $= V_A = V_B = V_C = 1.9\text{ V}$

Figure 3: *The total e.m.f. of two identical batteries in parallel will follow the same rule as for cells — see right.*

Tip: In this example, cell C has twice the amount of charge passing through it per second, compared to A or B. So cell C will transfer twice the amount of energy per second to charge passing through it than either A or B. This means cell C will go flat before A and B.

Tip: For a recap on lost volts and e.m.f., see pages 61-63.

Practice Questions — Application

Q1 A battery of negligible resistance is connected in a circuit as shown to the right.

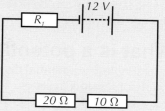

   a) The total resistance of the circuit is 40 Ω. What is the resistance of the resistor marked R_1?

   b) The current flowing through the battery is 0.4 A. What is the current flowing through the 10 Ω resistor?

Q2 The circuit below contains three identical cells, A, B and C. Each cell has an e.m.f. of 3 V and negligible internal resistance.

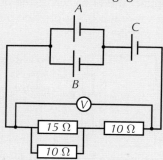

   a) Calculate the total e.m.f. of the cells.

   b) What is the total p.d. across the resistors? Explain your answer.

   c) Calculate the total resistance of the circuit.

Q3 Will the current through 3 identical cells connected in parallel be bigger or smaller than the current through the same cells connected in series in the same circuit?

Q4 The battery in the circuit below has a negligible internal resistance. The total resistance in the circuit is 10 Ω.

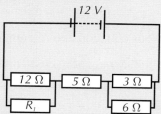

   a) Calculate the resistance of R_1.

   b) Calculate the potential difference across the 5 Ω resistor.

   c) Calculate the current through the 6 Ω resistor.

> **Tip:** Remember to calculate the resistance of resistors in parallel differently to the way you calculate resistors in series.

Practice Questions — Fact Recall

Q1 State Kirchhoff's first law.

Q2 State Kirchhoff's second law.

Q3 How are the resistors R_1 and R_2 connected if their total resistance is equal to $R_1 + R_2$?

Q4 Which type of circuit is $\frac{1}{R_{total}} = \frac{1}{R_1} + \frac{1}{R_2} + \frac{1}{R_3}$ true for?

Learning Objectives:

- Understand how a potential divider can be used to supply variable p.d.

- Understand how you can use a thermistor or LDR in a potential divider to create a sensor.

- Know that potential dividers have many applications, e.g. as audio 'volume' controls.

Specification Reference 3.1.3

9. The Potential Divider

Potential dividers can be used to supply a varying potential difference. If only that was all you needed to know about them, but I'm afraid there's a bit more...

What is a potential divider?

At its simplest, a **potential divider** is a circuit with a voltage source and a couple of resistors in series. The potential difference across the voltage source (e.g. a battery) is divided across the resistors in the ratio of the resistances (see page 66).

You can use potential dividers to supply a potential difference, V_{out}, between zero and the potential difference across the power supply. This can be useful, e.g. if you need a varying p.d. supply (see page 71) or one that is at a lower p.d. than the power supply.

Tip: V_{out} is equal to the voltage across R_2.

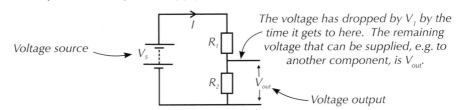

Voltage source — V_s

R_1

The voltage has dropped by V_1 by the time it gets to here. The remaining voltage that can be supplied, e.g. to another component, is V_{out}.

R_2 — V_{out}

Voltage output

Figure 1: *A simple potential divider made up of two fixed resistors.*

Tip: R_1 is whichever resistor the current travels through first — see Figure 1.

You can find an equation relating V_s and V_{out} using $V = IR$ (see page 50). The total resistance in the external circuit is $R = R_1 + R_2$, as the resistors are in series (see page 66). The total voltage across the resistors is V_s and the current through them is I, so $V_s = I(R_1 + R_2)$. Which when rearranged gives:

$$I = \frac{V_s}{R_1 + R_2}$$

You can also write I in terms of V_{out}, as $V_{out} = V_2$, and the resistance across R_2.

$$V_{out} = IR_2 \Rightarrow I = \frac{V_{out}}{R_2}$$

Substituting I into the previous equation and rearranging gives:

$$V_{out} = \frac{R_2}{R_1 + R_2} V_s$$

Tip: Make sure when you're using this equation that you plug in R_2 as the resistor that you're measuring the voltage over — otherwise you'll get completely the wrong answer.

Example

For the circuit in Figure 1, $V_s = 9$ V and $V_{out} = 6$ V. Suggest one set of possible values for R_1 and R_2.

First find what fraction V_{out} is of V_s:

$$\frac{V_{out}}{V_s} = \frac{6}{9} = \frac{2}{3} \Rightarrow V_{out} = \frac{2}{3}V_s$$

$$V_{out} = \frac{R_2}{R_1 + R_2} V_s, \text{ so } \frac{R_2}{R_1 + R_2} = \frac{2}{3}$$

This multiplies out to give $3R_2 = 2R_1 + 2R_2 \Rightarrow R_2 = 2R_1$

So you could have, say, $R_2 = 200\ \Omega$ and $R_1 = 100\ \Omega$.

In Figure 1, having R_1 as a variable resistor would allow you to vary V_{out}. This has many useful applications — see the next page.

Light and Temperature Sensors

As you may remember from page 55, a light-dependent resistor (LDR) has a very high resistance in the dark, but a lower resistance in the light. An NTC thermistor has a high resistance at low temperatures, but a much lower resistance at high temperatures (it varies in the opposite way to a normal resistor, only much more so). Either of these can be used as one of the resistors in a potential divider, giving an output voltage that varies with the light level or temperature.

Example

The diagram shows a sensor used to detect light levels.

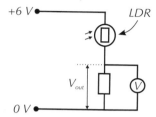

When light shines on the LDR its resistance decreases, so V_{out} increases.

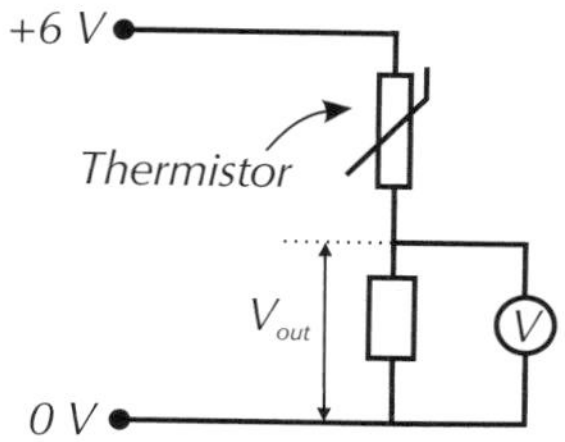

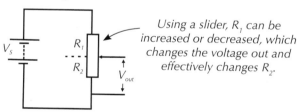

Figure 2: A sensor used to detect temperature changes — as temperature increases, V_{out} increases.

You can include LDRs and thermistors in circuits that control switches, e.g. to turn on a light or a heating system.

Potentiometers

A potentiometer has a variable resistor replacing R_1 and R_2 of the potential divider (see Figure 3), but it uses the same idea (it's even sometimes called a potential divider just to confuse things).

Using a slider, R_1 can be increased or decreased, which changes the voltage out and effectively changes R_2.

Figure 3: A potentiometer.

Tip: If you continually increase R_1, R_2 will eventually reach zero. When this happens, V_{out} will effectively be zero too. Decreasing R_1 until it is zero would mean $V_{out} = V_s$. This can be shown using the formula:
$$V_{out} = \frac{R_2}{R_1 + R_2} V_s.$$

You move a slider or turn a knob to adjust the relative sizes of R_1 and R_2. That way you can vary V_{out} from 0 V up to the source voltage. This is dead handy when you want to be able to change a voltage continuously, like in the volume control of a stereo...

Example

Here, V_s is replaced by the input signal (e.g. from a CD player) and V_{out} is the output to the amplifier and loudspeaker.

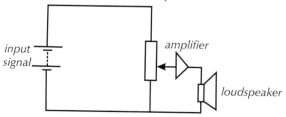

Figure 4: A rotary potentiometer.

Tip: Another common use of this type of potential divider is in old-style dimmer switches.

Q1 The circuit below shows a simple potential divider.

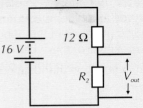

a) What would the output voltage be if $R_2 = 3.0\ \Omega$?

b) What would the resistance of R_2 have to be for V_{out} to be 5 V?

Q2 The potential divider below has the values of the resistors missed off.

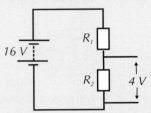

Give one set of possible values for resistors R_1 and R_2.

Q3 The circuit diagram below shows part of a temperature sensor for a greenhouse.

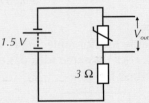

Tip: Watch out for the direction the current is flowing in. In Q3, the current will flow anticlockwise round the circuit — it's all to do with the direction of the cells.

When the greenhouse gets too hot this temperature sensor sets off an alarm.

a) The resistance of the thermistor when the alarm first starts to go off is 1.5 Ω. Calculate the voltage output of the circuit at this point.

b) The gardener starts to grow tropical plants in his greenhouse. He wants the alarm to go off when the voltage drops to 0.3 V. Calculate the new resistance of the thermistor when the alarm first starts to go off.

Q1 What is a potential divider?

Q2 Write down the equation you would use to work out the voltage output of a potential divider.

Q3 How can you make a light sensor using a potential divider?

Q4 What is a potentiometer?

Q5 Give two applications of a potentiometer.

10. Alternating Current

Here's a nice simple topic to end the section, thank goodness. You'll probably remember this stuff from GCSE, but here it is again in a bit more detail.

Oscilloscopes

An **alternating current** or voltage is one that changes with time. The voltage goes up and down in a regular pattern — some of the time it's positive and some of the time it's negative.

An oscilloscope is basically just a voltmeter. The trace you see is made by an electron beam moving across a screen. The time base controls how fast the beam is moved across the screen. You can set this using a dial on the front of the oscilloscope.

The vertical height of the trace at any point shows the input voltage at that point. The oscilloscope screen has a grid on it — you can select how many volts per division you want the y-axis scale to represent using the Y-input control dial, e.g. 5 V per division. On some oscilloscopes, the height of each square on the grid is 1 cm, so the scale may be set in terms of V per cm (Vcm⁻¹).

Learning Objectives:

- Know that an oscilloscope can be used as a d.c. and a.c. voltmeter, to measure time intervals and frequencies, and to display a.c. waveforms.

- Know that for sinusoidal waveforms:

  $I_{rms} = \dfrac{I_0}{\sqrt{2}}$ and

  $V_{rms} = \dfrac{V_0}{\sqrt{2}}$.

- Be able to calculate the mains electricity peak voltage and peak-to-peak voltage values.

  Specification Reference 3.1.3

--- Example ---

Oscilloscope settings:
Y-gain = 2 V per division,
time base = 1 ms per division

Oscilloscope settings:
Y-gain = 2 V per division,
time base turned off

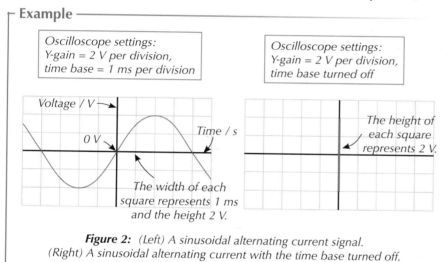

Voltage / V
0 V
Time / s
The height of each square represents 2 V.
The width of each square represents 1 ms and the height 2 V.

Figure 2: *(Left) A sinusoidal alternating current signal. (Right) A sinusoidal alternating current with the time base turned off.*

An alternating current (a.c.) source gives a regularly repeating waveform (see Figure 2). A direct current (d.c.) source is always at the same voltage, so you get a horizontal line (see Figure 3). You'd get a dot on the voltage axis (at the input voltage) if the time base was turned off (see Figure 3).

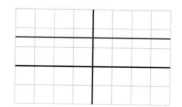

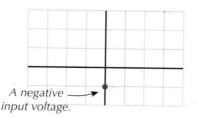

A negative input voltage.

Figure 3: *(Left) A d.c. supply shown on an oscilloscope. (Right) A different d.c. supply shown on an oscilloscope with the time base turned off.*

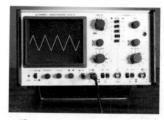

Figure 1: *An oscilloscope showing a wave form. The control dials can be used to change how the wave is displayed.*

Tip: If something is sinusoidal it means it varies like a sine curve. A sine curve is a smooth, repetitive wave, like the one shown on the left in Figure 2.

Tip: There's more coming up on how to read an oscilloscope on the next page.

Analysing oscilloscopes

Tip: The peak voltage is useful to know, though it's often easier to measure the peak-to-peak voltage and halve it.

There are three basic pieces of information you can get from an oscillator trace — the time period, T, the peak voltage, V_0, and the peak-to-peak voltage (see Figure 4).

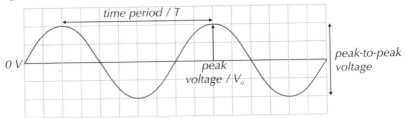

Figure 4: *A diagram showing the three basic pieces of information you can get from an oscillator trace.*

Measuring the distance between successive peaks along the time axis (the horizontal axis) gives you the time period (as long as you know the time base setting). You can use this to calculate the frequency:

Tip: You can use this formula to calculate the frequency of any type of wave (see page 140).

$$\text{frequency} = \frac{1}{\text{time period}}$$

$$f = \frac{1}{T}$$

Example

The diagram below shows the output on an oscilloscope of an alternating current.

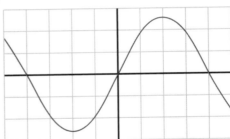

The Y-gain dial is set to 0.5 V per division and the time base is set to 1 s per division.

Calculate: a) the peak voltage of the wave,

b) the frequency of the wave.

a) The peak voltage is the height from the 0 V line to the top of the peak. The peak is 2.5 squares high.
So the peak voltage = 2.5 × 0.5 = 1.25 V

b) First you have to work out the time period of the wave.
The time base is set to 1 s, so every square on the grid represents 1 s. The time period of the wave is 8 squares = 8 seconds.

$$\text{frequency} = \frac{1}{\text{time period}} = \frac{1}{8} = 0.125\,\text{Hz}$$

Figure 5 region:

Figure 5: *A sine wave shown on an oscilloscope.*

Tip: A sine wave produces a sine curve on an oscilloscope (see previous page for more on sine curves).

Describing an alternating current

An a.c. supply with a peak voltage of 2 V will be below 2 V most of the time. That means it won't have as high a power output as a 2 V d.c. supply. To compare them properly, you need to average the a.c. voltage somehow. A normal average won't work, because the positive and negative bits cancel out. It turns out that something called the root mean square (r.m.s.) voltage does the trick. For a sine wave, you get this by dividing the peak voltage, V_0, by $\sqrt{2}$. You do the same to calculate the r.m.s. current I_{rms}:

$$V_{rms} = \frac{V_0}{\sqrt{2}}$$ $V_0 = peak$ voltage in volts (V)

$$I_{rms} = \frac{I_0}{\sqrt{2}}$$ $I_0 = peak$ current in amperes (A)

Tip: Even though this is only strictly true if the a.c. signal is a sine wave, it's also the only type of alternating signal that will come up in the exam, so I wouldn't worry too much about it.

If you want to work out the power for an a.c. supply, just replace I and V in the power formula, $P = VI$ (see page 58), with the r.m.s. values:

$$\text{Power} = V_{rms} \times I_{rms}$$

Tip: You'll get given the equations for V_{rms} and I_{rms} in your exam data and formulae book.

Example

A light is powered by a sinusoidal a.c. power supply with a peak voltage of 2.12 V and a root mean square current of 0.40 A.

a) Calculate the root mean square voltage of the power supply.

$$V_{rms} = \frac{V_0}{\sqrt{2}} = \frac{2.12}{\sqrt{2}} = 1.499... = 1.50 \text{ V (to 3 s.f.)}$$

b) Calculate the power of the power supply.

$$\text{Power} = V_{rms} \times I_{rms} = 1.499... \times 0.40 = 0.60 \text{ W (to 2 s.f.)}$$

Tip: Be careful when rounding, and make sure you don't use rounded answers in your calculations.

It's usually the r.m.s. voltage that's stated on a power supply. For example, the value of 230 V stated for the UK mains electricity supply is the r.m.s. value.

Example

To calculate the peak voltage or peak-to-peak voltage of the UK mains electricity supply, just rearrange $V_{rms} = \frac{V_0}{\sqrt{2}}$ into $V_0 = \sqrt{2}\, V_{rms}$:

$V_0 = \sqrt{2} \times V_{rms} = \sqrt{2} \times 230 = 325 \text{ V (to 3 s.f.)}$

$V_{\text{peak-to-peak}} = 2 \times V_0 = 651 \text{ V (to 3 s.f.)}$

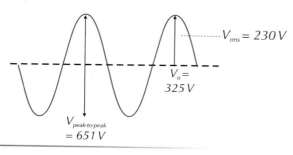

Figure 6: A two-pin electrical plug for North America. The mains electricity supply in North America has a root mean square voltage of 120 V.

It doesn't matter for calculating resistance, as the peak values and r.m.s. values will give you the same answer:

$$\text{Resistance}, R = \frac{V_{rms}}{I_{rms}} = \frac{V_0}{I_0}$$

Tip: See page 50 for more on resistance.

Practice Questions — Application

Q1 A sinusoidal a.c. supply provides a peak current of 8.2 A and a peak voltage of 9 V to a circuit.

a) Calculate the root mean square current provided by the supply.

b) Calculate the resistance of the circuit.

Q2 The USA mains power supply has an r.m.s. voltage of 120 V. It is used to power a heater. The heater has an r.m.s. current flowing through it of 20.0 A.

a) Calculate the peak voltage of the USA mains supply.

b) Calculate the power of the heater.

Q3 The diagram below shows an oscilloscope trace of a sinusoidal a.c. on a centimetre square grid.

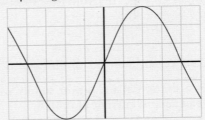

The time base of the oscilloscope is set to 20 ms cm^{-1} and the Y-input is set at 0.5 Vcm^{-1}.

a) Calculate the frequency of the wave.

b) Calculate the root mean square voltage of the a.c. current.

Practice Questions — Fact Recall

Q1 What is the trace on an oscilloscope created by?

Q2 What would an alternating current look like on an oscilloscope if the time base was turned off?

Q3 Why is it necessary to calculate the V_{rms} of an alternating power supply to be able to compare it to a d.c. power supply?

Q4 Write down the equation for calculating the root mean square current.

Exam Tip
Make sure you always include units with your answer — you could lose marks in the exam if you don't.

Section Summary

Make sure you know...

- The circuit symbols for basic electrical components.
- How to draw simple circuit diagrams.
- That electric current is the rate of flow of charge, $I = \Delta Q \div \Delta t$.
- That you can measure current using an ammeter, and that ammeters are always placed in series.
- That potential difference is the work done per unit charge, $V = W \div Q$.
- That you can measure potential difference using a voltmeter, and that voltmeters are always placed in parallel in a circuit.
- That resistance is defined as $R = V \div I$.
- That Ohm's law is a special case where $I \propto V$, and that conductors that follow Ohm's law are called ohmic conductors.
- What the characteristic I-V graph looks like for an ohmic conductor.
- How to interpret I-V graphs.
- How to collect data to plot a characteristic I-V graph for a component.
- What the characteristic I-V graph for a filament lamp looks like and why it has that shape.
- Why the resistance through a resistor increases as the temperature increases.
- Why semiconductors, like thermistors, diodes and LDRs, can make excellent sensors.
- What the characteristic I-V graphs look like for thermistors, diodes and LDRs, and what they show.
- That resistivity is defined as $\rho = (RA) \div L$, and how to calculate the resistivity of a material.
- What a superconductor is and some uses of superconducting wires.
- That the power of a component can be found using $P = VI$, $P = I^2R$ or $P = \dfrac{V^2}{R}$.
- That the energy transfer in a circuit can be found using $E = VIt$ and other equations too...
- Why starter motors in cars require very high currents to start car engines.
- What internal resistance and electromotive force (e.m.f.) are.
- That you can calculate the e.m.f. of a power source using $\varepsilon = E \div Q$.
- That you can calculate the internal resistance of a power source using $\varepsilon = I(R + r)$.
- Why car batteries need to have a very low internal resistance.
- How to measure the internal resistance and e.m.f. of a power source.
- That charge and energy are always conserved in circuits.
- That the total current entering a junction is equal to the total current leaving it.
- That the total e.m.f. around a series circuit is equal to the sum of the p.d.s across each component.
- How you find the resistance of, voltage across and current through components and cells connected in series and parallel.
- What a potential divider is and what it is used for.
- How to create a sensor using a potential divider.
- That you can use a variable resistor in a potential divider (a potentiometer) to provide a variable output voltage, e.g. for a stereo volume control.
- What an alternating current is.
- What an oscilloscope is and how to interpret a wave as shown by an oscilloscope.
- How to calculate the frequency and time period of a wave using $f = 1 \div T$.
- That for sinusoidal waves, $I_{rms} = I_0 \div \sqrt{2}$, $V_{rms} = V_0 \div \sqrt{2}$, $P = V_{rms} \times I_{rms}$ and $R = V_{rms} \div I_{rms} = V_0 \div I_0$.

Exam-style Questions

1   The circuit on the right has a cell attached in series to an ammeter, two resistors and a filament bulb.

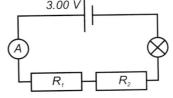

1 (a)   The current flowing through the cell is 0.724 A.

1 (a) (i)   Calculate the power of the cell.

(2 marks)

1 (a) (ii)   Calculate the charge passing through the cell in 5 minutes.

(2 marks)

1 (a) (iii)   It takes 56.5 J of energy to move the charge through resistor R_1 in 5 minutes. Calculate the potential difference across R_1.

(2 marks)

1 (a) (iv)   The ammeter and the cell have negligible resistances. The filament lamp has a resistance of 2.00 Ω. Calculate the potential difference across resistor R_2.

(3 marks)

1 (b)   The I-V graph for a filament lamp is shown on the right.

1 (b) (i)   Is the filament lamp an ohmic conductor? Explain your answer.

(1 mark)

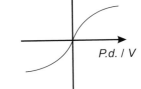

1 (b) (ii)   Explain why the I-V graph for a filament lamp has this characteristic shape.

(2 marks)

2   All batteries and power supplies have an internal resistance.

2 (a)   Explain why a battery has an internal resistance.

(1 mark)

2 (b)   Draw a labelled circuit diagram of a circuit that could be used to accurately determine the internal resistance of a battery.

(2 marks)

2 (c)   In an experiment to find the internal resistance of a battery, a student gathered the following data:

Terminal voltage (V)	Current (A)
1.00	2.82
3.00	2.38
4.00	1.18
6.00	1.75
8.00	1.30
9.00	1.13

2 (c) (i)   Draw a V-I graph of the data shown in the table.

(2 marks)

2 (c) (ii)   Use the graph to find the e.m.f. of the battery.

(1 mark)

2 (c) (iii)   Use the graph to determine the internal resistance of the battery.

(3 marks)

3   The circuit shown below contains a battery with an e.m.f. of 12 V with a negligible internal resistance. Component A will become superconducting at its transition temperature, 95 K.

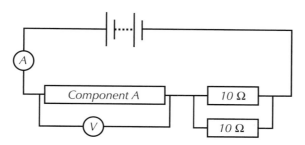

3 (a) (i)   Describe how the resistance of component A will change when it is cooled to 96 K.

(1 mark)

3 (a) (ii)   Give one application of superconducting wires.

(1 mark)

3 (b)   At 298 K the resistance of component A is 10 Ω.
3 (b) (i)   Calculate the total resistance in the circuit at 298 K.

(2 marks)

3 (b) (ii)   Calculate the current flowing through component A at 298 K.

(2 marks)

3 (c)   Component A is cooled to 96 K using liquid nitrogen.
The resistance of the component drops to 3.21 mΩ.
3 (c) (i)   Calculate the current flowing through component A at 96 K.

(2 marks)

3 (c) (ii)   Component A is a wire with a cross-sectional area of 3.05×10^{-6} m² and a length of 3.00 cm. Calculate the resistivity of the wire at 96 K. Give your answer to an appropriate number of significant figures.

(3 marks)

3 (c) (iii)   Describe what will happen to the current flowing through component A when its temperature reaches its transition temperature. Explain your answer.

(2 marks)

1. Scalars and Vectors

Vectors are quantities with both a size and a direction. You need to be able to split them into components or add them to find a resultant vector.

The difference between scalars and vectors

- A **scalar** quantity has no direction — it's just an amount of something, like the mass of a sack of potatoes.
- A **vector** quantity has magnitude (size) and direction — like the speed and direction of a car.

The table below shows some examples of vector and scalar quantities.

Scalars	Vectors
mass, temperature, time, distance, speed, energy	displacement, force, velocity, acceleration, momentum

Adding vectors together

Adding two or more vectors together is called finding their resultant. There are two ways of doing this you need to know about.

Finding resultant vectors using scale diagrams

You can find the **resultant vector** of two vectors by drawing a scale drawing of them 'tip-to-tail' (if they're not already) then measuring the length and angle of the resultant vector on the diagram.

---- Example ----

A man walks 4 m north and 3 m east. Find the magnitude and direction of his displacement, *s*.

Start by drawing a scale diagram for how far the man's walked:

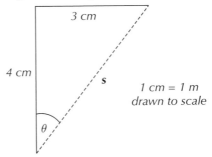

Then just measure the missing side with a ruler and the missing angle with a protractor: **s** = 5 cm and θ = 37°

So the man's displacement is 5 m, on a bearing of 037°.

Finding resultant vectors using trigonometry

If two vectors are perpendicular to each other, like in Figure 1, you can calculate the size and angle of the resultant vector using trigonometry.

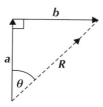

Figure 1: A right-angled triangle representing two vectors 'a' and 'b', and the resultant vector 'R'.

You can calculate the size of the resultant vector **R** using the formula:

$$R = \sqrt{a^2 + b^2}$$

You can calculate the size of the angle θ using the formula:

$$\theta = \tan^{-1}\left(\frac{b}{a}\right)$$

This comes from SOH CAH TOA. For any right-angled triangle where you know two sides, you can work out the size of an angle with one of three formulas.

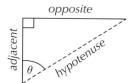

$$\sin\theta = \frac{opp}{hyp} \qquad \cos\theta = \frac{adj}{hyp} \qquad \tan\theta = \frac{opp}{adj}$$

Figure 2: SOH CAH TOA for a right-angled triangle.

Example

A remote-controlled aeroplane flies with a velocity of 14 ms⁻¹ east while being pushed north by a 8 ms⁻¹ wind. What is its resultant velocity?

Start by sketching a diagram:

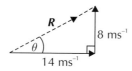

Then find R:
$R = \sqrt{14^2 + 8^2} = 16$ ms⁻¹ (to 2 s.f.)

Then find θ:
$\theta = \tan^{-1}\frac{8}{14} = 30°$ (to 2 s.f.)

So the resultant velocity is 16 ms⁻¹, on a bearing of 060°.

Figure 3: Boats crossing a river can't just head for their destination — their actual movement will be the resultant of their own velocity relative to the water and the velocity of the water.

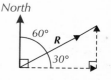

Resolving vectors into components

Tip: The components are normally horizontal and vertical. If you're working with an object on an inclined plane, it might be easier to use components that are parallel and at right angles to the plane (see below and next page).

Tip: You could resolve a vector into non-perpendicular components if you really wanted to... but it wouldn't be very useful.

Tip: This uses SOH CAH TOA as well (p.81).

Resolving vectors is the opposite of finding the resultant — you start from the resultant vector and split it into two components at right angles to each other. You're basically working backwards from the examples on pages 80-81.

Resolving a vector into horizontal and vertical components

The components of a vector are perpendicular to each other, so they form a right-angled triangle with the vector.

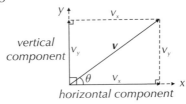

Figure 4: The vector **v** and its horizontal component v_x and vertical component v_y.

You just need to use a bit of trigonometry to find the components of the vector in each direction:

You get the horizontal component v_x like this:

$$\cos \theta = \frac{v_x}{v}$$

$$v_x = v \cos \theta$$

...and the vertical component v_y like this:

$$\sin \theta = \frac{v_y}{v}$$

$$v_y = v \sin \theta$$

Example

A hot air balloon is travelling at a speed of 5.0 ms⁻¹ at an angle of 60° up from the horizontal. Find the vertical and horizontal components.

First, sketch a diagram:

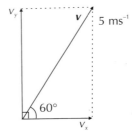

The horizontal component v_x is:
$$v_x = v \cos \theta = 5 \cos 60° = 2.5 \text{ ms}^{-1}$$

The vertical component v_y is:
$$v_y = v \sin \theta = 5 \sin 60° = 4.3 \text{ ms}^{-1} \text{ (to 2 s.f.)}$$

Exam Tip
$\cos 60° = \sin 30° = 0.5$. Remembering this will save time in the exam.

Tip: Turning the paper to an angle can help you see what's going on better in vector problems on a slope.

Resolving a vector on a slope

You should always resolve vectors in the directions that make the most sense for the situation you're dealing with. If you've got an object on a slope, choose your directions along the slope and at right angles to it.

Example

An apple with a weight of 1.5 N is at rest on a slope inclined at 30° to the horizontal, as shown in Figure 5. Find the component of its weight that acts along the slope.

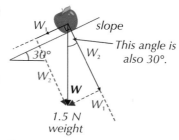

This time, instead of resolving the vector into vertical and horizontal components, you're resolving it into components parallel and perpendicular to the slope (W_1 and W_2).

To find W_1, use opp = $\sin\theta \times$ hyp

$$\Rightarrow W_1 = \sin 30° \times 1.5 = 0.75 \text{ N}$$

Figure 5: An apple with a weight of 1.5 N at rest on a slope.

Exam Tip
Examiners like to call a slope an 'inclined plane'.

Tip: Weight always acts vertically downwards.

Tip: Angle rules were used to work out that the angle between W and W_2 was 30° too.

Resolving is dead useful because two perpendicular components of a vector don't affect each other. This means you can deal with the two directions completely separately. When you have a force that affects only one of the vectors, you can just ignore the other.

Example

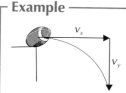

A ball is kicked horizontally off a ledge. Gravity will cause it to accelerate towards the ground (page 104) and its vertical velocity v_y will increase. But its horizontal velocity v_x will stay the same.

Tip: This is a case of projectile motion — there's more on this coming up on page 106.

Practice Questions — Application

Q1 Find the magnitude and direction of a paper plane's resultant velocity **v**, shown below.

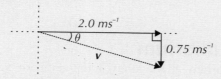

Q2 Find the horizontal and vertical components of this force.

Q3 Use a scale diagram to find the resultant of a 2.9 N force north and a 4.1 N force east.

Q4 A brick with a weight of 20 N is on a slope at 25° to the horizontal.
   a) Find the size of the force acting on it down the slope.
   b) Find the size of the reaction force exerted on it by the slope.

Tip: The reaction force is always perpendicular to the surface, and equal in size to the object's weight in the opposite (but parallel) direction.

Practice Questions — Fact Recall

Q1 What's the difference between a scalar and a vector?

Q2 What name is given to a vector formed by adding vectors together?

Tip: There's more on forces and their effect on page 102.

2. Forces in Equilibrium

All the forces acting on an object can be shown on a free-body force diagram. When all the forces are balanced, the body is in equilibrium.

Free-body force diagrams

Free-body force diagrams show a single body on its own. The diagram should include all the forces that act on the body, but not the forces it exerts on the rest of the world.

Remember, forces are vector quantities, so the arrow labels should show the size and direction of the forces.

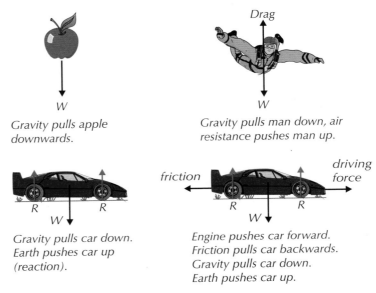

Gravity pulls apple downwards.

Gravity pulls man down, air resistance pushes man up.

Gravity pulls car down. Earth pushes car up (reaction).

Engine pushes car forward. Friction pulls car backwards. Gravity pulls car down. Earth pushes car up.

Figure 1: *Some free-body force diagrams.*

Forces in equilibrium

If an object is in **equilibrium**, all the forces acting on it are balanced and cancel each other out. In other words, there's no resultant force on an object in equilibrium. When only two forces act on an object, the object is in equilibrium if they're equal and opposite.

There are two ways you can go about solving equilibrium problems:

Force vectors in a closed loop

Forces acting on an object in equilibrium form a closed loop when you draw them tip-to-tail. This is sometimes called a vector triangle (or a vector polygon if more than 3 forces are involved).

Figure 2: *Three balanced vectors shown acting from a point and in a closed triangle.*

Figure 3 shows all the forces acting on a particle. Given that the particle is in equilibrium, find the magnitude of the missing force P.

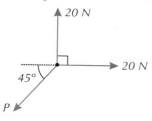

Figure 3: *Three balanced forces acting on a particle.*

The particle is in equilibrium, so the forces will form a closed loop when drawn tip-to-tail.

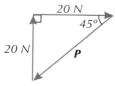

This means you can use trigonometry to find the magnitude of **P**.

$$\cos 45° = \frac{20}{P}$$

$$P = \frac{20}{\cos 45°}$$

$$= 28 \text{ N (to 2 s.f.)}$$

Figure 4: *These acrobats are in a state of equilibrium — all the forces on them must cancel out for them to be balanced. This is true for all balanced objects.*

Resolving forces in two perpendicular directions

You saw how to resolve forces into perpendicular components earlier in this section, and it's no different for objects in equilibrium. If an object is in equilibrium, the sum of the components in any direction must be equal to zero. To find the components of each force in a direction, just use trigonometry:

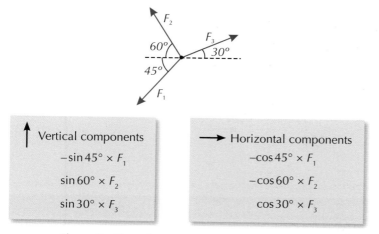

Vertical components	Horizontal components
$-\sin 45° \times F_1$	$-\cos 45° \times F_1$
$\sin 60° \times F_2$	$-\cos 60° \times F_2$
$\sin 30° \times F_3$	$\cos 30° \times F_3$

Figure 5: *Three forces acting at a point, and their horizontal and vertical components.*

─ **Example** ───────────────────────────

Figure 6 shows all the forces on a particle in equilibrium.
Find the magnitudes of the missing forces *P* and *Q*.

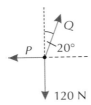

Figure 6: *The forces acting on a particle in equilibrium.*

Start by choosing a direction to resolve the vectors in. Starting with the horizontal direction would leave you with two unknown forces, so you need to start with the vertical direction:

Vertical components:

$$(\cos 20° \times Q) - 120 = 0$$

$$\Rightarrow Q = \frac{120}{\cos 20°}$$

$$= 127.7... = 128 \text{ N (to 3 s.f.)}$$

Now that you have the magnitude of *Q*, you can resolve the horizontal components to find the magnitude of *P*.

Horizontal components:

$$(\sin 20° \times Q) - P = 0$$

$$\Rightarrow P = \sin 20° \times 127.7...$$

$$= 43.7 \text{ N (to 3 s.f.)}$$

Tip: You could also use $\cos 70°$ here (instead of $\sin 20°$).

Practice Questions — Application

Q1 Show with a vector triangle that an object's in equilibrium if only these forces are acting on it: 12 N east, 5 N north, 13 N at 23° anticlockwise from west.

Q2 The three forces shown below are in equilibrium. Find the magnitude of the unknown force **F**.

F

7.1 N   64°

14.6 N

Practice Question — Fact Recall

Q1 If a body's in equilibrium, what's the sum of all the forces acting on it?

3. Moments

A moment is the turning effect of a force around a pivot. When moments cause a rotation, they are usually called torque.

Mass and weight

The **mass** of an object is the amount of 'stuff' (or matter) in it. It's measured in kg. The greater an object's mass, the greater its resistance to a change in velocity (called its inertia). The mass of an object doesn't change if the strength of the gravitational field changes.

Weight is a force. It's measured in newtons (N), like all forces. Weight is the force experienced by a mass due to a gravitational field. The weight of an object does vary according to the size of the gravitational field acting on it:

weight = mass × gravitational field strength ($W = mg$)

Figure 1 shows an example of how mass and weight vary for different values of **g**.

Name	Quantity	Earth ($g = 9.81$ Nkg^{-1})	Moon ($g = 1.6$ Nkg^{-1})
Mass	Mass (scalar)	150 kg	150 kg
Weight	Force (vector)	1471.5 N	240 N

Figure 1: *The mass and weight of a lion on the Earth and on the Moon*

Example

An astronaut has a mass of 85 kg. What would his weight be on Mars, where the value of g is 3.75 Nkg^{-1}?

weight = mass × gravitational field strength
= 85 × 3.75 = 319 N (to 3 s.f.)

Moments and turning effects

A moment is the turning effect of a force around a turning point. The **moment**, or torque, of a force depends on the size of the force and how far the force is applied from the **turning point**:

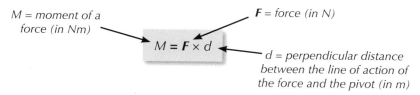

M = moment of a force (in Nm)

F = force (in N)

$M = F \times d$

d = perpendicular distance between the line of action of the force and the pivot (in m)

The principle of moments states that for a body to be in equilibrium, the sum of the clockwise moments about any point equals the sum of the anticlockwise moments about the same point. If the moments aren't balanced, the object will turn.

Learning Objectives:

- Be able to calculate the moment of a force about a point.

- Be able to state the principle of moments and use it to solve problems involving moments.

- Be able to define what a couple is, and know that it provides torque.

Specification Reference 3.2.1

Tip: $g = 9.81$ Nkg^{-1} on Earth.

Figure 2: *The value of g decreases as you move away from a planet — which is important for satellite calculations.*

Tip: The perpendicular distance means the distance along a line that makes a right angle with the line of action of the force (i.e. the shortest possible distance between the line of action of the force and the pivot).

Two children sit on a seesaw as shown in Figure 3. An adult balances the seesaw at one end. Find the size and direction of the force that the adult needs to apply.

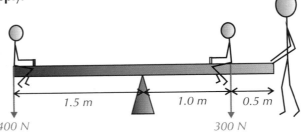

Figure 3: Two children sat on a balanced seesaw.

In equilibrium, $\sum$ anticlockwise moments = $\sum$ clockwise moments

$$400 \times 1.5 = (300 \times 1) + 1.5F$$
$$600 = 300 + 1.5F$$
$$F = \frac{600 - 300}{1.5} = 200 \text{ N downwards}$$

Tip: $\sum$ means "the sum of".

Tip: We know the force is downwards because it is positive.

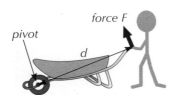

Figure 4: A wheelbarrow is a type of lever used to reduce the force needed to lift a heavy load.

Moments in levers

In a **lever**, an effort force acts against a load force by means of a rigid object rotating around a pivot. Levers are really useful in situations where you need a larger turning effect. Examples include spanners, wheelbarrows and scissors. They increase the distance from the pivot a force is applied, so you need less force to get the same moment. You can use the principle of moments to answer lever questions:

Example

Find the force exerted by the biceps in holding a bag of gold still. The bag of gold weighs 100 N and the forearm weighs 20 N.

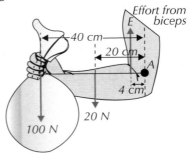

Figure 5: A biceps muscle providing the clockwise moment needed to balance the anticlockwise moments.

Take moments about A.

In equilibrium:

$$\sum \text{ anticlockwise moments } = \sum \text{ clockwise moments}$$
$$(100 \times 0.4) + (20 \times 0.2) = 0.04E$$
$$40 + 4 = 0.04E$$
$$E = \frac{40 + 4}{0.04} = 1100 \text{ N}$$

Figure 6: Heavy-duty spanners are a type of lever. They have long handles for larger turning effects.

Couples

A **couple** is a pair of forces of equal size which act parallel to each other, but in opposite directions. A couple doesn't cause any resultant linear force, but does produce a turning force (usually called a torque rather than a moment). The size of this torque depends on the size of the forces and the distance between them.

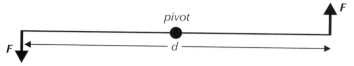

Figure 7: *Vehicle motors provide torque across the gears, which makes the wheels turn.*

Figure 8: *A couple acting across a pivot.*

T = torque of a couple (in Nm)

$$T = F \times d$$

F = size of the forces (in N)

d = perpendicular distance between the forces (in m)

Tip: The torque of a couple might also be referred to as the moment of the couple.

Example

A cyclist turns a sharp right corner by applying equal but opposite forces of 20 N to the ends of the handlebars. The length of the handlebars is 0.6 m. Calculate the torque applied to the handlebars.

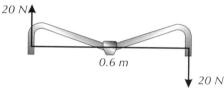

20 N

0.6 m

20 N

Figure 9: *Torque being applied across bicycle handlebars.*

torque = size of the forces × perpendicular distance between the forces
   = 20 × 0.6 = 12 Nm

Tip: Remember... for torque you use the perpendicular distance between the forces — not the distance from the force to the pivot.

Practice Questions — Application

Q1 Find the moment provided by a force of 73.1 N acting at a perpendicular distance of 0.25 m from a pivot.

Q2 The diagram below shows two children on a seesaw. If the child on the left stays where they are, how far from the pivot should the child on the right sit to balance the seesaw?

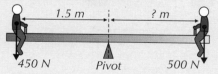

1.5 m   ? m

450 N   Pivot   500 N

Q3 An airtight chamber is kept shut by a release wheel with a diameter of 0.35 m. The release wheel won't open unless a torque of at least 50 Nm is applied across it. What's the minimum force needed to open the chamber door?

Tip: You'll need to rearrange the formula for torque here.

Practice Questions — Fact Recall

Q1 What is a moment?

Q2 What name is given to the moment applied by a couple?

Moments are important in working out the stability of objects because if something has a net moment in a particular direction, it will fall (topple) in that direction.

Centre of mass

The **centre of mass** (or centre of gravity) of an object is the single point that you can consider its whole weight to act through (whatever its orientation). The object will always balance around this point, although in some cases the centre of mass falls outside the object.

Centre of mass   Centre of mass   Centre of mass

Figure 1: *The centres of mass of three objects.*

Finding the centre of mass

You can find the centre of mass of a flat object using a simple experiment:

- Hang the object freely from a point (e.g. one corner).
- Draw a vertical line downwards from the point of suspension — use a plumb bob to get your line exactly vertical.
- Hang the object from a different point, and draw another vertical line.
- The centre of mass is where the two lines cross.

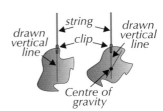

Figure 2: *The experimental set-up for finding the centre of mass of a flat object.*

Centre of mass and stability

An object will be nice and stable if it has a low centre of mass and a wide base area. This idea is used a lot in design, e.g. Formula 1 racing cars.

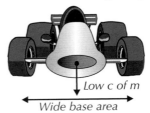

Low c of m
Wide base area

Figure 4: *Formula 1 cars have a wide base and a low centre of mass.*

Figure 3: *Cranes need a wide, heavy base to stop them toppling.*

The higher the centre of mass, and the smaller the base area, the less stable the object will be. An object will topple over if the line of action of its weight (drawn down from the centre of mass) falls outside its base area. The angle at which the object is on the brink of stability is called the critical angle.

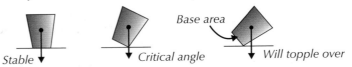

Stable   Critical angle   Base area   Will topple over

Figure 5: *An object shown when stable, on the brink of toppling, and toppling.*

Toppling and moments

When the line of action of an object's weight falls outside of its base, a resultant moment occurs, which provides a turning force. This is what causes an object to topple — it's just rotating around the base until it's stable again.

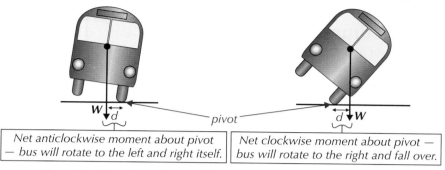

| Net anticlockwise moment about pivot — bus will rotate to the left and right itself. | Net clockwise moment about pivot — bus will rotate to the right and fall over. |

Figure 6: *A bus shown in a stable position and in an unstable position.*

Tip: If the centre of mass is directly over the pivot, there'll be no resultant moment in either direction. Any external force will then cause it to topple in the direction of the force.

Forces on supports

If an object is being held up by supports (e.g. chair legs, car tyres, etc.), the force acting on each support won't always be the same. The closer the object's centre of mass is to a support, the stronger the force on the support. It's all to do with the principle of moments — the anticlockwise and clockwise moments must be equal. So a support closer to the centre of mass will experience a larger force.

Exam Tip
Make sure you understand why different amounts of force can act on different supports, as you might be asked about it in the exam.

Example

A plank with a weight of 40 N is resting on two supports 3 m and 1 m from the plank's centre of mass. Find the upwards force provided by each support.

Start by treating one of the supports as the pivot and finding how much force is needed to balance the moments provided by the weight of the plank:

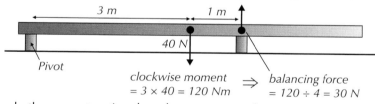

clockwise moment $\Rightarrow$ balancing force
$= 3 \times 40 = 120$ Nm $= 120 \div 4 = 30$ N

Then do the same, treating the other support as the pivot:

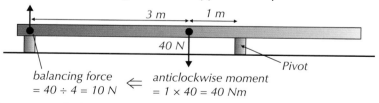

balancing force $\Leftarrow$ anticlockwise moment
$= 40 \div 4 = 10$ N $= 1 \times 40 = 40$ Nm

So the support furthest from the centre of mass provides 10 N of force, while the support closest to the centre of mass provides 30 N of force.

Tip: The balancing force is found by rearranging $M = \textbf{F} \times d$ to $\textbf{F} = M \div d$.

Tip: This is the force the supports experience too.

Practice Questions — Fact Recall

Q1 What is the centre of mass of an object?
Q2 Where should the centre of mass of an object lie so it doesn't topple?

Learning Objectives:

- Understand what is meant by displacement, velocity and acceleration.
- Be able to use the equations for uniform acceleration.

Specification Reference 3.2.1

5. Uniform Acceleration

There's a set of famous equations that you can use to work out an object's displacement, acceleration and starting and finishing velocity. These equations work for an object in uniform acceleration, and are really useful in mechanics.

Displacement, velocity and acceleration

You won't get far in mechanics without coming across **speed**, **displacement**, **velocity** and **acceleration**. Displacement, velocity and acceleration are all vector quantities (page 80), so the direction matters.

> **Speed** — How fast something is moving, regardless of direction.
>
> **Displacement** — How far an object's travelled from its starting point in a given direction.
>
> **Velocity** — The rate of change of an object's displacement (its speed in a given direction).
>
> **Acceleration** — The rate of change of an object's velocity.

There are four main equations that you use to solve problems involving uniform (constant) acceleration. You need to be able to use them, but you don't have to know how they're derived — it's just shown here to help you learn them. The equations use 5 different letters:

Tip: Acceleration could mean a change in speed or direction or both — since velocity is speed in a given direction.

s — displacement (in m) u — initial velocity (in ms^{-1})
v — final velocity (in ms^{-1}) a — acceleration (in ms^{-2}) t — time (in s)

- Acceleration is the rate of change of velocity. From this you get:

$$a = \frac{(v - u)}{t} \quad \text{so} \quad \boxed{v = u + at} \quad \text{①}$$

- Displacement = average velocity × time. If acceleration is constant, the average velocity is just the average of the initial and final velocities, so:

$$\boxed{s = \frac{(u + v)}{2} \times t} \quad \text{②}$$

Figure 1: *All objects fall through a vacuum with the same acceleration (g). There's more on this on pages 104-105.*

- Substitute the expression for v from equation 1 into equation 2 to give:

$$s = \frac{(u + u + at) \times t}{2} = \frac{2ut + at^2}{2} \Rightarrow \boxed{s = ut + \tfrac{1}{2}at^2} \quad \text{③}$$

- You can derive the fourth equation from equations 1 and 2:

Use equation 1 in the form: $a = \dfrac{(v - u)}{t}$

Multiply both sides by s, where: $s = \dfrac{(u + v)}{2} \times t$

This gives us: $as = \dfrac{(v - u)}{t} \times \dfrac{(u + v)t}{2}$

The t's on the right cancel, so: $2as = (v - u)(v + u)$
$$= v^2 - uv + uv - u^2$$

Tip: These equations are sometimes called 'suvat equations'.

so: $\boxed{v^2 = u^2 + 2as} \quad \text{④}$

A tile falls from a roof 25 m high. Calculate its speed when it hits the ground and how long it takes to fall. Take $g = 9.8$ ms^{-2}.

First of all, write out what you know:

$s = 25$ m
$u = 0$ ms^{-1} (since the tile's stationary to start with)
$a = 9.8$ ms^{-2} (due to gravity)
$v = ?$ $t = ?$

Then, choose an equation with only one unknown quantity.
So start with $v^2 = u^2 + 2as$:

$v^2 = 0 + 2 \times 9.8 \times 25$
$v^2 = 490$
$\Rightarrow v = 22$ ms^{-1} (to 2 s.f.)

Now find t using $s = ut + \frac{1}{2}at^2$:

$25 = 0 + (\frac{1}{2} \times 9.8 \times t^2)$
$\Rightarrow t^2 = \frac{25}{4.9} \Rightarrow t = 2.3$ s (to 2 s.f.)

> **Tip:** Usually you take upwards as the positive direction. In this question it's probably easier to take downwards as positive, so you get $g = +9.8$ ms^{-2} instead of $g = -9.8$ ms^{-2}.

Example ─────────────────────────────

A car accelerates steadily from rest at a rate of 4.2 ms^{-2} for 6 seconds. Calculate the final speed.

As before, start by writing down what you know:

$u = 0$ ms^{-1}
$a = 4.2$ ms^{-2} Then choose the right equation... $v = u + at$
$t = 6$ s $v = 0 + (4.2 \times 6) = 25.2$ ms^{-1}
$v = ?$

Calculate the distance travelled in 6 seconds.

$u = 0$ ms^{-1} You can use: $s = \frac{(u + v)t}{2}$ or: $s = ut + \frac{1}{2}at^2$
$v = 25.2$ ms^{-1} $\Downarrow$ $\Downarrow$
$a = 4.2$ ms^{-2}
$t = 6$ s $s = \frac{(0 + 25.2) \times 6}{2}$ $s = 0 + (\frac{1}{2} \times 4.2 \times 6^2)$
$s = ?$ $\Downarrow$ $\Downarrow$
                                    $s = 75.6$ m $s = 75.6$ m

---

Practice Questions — Application

Q1 A cat runs with uniform acceleration from rest to 10 ms^{-1} in 20 s. What's its displacement after this time?

Q2 The brakes are applied to a train travelling at 25 ms^{-1} and it takes 20 s to stop with uniform deceleration. What is its deceleration?

Q3 An electric tram sets off from rest and travels 100 m in 9.8 seconds. Calculate its acceleration during this time, assuming it was uniform.

> **Tip:** Deceleration is the same as negative acceleration.

Practice Questions — Fact Recall

Q1 What's the velocity of an object?

Q2 What's the acceleration of an object?

Q3 What are the 4 'suvat equations' for constant acceleration?

6. Displacement-Time Graphs

Displacement-time graphs show an object's position relative to its starting point over a period of time. They're useful because they can be used to describe an object's motion as well as find its velocity at a given point.

Learning Objectives:

- Be able to plot displacement-time graphs.
- Be able to describe the motion of an object by using its displacement-time graph.
- Be able to find an object's velocity using its displacement-time graph.

Specification Reference 3.2.1

Plotting displacement-time graphs

You need to be able to plot displacement-time graphs for moving objects. The suvat equations from the last topic can be used to work out values to plot. Displacement is plotted on the *y*-axis and time on the *x*-axis.

┌─ **Example** ─────────────────────────────

Plot a displacement-time graph for a panther who accelerates constantly from rest at 2 ms⁻² for 5 seconds.

You want to find **s**, and you know that:

$$a = 2 \text{ ms}^{-2}$$
$$u = 0 \text{ ms}^{-2}$$

Use $s = ut + \frac{1}{2}at^2$ to find values of *t* and *s* to plot on the graph. If you substitute in **u** and **a**, this simplifies to:

$$s = (0 \times t) + (\tfrac{1}{2} \times 2t^2)$$
$$= t^2$$

Now pick values of *t* between 0 and 5 seconds and work out **s** at those points with $s = t^2$: ...then plot the graph:

t (s)	s (m)
0	0
1	1
2	4
3	9
4	16
5	25

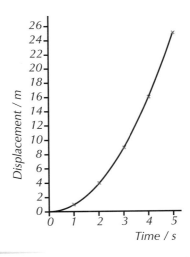

Tip: Try to use time intervals that make plotting the graph easier. In this example, using intervals of 1 second gives you 6 points to plot, which is enough for a neat curve.

Figure 1: *GPS and displacement-time graphs can be used to track a sea turtle's movement between mating seasons.*

Acceleration on displacement-time graphs

A graph of displacement against time for an accelerating object always produces a curve. If the object's accelerating at a uniform rate, then the rate of change of the gradient will be constant. Acceleration is shown by a curve with an increasing gradient (like the one in the example above). Deceleration is shown by a curve with a decreasing gradient.

Changing the acceleration of the panther in the example on page 94 would change the gradient of the displacement-time graph like this:

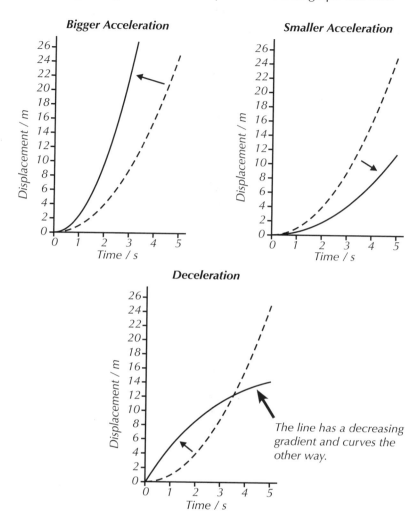

Figure 2: *The effect of changing the acceleration on the gradient of a displacement-time graph.*

The line has a decreasing gradient and curves the other way.

Tip: Note that in the case of deceleration, the panther must have been already moving at $t = 0$. Otherwise it would start moving backwards and its displacement would be negative.

Finding the velocity

When the velocity is constant, the displacement-time graph is a diagonal straight line. As you saw on page 92, velocity is defined as:

$$\text{velocity} = \frac{\text{change in displacement}}{\text{time}}$$

On the graph, this is $\dfrac{\text{change in } y \ (\Delta y)}{\text{change in } x \ (\Delta x)}$, i.e. the gradient.

So to get the velocity from a displacement-time graph, just find the gradient.

Tip: If a section of a displacement-time graph is horizontal (gradient = 0), the object's velocity is zero — it's not moving.

Tip: A negative gradient means the object's moving backwards.

The graph below shows a car's displacement over time. What's the car's velocity between 0 and 6 seconds?

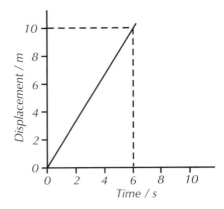

To work out the velocity, find the change in displacement and the change in time during the period given in the question:

$$v = \frac{\Delta y}{\Delta x} = \frac{10 - 0}{6 - 0} = \frac{10}{6} = 1.7 \, \text{ms}^{-1} \, (\text{to 2 s.f.})$$

Tip: Although it might seem pointless subtracting zero, the section of the graph you're working with won't always start at 0.

Velocity and curved displacement-time graphs

If the gradient isn't constant (i.e. if it's a curved line), it means the object is accelerating. To find the velocity at a certain point, you need to draw a tangent to the curve at that point to find its gradient.

Example

The graph below shows the displacement of a ball rolling down a slope over time. Find its velocity at 5.5 s.

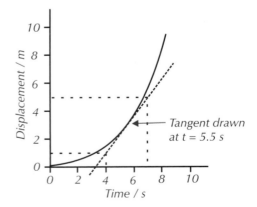

Tangent drawn at t = 5.5 s

Figure 3: *A displacement-time graph of a runner during a race can be used to work out their velocity at any point in the race.*

Start by drawing a tangent to the curve at 5.5 s (this has been done already). You can then draw horizontal and vertical lines from the tangent to the axes to find values for Δy and Δx.

$$v = \frac{\Delta y}{\Delta x} = \frac{5 - 1}{7 - 4} = \frac{4}{3} = 1.3 \, \text{ms}^{-1} \, (\text{to 2 s.f.})$$

Practice Questions — Application

Q1 Use the data in the table below to plot a displacement-time graph.

t (s)	s (m)
2	6
2.5	7.5
3.5	10.5
5	15
7	21
8	24

Q2 The graph below shows the displacement of a cyclist during a journey. Describe what's happening in parts a), b), c) and d).

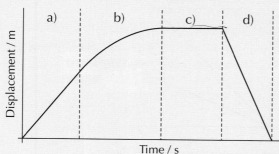

Figure 4: *The graph in Q2 might describe a cyclist's journey as they travel to the top of a hill and back.*

Q3 A rocket accelerates constantly from rest to 100 ms⁻¹ in 5 seconds. Plot a displacement-time graph for the rocket during this time.

Tip: Start by finding the rocket's displacement at various times.

Q4 a) Use the data in the table below to plot a displacement-time graph.

t (s)	s (m)
0	0
1	1.5
2	6
3	13.5
4	24
5	37.5

b) What's the velocity of the object at 3 s?

Practice Questions — Fact Recall

Q1 What kind of motion does a curved displacement-time graph show?

Q2 What kind of motion does a straight line on a displacement-time graph show?

Q3 How would you calculate the velocity of an object from its displacement-time graph?

7. Velocity-Time Graphs

Velocity-time graphs show, as the name suggests, an object's velocity over time. As with displacement-time graphs, their shape can be used to find out about an object's movement at different points in time.

Finding the acceleration

The gradient of a velocity-time graph tells you the acceleration, since:

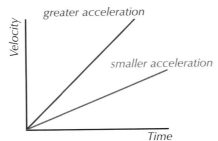

$$acceleration = \frac{change\ in\ velocity}{time\ taken}$$

Uniform acceleration is always a straight line. The steeper the gradient, the greater the acceleration:

greater acceleration

Velocity

smaller acceleration

Time

Figure 1: *A velocity-time graph showing the gradients of two different accelerations.*

Learning Objectives:

- Be able to plot velocity-time graphs.
- Be able to describe the motion of an object by looking at its velocity-time graph.
- Be able to find an object's acceleration by measuring the gradient of its velocity-time graph.
- Understand that the area under a velocity-time graph is displacement.

Specification Reference 3.2.1

─ Example ───────────────────

A lion walks at 1.5 ms⁻¹ for 4 s and then accelerates uniformly at a rate of 2.5 ms⁻² for 4 s. Plot this information on a velocity-time graph.

Start by finding the lion's velocity at intervals between 0 and 8 s — it's 1.5 ms⁻¹ for the first 4 seconds, then it increases by 2.5 ms⁻¹ every second.

t (s)	v (ms⁻¹)
0 – 4	1.5
5	4.0
6	6.5
7	9.0
8	11.5

Then just plot a graph with time on the x-axis and velocity on the y-axis:

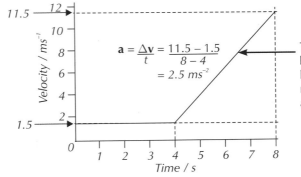

$$a = \frac{\Delta v}{t} = \frac{11.5 - 1.5}{8 - 4}$$
$$= 2.5\ ms^{-2}$$

The gradient is constant between 4 and 8 s and has a value of 2.5 ms⁻², representing the acceleration of the lion.

Tip: In questions like this you could use the equations of motion to find the object's velocity at various times — in a similar way to the displacement-time graph example on page 94.

Finding displacement

A speed-time graph is very similar to a velocity-time graph. The big difference is that velocity-time graphs can have negative regions to show something travelling in the opposite direction.

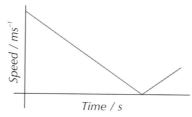

Figure 2: *The velocity-time and speed-time graphs for a ball being thrown up into the air.*

Tip: When the ball slows down and starts falling, its velocity will become negative but its speed will start increasing again.

The area under a velocity-time graph represents the displacement of an object, since displacement, **s**, of an object with uniform acceleration can be found using:

$$s = \left(\frac{u + v}{2}\right)t = \text{average velocity} \times \text{time}$$

Tip: For velocity-time graphs, the areas under any negative parts of the graph count as 'negative areas', as they show the object moving back to its start point.

You can find the total distance travelled by an object using:

$$\text{distance travelled} = \text{average speed} \times \text{time}$$

Therefore the area underneath a speed-time graph is the distance travelled.

Tip: The examples below show the link between these equations and the area under a speed-time or velocity-time graph.

Examples

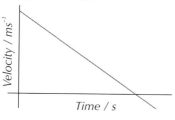
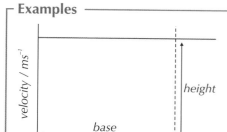

Figure 3: *The displacement for a rectangular velocity-time graph is just base × height.*

Area under graph
= base × height
= average velocity × time

Average velocity = $\frac{(u + v)}{2}$

But velocity is constant, so **u** = **v**.
So:
Area under graph
= **v** × t
= displacement

Tip: The initial and final velocity are the same, so the average velocity is **v**.

Tip: Displacement is the same as distance travelled here, because the velocity-time graph has no negative parts.

Figure 4: *The distance travelled for a triangular speed-time graph is ½ × base × height.*

Area under graph
= ½ × base × height
= average speed × time

Average speed = $\frac{(u + v)}{2}$

So:
Area under graph
= (½ × **v**) × t
= distance travelled

Tip: The initial speed is zero, so the average speed is just ½ × **v**.

─ **Example** ───────────────────────────────

A racing car accelerates uniformly from rest to 40 ms⁻¹ in 10 s. It maintains this speed for a further 20 s before coming to rest by decelerating at a constant rate over the next 15 s. Draw a velocity-time graph for this journey and use it to calculate the total distance travelled by the racing car.

Start by drawing the graph and then splitting it up into sections:

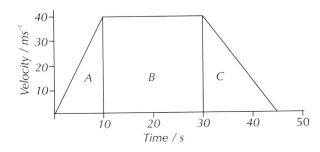

Calculate the area of each section and add the three results together.

A: Area = ½ × base × height = ½ × 10 × 40 = 200 m

B: Area = base × height = 20 × 40 = 800 m

C: Area = ½ base × height = ½ × 15 × 40 = 300 m

Total distance travelled = 200 + 800 + 300 = 1300 m

Tip: Remember, uniform acceleration and deceleration are shown by a straight line on a velocity-time or speed-time graph.

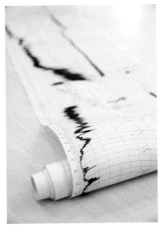

Figure 5: *A speed-time graph of wind during a hurricane.*

Non-uniform acceleration

If the acceleration is changing, the gradient of the velocity-time graph will also be changing — so you won't get a straight line. Increasing acceleration is shown by an increasing gradient – like in curve ① below. Decreasing acceleration is shown by a decreasing gradient — like in curve ② below.

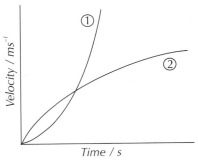

Figure 6: *Non-uniform acceleration on a velocity-time graph.*

Drawing graphs using ICT

Instead of gathering distance and time data using traditional methods, e.g. a stopwatch and ruler, you can be a bit more high-tech.

A fairly standard piece of kit you can use for motion experiments is an ultrasound position detector. This is a type of data-logger that automatically records the distance of an object from the sensor several times a second. If you attach one of these detectors to a computer with graph-drawing software, you can get real-time displacement-time and velocity-time graphs.

The main advantages of data-loggers over traditional methods are:

▪ The data is more accurate — you don't have to allow for human reaction times.

▪ Automatic systems have a much higher sampling rate than humans — ultrasound position detectors can take a reading ten times every second.

▪ You can see the data displayed in real time.

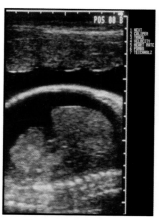

Figure 7: *Ultrasound position tracking is used to obtain medical images in real time.*

Practice Questions — Application

Q1 Use the data in the table below to plot a velocity-time graph.

t (s)	v (ms^{-1})
0	2
1	3
2	6
3	11
4	18
5	27

Q2 The graph below shows the velocity of a car over 10 seconds. Use the graph to find the displacement of the car in this time.

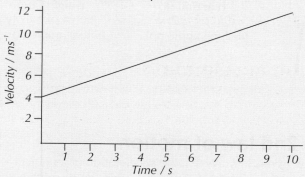

Tip: To find the area of a non-standard shape, try splitting it into two easier shapes (e.g. a rectangle and a triangle).

Q3 a) A cyclist goes down a hill with increasing acceleration. Use the table below to plot a velocity-time graph of the cyclist.

t (s)	v (ms^{-1})
0	0
1	1
2	4
3	9
4	16

b) Use the graph to find the acceleration at 2 seconds.

Practice Questions — Fact Recall

Q1 What does the gradient of a velocity-time graph tell you?

Q2 How is uniform acceleration shown on a velocity-time graph?

Q3 What does the area under a velocity-time graph tell you?

Q4 How is non-uniform acceleration shown on a velocity-time graph?

Newton's laws of motion describe the relationship between the forces acting on an object and its motion. You might have already met these ideas at GCSE — they're really important in mechanics, so they crop up a lot in physics.

Newton's 1st law of motion

Newton's 1st law of motion states that:

> *"The velocity of an object will not change*
> *unless a resultant force acts on it."*

This means a body will stay still or move in a straight line at a constant speed, unless there's a resultant force acting on it. If the forces aren't balanced, the overall resultant force will make the body accelerate. This could be a change in direction, speed, or both (see Newton's 2nd law below).

> **Example**
>
> An apple sitting on a table won't go anywhere because the forces on it are balanced.
>
>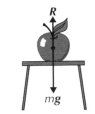
>
> | reaction (*R*) | = | weight (*mg*) |
> | (force of table pushing apple up) | | (force of gravity pulling apple down) |

Figure 1: *Sir Isaac Newton, the British physicist who devised the three laws of motion still used in modern mechanics.*

Newton's 2nd law of motion

Newton's 2nd law of motion says that the acceleration of an object is proportional to the resultant force acting on it. This can be written as the well-known equation:

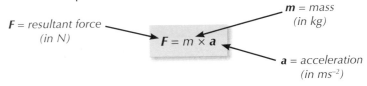

$$F = m \times a$$

F = resultant force (in N)

m = mass (in kg)

a = acceleration (in ms^{-2})

This equation says that the more force you have acting on a certain mass, the more acceleration you get. It also says that for a given force, the more mass you have, the less acceleration you get.

Try to remember:

- The resultant force is the vector sum of all the forces (page 80).

- The force is always measured in newtons.

- The mass is always measured in kilograms.

- The acceleration is always in the same direction as the resultant force and is measured in ms^{-2}.

Newton's 3rd law of motion

There are a few different ways of stating **Newton's 3rd law**, but the clearest way is:

> *"If an object A exerts a force on object B, then object B exerts an equal but opposite force on object A."*

You'll also hear the law as "every action has an equal and opposite reaction". But this can wrongly sound like the forces are both applied to the same object. (If that were the case, you'd get a resultant force of zero and nothing would ever move anywhere.)

The two forces actually represent the same interaction, just seen from two different perspectives:

- If you push against a wall, the wall will push back against you, just as hard. As soon as you stop pushing, so does the wall.

- If you pull a cart, whatever force you exert on the rope, the rope exerts the exact opposite pull on you.

- When you go swimming, you push back against the water with your arms and legs, and the water pushes you forwards with an equal-sized force.

Newton's 3rd law applies in all situations and to all types of force. But the pairs of forces are always the same type, e.g. both gravitational or both electrical. Sometimes it looks like Newton's 3rd law is being applied, but it's not.

Figure 2: *A swimmer moves forwards because the water pushes back against them, as they push against the water.*

Example

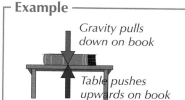

Gravity pulls down on book

Table pushes upwards on book

Both forces are acting on the book, and they're not of the same type. This is two separate interactions. The forces are equal and opposite, resulting in zero acceleration, so this is showing Newton's first law.

Tip: In this example, the resultant force is zero and the acceleration is zero, so Newton's second law is shown too.

Practice Questions — Application

Q1 Draw a diagram showing what forces are acting on a book when it's sitting still on the floor.

Q2 Why does a bird lift into the air when it flaps its wings?

Q3 How much resultant force is needed to accelerate a 24.1 kg mass by 3.5 ms^{-2}?

Q4 A resultant force of 18 N is applied to a toy car with a mass of 0.61 kg. What will the magnitude of the car's acceleration be?

Q5 Two ice skaters of mass 55 kg and 60 kg push against each other. The heavier ice skater accelerates away at 2.3 ms^{-2}. What will the magnitude of the lighter ice skater's acceleration be?

Exam Tip
Using ice skaters is a common way of saying there's no friction involved — the only force is from where they push against each other.

Practice Question — Fact Recall

Q1 State Newton's three laws of motion, and briefly explain what they mean.

9. Free Fall and Projectile Motion

Objects such as a thrown ball or a bullet leaving a gun have projectile motion. They follow a curved path and experience something called free fall.

What is free fall?

Free fall is when there's gravity acting on an object and nothing else.
It's defined as the motion of an object undergoing an acceleration of '**g**'.
You need to remember:

- Acceleration is a vector quantity — and '**g**' acts vertically downwards.
- The magnitude of '**g**' is usually taken as 9.81 ms^{-2}, though it varies slightly at different points on the Earth's surface.
- The only force acting on an object in free fall is its weight.
- Objects can have an initial velocity in any direction and still undergo free fall as long as the force providing the initial velocity is no longer acting.

Galileo's free fall investigations

All objects in free fall accelerate to the ground at the same rate. It sounds simple enough, but it took a long time to understand this. For over 1000 years the generally accepted theory was that heavier objects would fall towards the ground quicker than lighter objects. It was challenged a few times, but it was finally overturned with Galileo's investigations into free fall.

The difference with Galileo was that he set up systematic and rigorous experiments to test his theories — just like in modern science. These experiments could be repeated and the results described mathematically and compared.

Galileo believed that all objects fall at the same rate. The problem in trying to prove it was that free-falling objects fell too quickly for him to be able to take any accurate measurement (he only had a water clock), and air resistance affects the rate at which objects fall. He measured the time a ball took to roll down a smooth groove in an inclined plane. Rolling the ball down a plane slowed down the ball's fall as well as reducing the effect of air resistance.

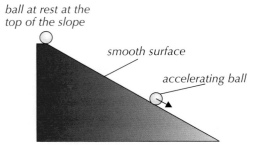

ball at rest at the top of the slope

smooth surface

accelerating ball

Figure 2: *A ball rolling down a smooth surface, the set-up used by Galileo to investigate free fall motion.*

By rolling the ball along different fractions of the total length of the slope, he found that the distance the ball travelled was proportional to the square of the time taken. The ball was accelerating at a constant rate. In the end it took Newton to bring it all together to show and explain why all free-falling objects have the same acceleration. He showed mathematically that all objects are attracted towards the Earth due to a force he called gravity.

Tip: Increasing the amount of time the ball takes to fall reduces the human error in recording the time.

Figure 1: *Galileo Galilei, Italian astronomer and physicist who investigated objects in free fall.*

Why do all objects fall at the same rate?

Newton's 2nd law (page 102) explains this nicely — consider two balls dropped at the same time, ball 1 being heavy and ball 2 being light. Then use Newton's 2nd law to find their acceleration:

Newton's 2nd law (page 102)

Examples

mass = m_1
resultant force = F_1
acceleration = a_1

By Newton's second law:

$$F_1 = m_1 a_1$$

Ignoring air resistance, the only force acting on the ball is weight, given by $W_1 = m_1 g$ (where g = gravitational field strength = 9.81 Nkg^{-1}).

So: $F_1 = m_1 a_1 = W_1 = m_1 g$

So: $m_1 a_1 = m_1 g$, then m_1 cancels out to give $a_1 = g$

mass = m_2
resultant force = F_2
acceleration = a_2

By Newton's second law:

$$F_2 = m_2 a_2$$

Ignoring air resistance, the only force acting on the ball is weight, given by $W_2 = m_2 g$ (where g = gravitational field strength = 9.81 Nkg^{-1}).

So: $F_2 = m_2 a_2 = W_2 = m_2 g$

So: $m_2 a_2 = m_2 g$, then m_2 cancels out to give $a_2 = g$

In other words, the acceleration is independent of the mass. It makes no difference whether the ball is heavy or light.

Tip: This only works if you ignore air resistance.

Figure 3: *Apollo 15 astronaut David Scott showing that a feather and a hammer fall at the same rate on the moon, where there is no air resistance.*

Free fall and the equations of motion

You need to be able to work out speeds, distances and times for objects moving vertically with an acceleration of g. As g is a constant acceleration you can use the equations of motion. But because g acts downwards, you need to be careful about directions. To make it clear, there's a sign convention: upwards is positive, downwards is negative.

Tip: See page 92 for the equations of motion.

Tip: See page 92 for the equations of motion.

- g is always downwards, so it's usually negative.
- t is always positive.
- u and v can be either positive or negative.
- s can be either positive or negative.

Tip: Make sure you learn these conventions — remember that direction is important when using vectors.

Case 1: No initial velocity

This means an object is just falling — initial velocity $u = 0$
Acceleration $a = g = -9.81$ ms^{-2}. Hence the equations of motion become:

$$v = gt \qquad v^2 = 2gs$$
$$s = \frac{1}{2}gt^2 \qquad s = \frac{vt}{2}$$

Case 2: An initial velocity upwards

This means it's projected up into the air. The equations of motion are just as normal, but with $a = g = -9.81$ ms^{-2}

Case 3: An initial velocity downwards

This is like case 2 — the equations of motion are as normal with
$a = g = -9.81 \text{ ms}^{-2}$.

┌─ Example ─────────────────────────────────

Alex throws a stone downwards from the top of a cliff. She throws it with a downwards velocity of 2 ms⁻¹. It takes 3 s to reach the water below. How high is the cliff?

You know $u = -2 \text{ ms}^{-1}$, $a = g = -9.81 \text{ ms}^{-2}$ and $t = 3$ s. You need to find s.

Use $s = ut + \frac{1}{2}gt^2 = (-2 \times 3) + (\frac{1}{2} \times -9.81 \times 3^2) = -50.145$ m.

So the cliff is 50.1 m high (to 3 s.f.).

Tip: s is negative because the stone ends up further down than it started. Height is a scalar quantity, so is always positive.

Projectile motion

Any object given an initial velocity and then left to move freely under gravity is a projectile. In projectiles, the horizontal and vertical components of the object's motion are completely independent. Projectiles follow a curved path because the horizontal velocity remains constant, while the vertical velocity is affected by the acceleration due to gravity, g.

Exam Tip
If you're doing AS Maths, you'll probably cover projectiles in mechanics.

┌─ Example ─────────────────────────────────

Matteo fires a cannon ball horizontally with a velocity of 100 ms⁻¹ from 1.5 m above the ground. How long does it take to hit the ground, and how far does it travel? Assume the cannon ball acts as a particle, the ground is horizontal and there is no air resistance.

Start with the vertical motion — it's constant acceleration under gravity:

You know $u = 0$ (no vertical velocity at first), $s = -1.5$ m and $a = g = -9.81 \text{ ms}^{-2}$. You need to find t.

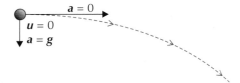

Use $s = \frac{1}{2}gt^2 \Rightarrow t = \sqrt{\frac{2s}{g}} = \sqrt{\frac{2 \times -1.5}{-9.81}} = 0.5530....$ s

So the ball hits the ground after 0.55 seconds (to 2 s.f.).

Then do the horizontal motion:

The horizontal motion isn't affected by gravity or any other force, so it moves at a constant speed. This means you can just use speed = $\frac{\text{distance}}{\text{time}}$.

Now $v_h = 100 \text{ ms}^{-1}$, $t = 0.5530....$ s and $a = 0$. You need to find s_h.

$s_h = v_h t = 100 \times 0.5530.... = 55$ m (to 2 s.f.)

Exam Tip
"Assume the [object] acts as a particle and there is no air resistance" means you don't need to worry about any forces other than the one caused by gravity (weight).

Tip: v_h is the horizontal velocity and s_h is the horizontal displacement.

Projectile motion at an angle

If something's projected at an angle (like, say, a javelin) you start off with both horizontal and vertical velocity. This can make solving problems trickier.

To solve this kind of problem, you need to use this method:

- Resolve the initial velocity into horizontal and vertical components.
- Use the vertical component to work out how long it's in the air and/or how high it goes.
- Use the horizontal component to work out how far it goes in the horizontal direction while it's in the air.

Example

A javelin is thrown with a velocity of 21 ms⁻¹ at an angle of 45° to the ground from a height of 1.8 m. How far does the javelin travel? Assume the javelin acts as a particle, the ground is horizontal and there is no air resistance.

Start by resolving the velocity into horizontal and vertical components:

$u_h = \cos 45° \times 21 = 14.84... \text{ ms}^{-1} = 14.8 \text{ ms}^{-1}$ (to 3 s.f.)
$u_v = \sin 45° \times 21 = 14.84... \text{ ms}^{-1} = 14.8 \text{ ms}^{-1}$ (to 3 s.f.)

Then find how long it's in the air for — start by finding v_v. The javelin starts from a height of 1.8 m and finishes at ground level, so use $s = -1.8$ m:

$v_v^2 = u_v^2 + 2gs_v \Rightarrow v_v = \sqrt{14.84...^2 + 2 \times (-9.81) \times (-1.8)} = -15.99... \text{ ms}^{-1}$

Then find the time it stays in the air:

$s_v = \dfrac{(u_v + v_v)}{2} \times t \Rightarrow t = \dfrac{s_v}{(u_v + v_v)} \times 2 = \dfrac{-1.8}{14.84... - 15.99...} \times 2 = 3.144... \text{ s}$

Now you can work out how far it travels horizontally in this time:

$s_h = u_h t + \dfrac{1}{2}a_h t^2 = 14.84... \times 3.144... + 0 = 46.7 \text{ m}$ (to 3 s.f.)

Tip: Resolving vectors was covered on p.82.

Tip: v_v is negative because the javelin is travelling downwards when it lands.

Figure 4: The only thing carrying a javelin forwards after it's been thrown is the initial horizontal velocity given to it by the thrower.

Practice Questions — Application

Q1 A ball is dropped from the top of a cliff and takes 6.19 s to hit the ground. Assuming there's no air resistance, how tall is the cliff?

Q2 A spanner is dropped from a height of 6.83 m. Assuming there's no air resistance, how fast will it be going when it hits the ground?

Q3 A gun fires a bullet at 502 ms⁻¹ horizontally. If the gun was held 1.61 m above the ground, how far will the bullet travel? Assume there's no air resistance and the ground is horizontal.

Q4 A catapult hurls a rock from ground level at 25 ms⁻¹, 60° to the horizontal. Assuming there's no air resistance and that the ground is horizontal, calculate:

  a) The amount of time the rock stays in the air.

  b) How far away from the catapult the rock will land.

Practice Questions — Fact Recall

Q1 What's the only force present in free-fall motion?

Q2 What's free-fall motion called when the object is given an initial velocity?

Figure 5: A bullet acts as a projectile in free fall after leaving the gun (if you ignore air resistance).

When an object moves it feels a resistive force called friction (or drag for a fluid) that opposes its motion. When the friction forces equal the driving forces, the object stops accelerating and reaches its terminal speed.

Friction

Friction is a force that opposes motion. There are two main types of friction — contact and fluid friction.

Contact friction happens between solid surfaces (which is what we usually mean when we just use the word 'friction').

'Fluid' is a word that means either a liquid or a gas — something that can flow. Fluid friction is known as **drag**, or fluid resistance or air resistance. Three things affect fluid friction:

- The force depends on the thickness (or viscosity) of the fluid.
- The force increases as the speed increases (for simple situations it's directly proportional, but you don't need to worry about the mathematical relationship).
- The force depends on the shape of the object moving through it — the larger the area pushing against the fluid, the greater the resistance force.

There are three things you need to remember about frictional forces:

- They always act in the opposite direction to the motion of the object.
- The can never speed things up or start something moving.
- They convert kinetic energy into heat.

Terminal speed

Terminal speed (or terminal velocity) happens when frictional forces equal the driving force. An object will reach a terminal speed at some point if there's a driving force that stays the same all the time, and a frictional or drag force (or collection of forces) that increases with speed. There are three main stages to reaching terminal speed:

┌─ **Example** ─────────────────────────

The car accelerates from rest using a constant driving force.

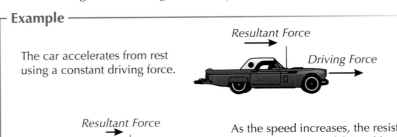

As the speed increases, the resistance forces increase (because of things like turbulence). This reduces the resultant force on the car and hence reduces its acceleration.

Eventually the car reaches a speed at which the resistance forces are equal to the driving force. There is now no resultant force and no acceleration, so the car carries on at a constant speed.

Motion graphs for terminal velocity

You need to be able to recognise and sketch the graphs for velocity against time and acceleration against time for the terminal velocity situation.

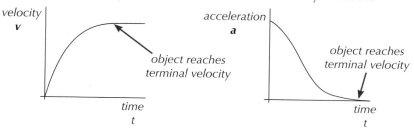

Figure 1: *The velocity-time and acceleration-time graphs for an object reaching terminal velocity.*

> **Exam Tip**
> These graphs might come up in the exam, so make sure you get lots of practice with them — try shutting the book and sketching them from memory.

Terminal speed in a fluid

Things falling through a fluid reach a terminal speed or velocity too. When something's falling through air, the weight of the object is a constant force accelerating the object downwards. Air resistance is a frictional force opposing this motion, which increases with speed. So before a parachutist opens the parachute, exactly the same thing happens as with the car:

Example

A skydiver leaves a plane and will accelerate until the air resistance equals his weight.

He will then be travelling at a terminal speed. But the terminal speed of a person in free fall is too great to land safely — so he needs to increase the upwards force of air resistance, to slow him down to a lower speed.

Before reaching the ground he will open his parachute, which immediately increases the air resistance so it is now bigger than his weight.

This slows him down until his speed has dropped enough for the air resistance to be equal to his weight again. This new terminal speed is small enough to survive landing.

Figure 2: *A parachute increases the drag acting on a skydiver, so they hit the ground at a slower speed.*

The velocity-time graph for this situation is a bit different, because you have a new terminal velocity being reached after the parachute is opened:

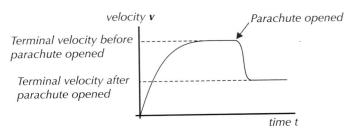

Figure 3: *The velocity-time graph for a skydiver who releases his parachute after reaching terminal velocity.*

Practice Question — Application

Q1 A ball is dropped above a cylinder of water. It falls through the air and lands in the water after 1.2 seconds. It then reaches a terminal velocity after 4.2 seconds. Its motion is shown by the graph below.

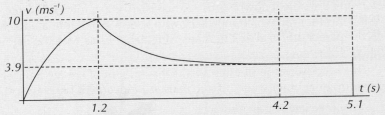

Tip: Falling into water has a similar effect on the ball's velocity to opening a parachute.

a) Describe the ball's acceleration from when it's dropped to when it reaches the bottom of the cylinder (at 5.1 seconds).

b) Sketch a velocity-time graph for the same ball if it were dropped straight into the water (without falling through air first). Include the ball's terminal velocity in your sketch.

Practice Questions — Fact Recall

Q1 In what direction does a frictional force act?

Q2 What is friction caused by a fluid called?

Q3 What can you say about the frictional forces and the driving forces acting on an object when it reaches terminal velocity?

Q4 Which of these graphs shows the velocity-time graph for an object falling through air and reaching a terminal velocity?

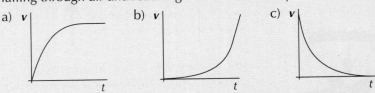

Q5 How does a skydiver reduce his or her terminal velocity?

11. Work and Power

You'll have met work and power at GCSE. In physics, they have specific meanings, and they can be calculated with a set of equations.

What is work?

Work is done whenever energy is transferred — it's just two ways of saying the same thing. Here are some examples of work being done:

Activity	Work done against	Final energy form
Lifting up a box.	Gravity	Gravitational potential energy
Pushing a chair across level floor.	Friction	Heat
Pushing two magnetic north poles together.	Magnetic Force	Magnetic energy
Stretching a spring.	Stiffness of spring	Elastic potential energy

Figure 1: *A table showing examples of work being done and the energy change that happens.*

Usually you need a force to move something because you're having to overcome another force. The thing being moved has **kinetic energy** while it's moving, which is transferred to other forms of energy when the movement stops.

The word 'work' in physics means the amount of energy transferred from one form to another when a force causes a movement of some sort.

Calculating work done

When a car tows a caravan, it applies a force to the caravan to move it to where it's wanted. To find out how much work has been done, you need to use the equation:

W = work done in J $W = Fs$ *F* = force causing motion in N
s = distance moved in m

- Work is the energy that's been changed from one form to another — it's not necessarily the total energy. E.g. moving a book from a low shelf to a higher one will increase its gravitational potential energy, but it had some potential energy to start with. Here, the work done would be the increase in potential energy, not the total potential energy.

- Remember the distance needs to be measured in metres — if you have distance in cm or km, you need to convert it to metres first.

- The force *F* will be a fixed value in any calculations, either because it's constant or because it's the average force.

- The equation assumes that the direction of the force is the same as the direction of movement.

- The equation gives you the definition of the joule (symbol J): 'One joule is the work done when a force of 1 newton moves an object through a distance of 1 metre'.

Learning Objectives:
- Know what is meant by work.
- Be able to calculate the work done by a force moving an object, using $W = Fs$ or $W = Fs\cos\theta$.
- Be able to calculate the power of something using $\Delta W / \Delta t$.
- Be able to calculate the power output of a moving object using $P = Fv$.

Specification Reference 3.2.1

Figure 2: *The engine of the towboat does work against the drag acting on the container.*

Tip: Remember force is a vector, so you can resolve it into components (page 82).

Forces at an angle

Sometimes the direction of movement of an object is different from the direction of the force acting on it. In this case you need to find the component of the force that acts in the direction of the movement:

Example

A girl pulls a sledge with a force of 51.9 N for 100 m. The string she uses to pull the sledge is at an angle of 19.3° to the ground. Calculate the work she does in pulling the sledge over this distance.

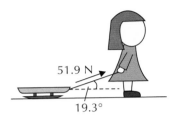

51.9 N

19.3°

To calculate the work done in a situation like the one above, you need to consider the horizontal and vertical components of the force. The only movement is in the horizontal direction. This means the vertical force is not causing any motion (and hence not doing any work) — it's just balancing out some of the weight, meaning there's a smaller reaction force.

The horizontal force is causing the motion, so to calculate the work done, this is the only force you need to consider. So resolving the force to find the horizontal component we get:

$$F_h = 51.9 \times \cos 19.3° = 48.98... \text{ N}$$

$$\Rightarrow W = F_h \times s = 48.98... \times 100 = 4900 \text{ J (to 3 s.f.)}$$

Tip: θ is the angle the line of action of the force makes with the direction of motion.

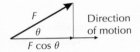

F

θ

$F \cos \theta$

Direction of motion

Because you only need to worry about the component of the force in the direction of the motion, you only ever need to resolve it in that direction. In general for a force at an angle to the direction of motion, you can find the work with this equation:

$$W = Fs\cos\theta$$

θ = angle at which the force acts from the direction of motion

Power and work

Power means many things in everyday speech, but in physics it has a special meaning. Power is the rate of doing work — in other words it is the amount of energy transformed from one form to another per second.

You calculate the power from this equation:

$$P = \frac{\Delta W}{\Delta t}$$

P = power in W

W = work done in J

t = time in s

Figure 3: A flea's legs transfer a small amount of energy, but in a very short time — this makes them very powerful.

The **watt** (symbol W) is defined as a rate of energy transfer equal to 1 joule per second (Js^{-1}). Make sure you learn this definition.

Power of a moving object

Sometimes, for a moving object, it's easier to use another version of the power equation. It's derived like this:

- You know $P = \frac{W}{t}$.

- You also know $W = Fs$, which gives $P = \frac{Fs}{t}$.

- But $v = \frac{s}{t}$, which you can substitute into the above equation to give:

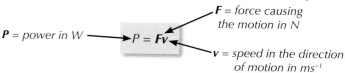

P = power in W ⟶ $P = Fv$

F = force causing the motion in N

v = speed in the direction of motion in ms⁻¹

Exam Tip
You'll be given this equation in your exam data booklet.

It's easier to use this if you're given the speed in the question. Learn this equation as a shortcut to link power and speed.

Example

A car is travelling at a speed of 10 ms⁻¹ and is kept going against the frictional force by a driving force of 500 N in the direction of motion. Find the power supplied by the engine to keep the car running.

Use the shortcut $P = Fv$, which gives:

$P = 500 \times 10 = 5000$ W

If the force and motion are in different directions, you can replace F with $F\cos\theta$ to get:

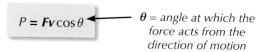

$P = Fv\cos\theta$ ⟵ θ = angle at which the force acts from the direction of motion

Exam Tip
This equation doesn't appear on your formula sheet. Make sure you know how to find the power of a moving object when the force isn't in the direction of the object's motion.

Practice Questions — Application

Q1 John pushes a desk 2.81 m across a flat floor. If he pushes with a steady force of 203 N, how much work does he do?

Q2 Alan pulls a desk 1.39 m across the floor by pulling a rope attached to it at 13.1° to the horizontal. If he pulls with a steady force of 371 N, how much work does he do?

Q3 A car operating at a power of 60.1 kW is travelling at a steady 34.7 ms⁻¹. How much force is being provided by the engine?

Q4 A child is pulling a cart along by a string at 15.2° to the horizontal. The child is pulling with a constant force of 83.1 N and the cart is moving horizontally at 2.99 ms⁻¹. What is the power of the child?

Practice Questions — Fact Recall

Q1 What's transferred when work is done?

Q2 Power is the rate of doing what?

12. Conservation of Energy

Learning Objectives:

- Be able to recall the principle of conservation of energy.
- Be able to calculate the efficiency of a machine.
- Be able to calculate the kinetic energy of a moving object.
- Be able to calculate the change in gravitational potential energy of an object.
- Be able to solve conservation of energy problems involving kinetic and gravitational potential energy.

Specification Reference 3.2.1

You'll no doubt have already met the idea that energy can be transformed from one type to another. Some energy transfers are useful, but others aren't.

The principle of conservation of energy

The **principle of conservation of energy** states that:

> Energy cannot be created or destroyed. Energy can be transferred from one form to another but the total amount of energy in a closed system will not change.

--- Example ---

Not all the energy input into a motor is converted to useful energy (e.g. kinetic energy) — it's not destroyed, but it is converted to less useful forms of energy (like sound, heat, etc.)

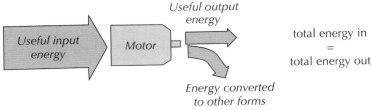

Figure 1: *The useful energy input is equal to the useful energy output + energy converted to useless forms.*

You can talk about how well energy is transferred in terms of **efficiency**. The more useful energy you get out of a machine for what you put into it, the more efficient it is:

$$\text{efficiency} = \frac{\text{useful energy given out by the machine}}{\text{energy supplied to the machine}}$$

You can write the efficiency of a machine in terms of power:

$$\text{efficiency} = \frac{\text{useful power output}}{\text{power input}}$$

--- Example ---

A meat grinder has a useful power output of 50.7 W. If its efficiency is 89.1%, work out its power input.

You know that: $\text{efficiency} = \dfrac{\text{useful power output}}{\text{power input}}$

Which you can rearrange to make: $\text{power input} = \dfrac{\text{useful power output}}{\text{efficiency}}$

Efficiency needs to be between 0 and 1, so when you have a percentage divide it by 100 first.

$$\text{power input} = \frac{50.7}{0.891} = 56.9 \text{ W (to 3 s.f.)}$$

Figure 2: *A steam engine outputs a large proportion of its input energy in "useless" forms (e.g. heat out of the chimney and sound).*

Tip: It goes the other way too — you might need to multiply efficiency by 100 to give it as a percentage.

Kinetic and potential energy

The principle of conservation of energy nearly always comes up when you're doing questions about changes between kinetic and potential energy.

Kinetic energy is the energy of anything moving, which you work out from:

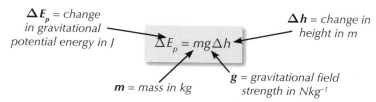

E_k = kinetic energy in J

m = mass in kg

$$E_k = \frac{1}{2}mv^2$$

v = speed in ms⁻¹

Example

A car with a mass of 903 kg is cruising at a steady 20.6 ms⁻¹. How much kinetic energy does it have?

Just put the numbers into the equation:

$$E_k = \frac{1}{2}mv^2 = \frac{1}{2} \times 903 \times 20.6^2 = 192 \text{ kJ (to 3 s.f.)}$$

Tip: A kilojoule (kJ) is equal to 1000 joules (J).

There are different types of potential energy, e.g. gravitational and elastic. **Gravitational potential energy** is the energy something gains if you lift it up. You work it out using:

ΔE_p = change in gravitational potential energy in J

Δh = change in height in m

$$\Delta E_p = mg\Delta h$$

m = mass in kg

g = gravitational field strength in Nkg⁻¹

Tip: An object loses gravitational potential energy when it falls.

Example

A man with a mass of 82.5 kg climbs up a cliff and gains 28.5 kJ of gravitational potential energy. How high did he climb?
(assume g = 9.81 Nkg⁻¹)

You can rearrange $\Delta E_p = mg\Delta h$ to get $\Delta h = \dfrac{\Delta E_p}{mg}$

Then just put the numbers in:

$$\Delta h = \frac{28\,500}{82.5 \times 9.81} = 35.2 \text{ m (to 3 s.f.)}$$

Elastic potential energy (elastic stored energy) is the energy you get in, say, a stretched rubber band or spring. You work this out using:

E = Elastic potential energy in J

$$E = \frac{1}{2}k(\Delta L)^2$$

ΔL = extension of the material in m

k = stiffness constant in Nm⁻¹

Figure 3: A loaded slingshot has elastic potential energy.

Transfers between kinetic and potential energy

Often when an object moves, energy is being transferred from one type to another. For example, kinetic can be transferred to potential energy by doing work, and vice versa.

Examples

Figure 4: *Some examples of energy transfers between kinetic and potential energy.*

1. As Becky throws the ball upwards, kinetic energy is converted into gravitational potential energy. When it comes down again, that gravitational potential energy is converted back into kinetic energy.

2. As Dominic goes down the slide, gravitational potential energy is converted into kinetic energy.

3. As Vina bounces upwards from the trampoline, elastic potential energy is converted into kinetic energy, to gravitational potential energy. As she comes back down again, that gravitational potential energy is converted back to kinetic energy, to elastic potential energy, and so on.

Figure 5: *Rollercoasters transfer gravitational potential energy to kinetic energy and vice versa.*

In real life there are also frictional forces — Vina, in the example above, would have to use some force from her muscles to keep jumping to the same height above the trampoline each time. Each time the trampoline stretches, some heat is generated in the trampoline material.

You're usually told to ignore friction in exam questions — this means you can assume that the only forces are those that provide the potential or kinetic energy (in the example above that's Vina's weight and the tension in the springs and trampoline material).

If you're ignoring friction, you can say that the sum of the kinetic and potential energy is constant. So for a falling object with no air resistance, the gain in kinetic energy is equal to the loss in potential energy:

$$\frac{1}{2}mv^2 = mg\Delta h$$

Tip: In other words, the total energy in the trampoline example is always the same — it just alternates between potential and kinetic.

Solving problems with energy conservation

You need to be able to use conservation of mechanical energy (change in potential energy = change in kinetic energy) to solve problems. The classic example is the simple pendulum. In a simple pendulum, you assume that all the mass is in the bob at the end.

Example

A simple pendulum has a mass of 700 g and a length of 50 cm.
It is pulled out to an angle of 30° from the vertical.

(a) Find the gravitational potential energy stored in the pendulum bob
relative to it's lowest point.

Start by drawing a diagram.

You can work out the increase in height, h,
of the end of the pendulum using trig.

Gravitational potential energy

$$= mgh$$
$$= 0.7 \times 9.81 \times (0.5 - 0.5 \cos 30°)$$
$$= 0.460...$$
$$= 0.46 \text{ J (to 2 s.f.)}$$

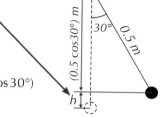

(0.5 cos 30°) m

30°

0.5 m

h

Tip: $0.5 \cos 30°$ is
the vertical side of the
triangle formed when
the pendulum swings,
so the change in height
is 0.5 (original height) −
$0.5 \cos 30°$ (new height).

(b) The pendulum is released. Find the maximum speed of the pendulum
bob as it passes the vertical position.

To find the maximum speed, assume no air resistance, then $mgh = \frac{1}{2}mv^2$.

So $\frac{1}{2}mv^2 = 0.460....$ Rearrange to find:

$$v = \sqrt{\frac{2 \times 0.460...}{0.7}} = 1.1 \text{ ms}^{-1} \text{ (to 2 s.f.)}.$$

OR cancel the ms and rearrange to give:

$$v^2 = 2gh$$
$$= 2 \times 9.81 \times (0.5 - 0.5 \cos 30°) = 1.3142...$$
$$\Rightarrow v = 1.1 \text{ ms}^{-1} \text{ (to 2 s.f.)}$$

Exam Tip
You could be asked to
apply this stuff to just
about anything in the
exam. Rollercoasters
are an exam favourite.

Practice Questions — Application

Q1 Describe the energy transfers involved when a catapult string is drawn
back and a pellet is fired out of the catapult.

Q2 Find the useful power output of a 20% efficient engine with a power
input of 29 kW.

Q3 a) How much gravitational potential energy does a falcon with a
mass of 650 g lose when it dives 103 m?

b) As it dives, 95% of its gravitational potential energy is converted to
kinetic energy. If it started stationary, how fast is it moving after
the dive?

c) The falcon misses its prey and soars back up, converting 80% of
its kinetic energy to gravitational potential energy. How high will
it climb before needing to flap its wings?

Figure 6: *Birds of prey are
highly streamlined so that
only a small amount of
energy is transferred to heat
through drag.*

Practice Questions — Fact Recall

Q1 What's the principle of conservation of energy?

Q2 How is the efficiency of a machine defined in terms of power?

Section Summary

Make sure you know...

- That scalars have only magnitude while vectors have magnitude and direction.
- How to add together two perpendicular vectors using a scale drawing.
- How to add together two perpendicular vectors using trigonometry.
- How to resolve a vector into two components at right angles to each other.
- That if all forces acting on an object cancel each other out, the object is in equilibrium.
- That the forces on an object in equilibrium can be drawn as a closed triangle (for 3 forces).
- How to show a body is in equilibrium by resolving the forces on it.
- How to calculate missing forces acting on an object in equilibrium.
- How to calculate the moment of a force about a point.
- What the principle of moments is and how it applies to balanced objects.
- What a couple is and how it applies a torque.
- How to calculate the torque of a pair of forces about a point.
- What the centre of mass of an object is.
- How the position of an object's centre of mass affects the object's stability.
- That displacement is how far an object has travelled from its starting point in a given direction.
- That velocity is the rate of change of displacement over time.
- That acceleration is the rate of change of velocity over time.
- How to use the equations of motion for constant acceleration.
- How to recognise acceleration on a displacement-time graph.
- How to find the velocity of an object using the gradient of its displacement-time graph.
- How to describe the motion of an object using its velocity-time graph.
- How to calculate acceleration on a velocity-time graph.
- How to calculate the displacement of an object using the area under a velocity-time graph.
- What Newton's three laws of motion are.
- That all objects in free fall have the same acceleration due to gravity, g.
- How to use the equations of motion for all objects in free fall.
- That projectile motion means that an object is left to move freely under gravity after it has started its motion.
- That the vertical and horizontal components of projectile motion are independent.
- What terminal speed is and how an object reaches it.
- That work is done whenever energy is transferred.
- That the work done in moving an object is calculated by multiplying the force by the distance moved.
- That power is the rate of doing work.
- The link between power, force and velocity.
- What the principle of conservation of energy is.
- How to find the efficiency of a machine using the ratio of useful power output to power input.
- How to find the kinetic energy of a moving object.
- How to find the change in gravitational potential energy of an object after a change in height.
- That energy is transferred between kinetic and gravitational potential energy when an object falls or climbs.

Exam-style Questions

1 (a) State one example of a vector quantity and one example of a scalar quantity.

(2 marks)

1 (b) **Figure 1** shows a cart with a mass of 3.75 kg attached to a wind sail.
The force of the wind on the sail pulls the cart along the smooth, horizontal ground.

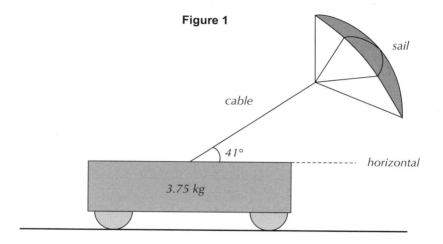

Figure 1

sail

cable

41°

horizontal

3.75 kg

1 (b) (i) The vertical force exerted on the cart by the cable balances the weight of the cart, so that it feels no reaction force from the ground.
Calculate the magnitude of the force exerted on the cart by the cable.

(3 marks)

1 (b) (ii) Assume there's no friction or air resistance. Calculate the forwards acceleration of the cart caused by the force from the cable.

(2 marks)

1 (c) When the cart is travelling at 12.5 ms^{-1}, it applies the brakes and comes to a stop after 15 seconds.

1 (c) (i) Calculate the kinetic energy of the cart just before it applies the brakes.

(2 marks)

1 (c) (ii) Assuming the cart undergoes uniform deceleration, calculate how far it will travel before coming to a stop.

(2 marks)

1 (c) (iii) Calculate the power of the brakes.

(2 marks)

2 (a)   **Figure 2** shows the displacement-time graph for a cyclist during a bike ride.
Describe the cyclist's motion in parts A, B, C and D of the graph.

Figure 2

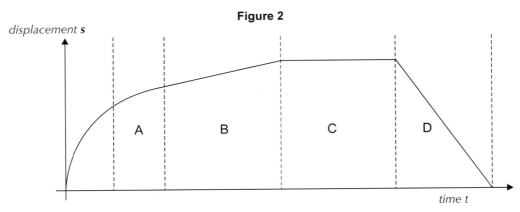

(2 marks)

2 (b)   Another cyclist starts from rest and accelerates at a rate of 1.5 ms⁻² for 4 seconds.
She then decelerates at a rate of 1 ms⁻² for 6 seconds. The table below shows the
cyclist's velocity during this time. Draw a graph of velocity against time for the cyclist

t (s)	0	1	2	3	4	5	6	7	8	9	10
v (ms⁻¹)	0	1.5	3	4.5	6	5	4	3	2	1	0

(5 marks)

2 (c)   She then allows herself to roll down a hill without pedalling. The top of the hill is
22.5 m above ground. The cyclist and bicycle have a mass of 64.8 kg.

Calculate how fast she will be going when she reaches the bottom of the hill.
Assume air resistance and other resistive forces are negligible.

(3 marks)

2 (d)   The cyclist throws a water bottle with a velocity of 6.5 ms⁻¹,
from a height of 1.31 m and at 29° above the horizontal.

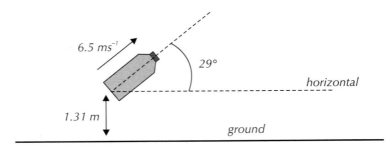

2 (d) (i)   Calculate the vertical component of the velocity of the bottle when it hits the ground.

(2 marks)

2 (d) (ii) Calculate how long the bottle will take to hit the ground.

(2 marks)

3 (a) Define the moment of a force about a point or pivot.

(2 marks)

(b) A truck is used to carry rocks. The truck has a mass of 21 000 N and is 4.75 m long. When it's carrying no load the centre of mass is 1.3 m from the front wheels and 2.4 m from the rear wheels. The truck is shown in **Figure 3**.

Figure 3

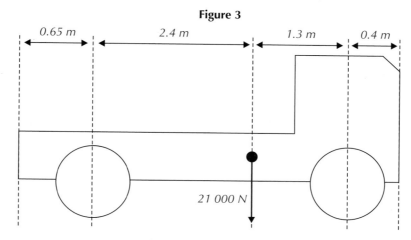

3 (b) (i) State and explain which set of wheels, front or back, will feel the most force when the truck is carrying no load.

(2 marks)

3 (b) (ii) A rock is placed on the very edge of the back of the truck and the front wheels remain on the ground but no longer feel any force from the truck. Calculate how much the rock weighs.

(3 marks)

4 (a) Define the centre of mass of an object.

(1 mark)

(b) **Figure 4** shows a flat toy parrot balanced on a branch. Is the head or the tail made from a heavier material? Explain your answer.

Figure 4

(2 marks)

drawn to scale

branch

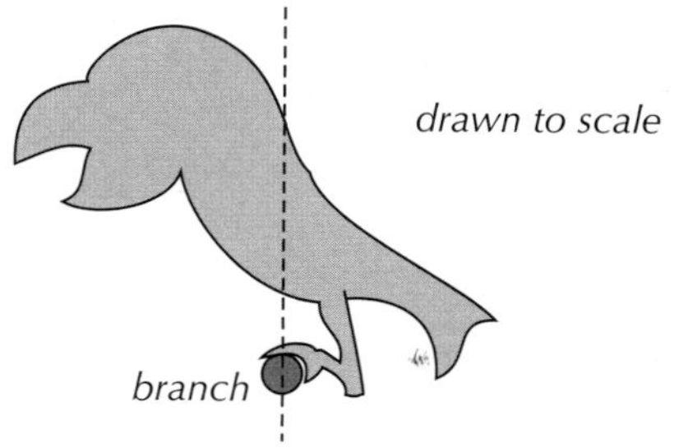

(c) Cranes are tall structures used to move heavy objects on construction sites. Describe the features the base of a crane must have and explain why these features are needed.

(3 marks)

Learning Objectives:

- Know what is meant by the density of a material.
- Be able to use the formula $\rho = \frac{m}{V}$ to calculate the density, mass or volume of an object.

Specification Reference 3.2.2

1. Density

Density is a property that all materials have, and different materials have different densities. For example, it'd be much easier to lift a balloon full of air than a lead balloon, because lead is much more dense than air.

What is density?

Density is a measure of the 'compactness' of a substance. It relates the mass of a substance to how much space it takes up. The density of a material is its mass per unit volume:

ρ = density in $kg\,m^{-3}$ ⟶ $\rho = \frac{m}{V}$ ⟵ m = mass in kg

V = volume in m^3

If you're given mass in g and volume in cm^3, you can work out the density of an object in $g\,cm^{-3}$.

Tip: The symbol for density is a Greek letter rho (ρ) — it looks like a p but it isn't.

Tip: It can be useful to remember that:
1 g cm^{-3} = 1000 kg m^{-3}.

─ **Example** ─────────

Aluminium has a density of 2.70 g cm^{-3}.
Calculate the volume of a 460 g solid object made out of aluminium.

Rearrange the formula $\rho = \frac{m}{V}$ to get $V = \frac{m}{\rho}$.

Substitute $m = 460$ g and $\rho = 2.70$ g cm^{-3} into the rearranged equation to find the volume of the object.

$$V = \frac{460}{2.70} = 170 \text{ cm}^3 \text{ (to 3 s.f.)}$$

The density of an object depends on what it's made of. Density of a material doesn't vary with size or shape. The average density of an object determines whether it floats or sinks. A solid object will float on a fluid if it has a lower density than the fluid.

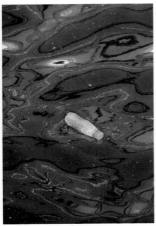

Figure 1: *Oil floats on water because it has a lower density. The bottle floats because the average density of the bottle and the air inside it combined is lower than the density of the water.*

Tip: You can work out the volume of a sphere using: $V = \frac{4}{3}\pi r^3$.

Practice Questions — Application

Q1 Find the density of an object with a mass of 360 kg and a volume of 0.45 m^3.

Q2 A gold pendant has a mass of 91.0 g. If gold has a density of 19.3 g cm^{-3}, what is the volume of the pendant?

Q3 A solid aluminium cylinder has a volume of 9.1×10^{-4} m^3. Aluminium has a density of 2700 kg m^{-3}. What is the mass of the cylinder?

Q4 An ice cube has a density of 0.92 g cm^{-3} and a mass of 4.1×10^{-3} kg. What is its volume?

Q5 A sphere has a mass of 0.80 kg and a radius of 0.020 m. What is its density?

2. Hooke's Law

Applying a force to a material can stretch it. When some materials are stretched, they follow Hooke's law — but only usually up to a certain point.

What is Hooke's law?

If a metal wire of original length L is supported at the top and then a weight attached to the bottom, it stretches. The weight pulls down with force F, producing an equal and opposite force at the support.

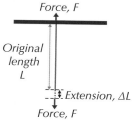

Force, F

Original length L

Extension, ΔL

Force, F

Figure 1: *A supported metal wire extending by ΔL when a weight is attached.*

Robert Hooke discovered in 1676 that the extension of a stretched wire, ΔL, is proportional to the load or force, F. This relationship is now called **Hooke's law**. Hooke's law can be written as:

$$k = \text{the stiffness constant in Nm}^{-1}$$

$$\mathbf{F} = \text{force in N} \longrightarrow F = k\Delta L \longleftarrow \mathbf{\Delta L} = \text{extension in m}$$

k is a constant that depends on the object being stretched.

Example

A force of 6.0 N is applied to a metal wire, which extends by 0.040 m. Calculate the stiffness constant of the wire.

Rearrange the formula $F = k\Delta L$ to get $k = \dfrac{F}{\Delta L}$.

Then substitute $F = 6.0$ N and $\Delta L = 0.040$ m into the rearranged equation to find the stiffness constant of the wire.

$$k = \frac{6.0}{0.040} = 150 \, \text{Nm}^{-1}$$

Hooke's law and springs

A metal spring also changes length when you apply a pair of opposite forces. The extension or compression of a spring is proportional to the force applied — so Hooke's law applies.

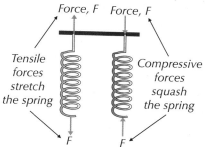

Force, F   Force, F

Tensile forces stretch the spring

Compressive forces squash the spring

F   F

Figure 2: *Metal springs with tensile and compressive forces acting on them.*

Tip: An object's <u>stiffness constant</u> is the force needed to extend it by 1 m. It depends on the material that it's made from, as well as its length and shape.

Exam Tip
If you're given a question like this in the exam, but with the extension in mm, change it to m.

Tip: If two things are proportional, it means that if one increases, the other increases by the same proportion.

Tip: A tensile force stretches something and a compressive force squashes it.

For springs, k in the formula $F = k\Delta L$ is usually called the spring stiffness or spring constant.

Hooke's law works just as well for **compressive forces** as **tensile forces**. For a spring, k has the same value whether the forces are tensile or compressive (though some springs and many other objects can't compress).

The limit of proportionality

There's a limit to the force you can apply for Hooke's law to stay true. Figure 3 shows load against extension for a typical metal wire.

The first part of the graph shows Hooke's law being obeyed — there's a straight-line relationship between load and extension and it goes straight through the origin. The gradient of the straight line is the stiffness constant, k.

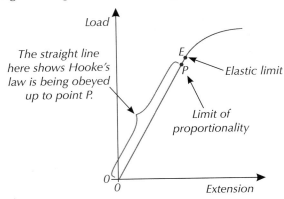

Figure 3: *The graph of load against extension for a typical metal wire.*

When the load becomes great enough, the graph starts to curve. The point marked **E** on the graph is called the **elastic limit**. If you increase the load past the elastic limit, the material will be permanently stretched. When all the force is removed, the material will be longer than at the start.

Metals generally obey Hooke's law up to the **limit of proportionality**, marked **P** on the graph, which is very near the elastic limit. The limit of proportionality is the point beyond which the force is no longer proportional to extension. The limit of proportionality is also known as the **Hooke's law limit**.

Be careful — there are some materials, like rubber, that only obey Hooke's law for really small extensions.

Example

Below is a load-extension graph for a spring.
Calculate the stiffness constant, k, in Nm^{-1} for the spring.

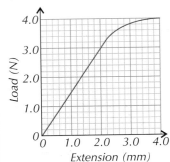

k is the gradient of the graph up to the limit of proportionality.

For this graph, this is shortly after the point where the load is 3.0 N and the extension is 2.0 mm.

Convert 2.0 mm into m, to get 0.002 m.

Then $k = \dfrac{\Delta F}{\Delta L} = \dfrac{3.0}{0.002} = 1500\,Nm^{-1}$.

Investigating extension

Figure 4 shows the experimental set-up you could use in the lab to investigate how the extension of an object varies with the force used to extend it.

The object under test should be supported at the top, e.g. using a clamp, and a measurement of its original length taken using a ruler. Weights should then be added one at a time to the other end of the object.

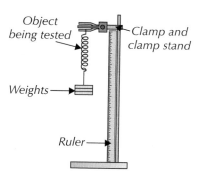

Figure 4: *An experimental set-up used to investigate how extension varies with force.*

The weights used will depend on the object being tested — you should do a trial investigation if you can to work out the range and size of weights needed. You want to be able to add the same size weight each time and add a large number of weights before the point the object breaks to get a good picture of how the extension of the object varies with the force applied to it.

After each weight is added, the extension of the object should be calculated. This can be done by measuring the new length of the object with a ruler, and then using:

> extension = new length – original length

Finally, a graph of load against extension should be plotted to show the results.

Tip: When carrying out this experiment, make sure you're stood up so you can move out of the way quickly if the weights fall. Ouch.

Tip: If you have unknown masses, rather than known weights, the object can be suspended by a <u>newton meter</u> — this will tell you the force being applied each time a mass is added.

Figure 5: *A student investigating how the extension of a rubber band varies with force.*

Elastic stretches

If a deformation is **elastic**, the material returns to its original shape once the forces are removed — so it has no permanent extension. Figure 6 shows a load-extension graph for an elastic material. Curve A shows the material being loaded and curve B shows the material being unloaded.

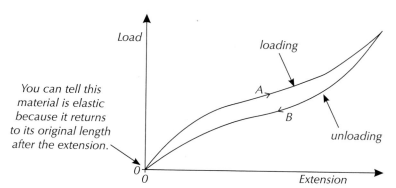

Figure 6: *A graph to show loading and unloading of an elastic material.*

Tip: 'Loading' just means increasing the force on the material and 'unloading' means reducing the force on the material.

Tip: You don't need to know why curves A and B aren't exactly the same — just that they start and end in the same place for elastic stretches.

When a material is put under tension, the atoms of the material are pulled apart from one another. Atoms can move small distances relative to their equilibrium positions without actually changing position in the material.

Once the load is removed, the atoms return to their equilibrium distance apart. For a metal, elastic deformation happens as long as Hooke's law is obeyed.

Plastic stretches

If a deformation is **plastic**, the material is permanently stretched (after the force has been removed). Some atoms in the material move position relative to one another. When the load is removed, the atoms don't return to their original positions. A metal stretched past its elastic limit shows plastic deformation.

Practice Questions — Application

Q1 A metal spring has a spring constant of 1250 Nm⁻¹. When a force is applied, the spring extends 1.60 cm. Calculate the force applied.

Tip: Remember, Hooke's law applies for compression as well as tension. Huzzah.

Q2 A spring is compressed 0.80 mm by a force of 20 N. Calculate the spring constant of the spring in Nm⁻¹.

Q3 The original length of a metal wire is 20.0 cm. A force of 55.0 N is applied and the wire extends to a new length of 22.0 cm. Assume that the limit of proportionality has not been reached.

  a) Calculate the extension of the wire in metres.

  b) Calculate the spring constant of the length of wire.

Q4 Below is a force-extension graph for an investigation into how extension varies with force for a rubber band. The band was loaded with weights, shown by curve A. The band was then unloaded, shown by curve B.

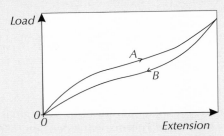

  a) Does the elastic band obey Hooke's law? Explain your answer.

  b) Is the rubber band elastic or plastic? Explain your answer.

Practice Questions — Fact Recall

Exam Tip
You'll be given the formula for Hooke's law in your formula booklet, so you don't need to know it off by heart.

Q1 What is Hooke's law?

Q2 Write down the formula for Hooke's law, defining all the symbols you use.

Q3 What is meant by the elastic limit of a material?

Q4 What is meant by the limit of proportionality for a material?

Q5 What does it mean if a material is deforming elastically?

Q6 What does it mean if a material is deforming plastically?

3. Stress and Strain

Two samples of the same material with different dimensions will stretch different amounts under the same force. Stress and strain are measurements that take into account the size of the sample, so a stress-strain graph is the same for any sample of a particular material.

Tensile stress and tensile strain

A material subjected to a pair of opposite forces might deform, i.e. change shape. If the forces stretch the material, they're tensile. If the forces squash the material, they're compressive.

Tensile stress is defined as the force applied, *F*, divided by the cross-sectional area, *A*:

$$\text{stress} = \frac{F}{A}$$

The units of stress are Nm^{-2} or pascals, Pa.

A stress causes a strain. **Tensile strain** is defined as the change in length, i.e. the extension, divided by the original length of the material:

$$\text{strain} = \frac{\Delta L}{L}$$

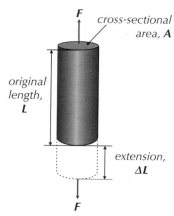

Figure 1: A pair of opposite tensile forces acting on an object.

Strain has no units — it's just a number.

It doesn't matter whether the forces producing the stress and strain are tensile or compressive — the same equations apply. The only difference is that you tend to think of tensile forces as positive, and compressive forces as negative.

Breaking stress

As a greater and greater tensile force is applied to a material, the stress on it increases.

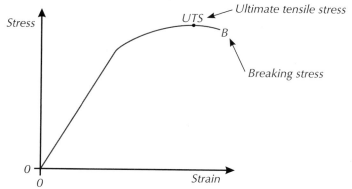

Figure 2: A stress-strain graph showing the ultimate tensile strength and breaking stress of a material.

The effect of the stress is to start to pull the atoms apart from one another. Eventually the stress becomes so great that atoms separate completely, and the material breaks. This is shown by point B on the graph in Figure 2. The stress at which this occurs is called the **breaking stress** — the stress that's big enough to break the material.

The point marked UTS on the graph in Figure 2 is called the **ultimate tensile stress**. This is the maximum stress that the material can withstand. Engineers have to consider the UTS and breaking stress of materials when designing a structure.

Figure 3: A material having its tensile stress tested by a machine.

Tip: 1 MPa is the same as 1×10^6 Pa.

┌ **Example** ─────────────────────────────

A rope has a cross-sectional area of 8.0×10^{-3} m². A tensile force is applied to the rope and slowly increased. The rope breaks when a force of 1.8×10^5 N is applied. Calculate the breaking stress of the material.

$$\text{stress} = \frac{F}{A} = \frac{1.8 \times 10^5}{8.0 \times 10^{-3}} = 2.3 \times 10^7 \,\text{Pa (or Nm}^{-2}\text{) (to 2 s.f.)}$$

You could also write 2.3×10^7 Pa as 23 MPa.

└──

Elastic strain energy

When a material is stretched, work has to be done in stretching the material. Before the elastic limit, all the work done in stretching is stored as potential energy in the material. This stored energy is called **elastic strain energy**. On a graph of force against extension, the elastic strain energy is given by the area under the graph — see Figure 4.

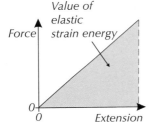

Figure 4: The area under a force-extension graph for a stretched material is the elastic strain energy stored by it.

┌ **Example** ─────────────────────────────

Shown to the right is a force-extension graph for a metal spring. Find the elastic strain energy stored in the spring when the extension is 0.3 m.

To find the elastic strain energy stored, you need to find the area under the graph shown highlighted below:

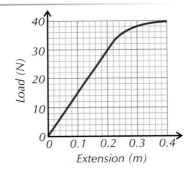

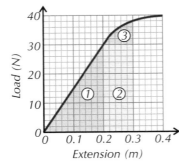

You can approximate the area using triangles and rectangles:

Area 1: ½ × 30 N × 0.2 m = 3 J
Area 2: 30 N × 0.1 m = 3 J
Area 3: ½ × 8 N × 0.1 m = 0.4 J
Total energy ≈ 3 J + 3 J + 0.4 J = 6.4 J

You can also approximate the area using the squares on the grid:

There are (approximately) 6 big squares, each worth: 10 N × 0.1 m = 1 J
So the total energy stored is ≈ 6 × 1 J = 6 J.

└──

Exam Tip
The examiners will accept a range of answers for questions like this, as it's tricky to get the area under a curve <u>exactly right</u>. But that doesn't mean you can be slapdash when working areas out — still do it carefully.

Tip: You could also count the number of small squares. Oh joy.

Calculating energy stored

Provided a material obeys Hooke's law, the potential energy stored inside it can be calculated quite easily using a formula. This formula can be derived using a force-extension graph and work done.

The energy stored by the stretched material is equal to the work done on the material in stretching it. So on a force-extension graph, the area underneath the straight line from the origin to the extension (ΔL) represents the energy stored (page 131) or the work done.

Work done is equal to force × displacement. But on a force-extension graph, the force acting on the material is not constant. Therefore you need to work out the average force acting on the material, from zero to F, which is $\frac{1}{2}F$. So it's the area underneath the straight line on a force-extension graph:

$$\text{work done} = \tfrac{1}{2}F \times \Delta L$$

And so the elastic strain energy, E, is:

$$E = \tfrac{1}{2}F\Delta L$$

Because Hooke's law is being obeyed, $F = k\Delta L$, which means F can be replaced in the equation to give:

$$E = \tfrac{1}{2}k(\Delta L)^2$$

If the material is stretched beyond the elastic limit, some work is done changing the positions of atoms. This will not be stored as strain energy and so isn't available when the force is released.

Tip: This is just the same as working out the area of a triangle: ($\frac{1}{2}$ × base × height).

Exam tip
In the exam, they might ask you to explain how the formula $E = \frac{1}{2}F\Delta L$ can be derived using a force-extension graph.

Practice Questions — Application

Q1 A force of 50 N is applied to wire with a cross-sectional area of 3.1×10^{-6} m². Calculate the stress on the wire.

Q2 A rope has an original length of 12.0 cm. After a force is applied, its length becomes 12.3 cm. Calculate the strain on the rope.

Q3 Calculate the energy stored in a spring when a force of 30 N has produced an extension of 1.2 cm.

Q4 A wire with a cross-sectional area of 1.2×10^{-7} m² has a breaking stress of 3.8×10^8 Pa. Calculate the minimum force you would need to apply to break the wire.

Tip: Watch out for the units in Q3 — to calculate the elastic strain energy, the force has to be in newtons and the extension has to be in metres.

Practice Questions — Fact Recall

Q1 What is meant by:
   a) tensile stress,
   b) tensile strain,
   c) breaking stress?

Q2 Explain how you would find the elastic strain energy stored by a stretched material using its force-extension graph.

Q3 Write down the formula relating the elastic strain energy, force and extension of a stretched material obeying Hooke's Law.

The Young modulus is a measure of how stiff a material is. It is really useful for comparing the stiffness of different materials, for example if you're trying to find out the best material for making a particular product.

Calculating the Young modulus

When you apply a load to stretch a material, it experiences a tensile stress and a tensile strain. Up to a point called the limit of proportionality, the stress and strain of a material are proportional to each other. So below this limit, for a particular material, stress divided by strain is a constant. This constant is called the **Young modulus, E**.

$$E = \frac{\text{tensile stress}}{\text{tensile strain}} = \frac{F/A}{\Delta L/L} = \frac{FL}{A\Delta L}$$

Where F = force in N, A = cross-sectional area in m², L = initial length in m and ΔL = extension in m. The units of the Young modulus are the same as stress (Nm⁻² or pascals), since strain has no units.

The Young modulus experiment

Figure 1 shows an experiment you could use to find out the Young modulus of a material:

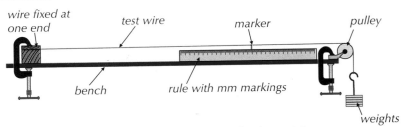

Figure 1: *Experimental set-up for determining the Young modulus of a test material.*

The test wire should be thin and as long as possible — at least over 1 m. The longer and thinner the wire, the more it extends for the same force. Start with the smallest weight necessary to straighten the wire. Measure the distance between the fixed end of the wire and the marker using a ruler — this is your unstretched length. If you then increase the weight, the wire stretches and the marker moves.

Increase the weight by steps, recording the marker reading each time — the extension is the difference between this reading and the unstretched length.

Once you've taken all your readings, use a micrometer to measure the diameter of the wire in several places. Take an average of your measurements, and use that to work out the average cross-sectional area of the wire. To make your results more accurate you could repeat your experiment.

The other standard way of measuring the Young modulus in the lab is using Searle's apparatus. This is a bit more accurate, but it's harder to do and the equipment's more complicated.

Finding the Young modulus using a graph

You can plot a graph of stress against strain from your results (page 130) — see Figure 3. The gradient of the graph gives the Young modulus, E.

$$E = \frac{\text{stress}}{\text{strain}} = \text{gradient}$$

The area under the graph gives the strain energy (or energy stored) per unit volume, i.e. the energy stored per 1 m³ of wire.

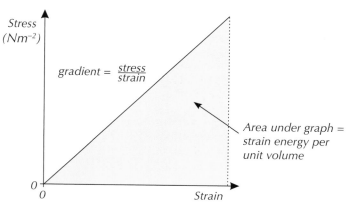

Figure 3: A stress-strain graph showing how to calculate the gradient and strain energy per unit volume.

The stress-strain graph is a straight line provided that Hooke's law is obeyed, so you can also calculate the energy per unit volume as:

energy per unit volume = ½ × stress × strain

Figure 2: Steel has a high Young modulus, which means under huge stress there's only a small strain. This makes it an ideal building material for things like bridges.

Tip: Remember, when using the gradient to work out the Young modulus, you can only use it up to the limit of proportionality (p.124). After then, the stress and strain are no longer proportional.

Practice Questions — Application

Q1 a) A copper wire has an original length of 1.0 m and an average diameter of 1.1 mm. What is the cross-sectional area of the wire?

    b) A force of 23 N is applied to the wire and it extends by 0.20 mm. Find the Young modulus of the copper.

Q2 A nylon wire with a cross-sectional area of 8.0×10^{-7} m² has a Young modulus of 3.5×10^8 Pa. A force of 100 N is applied to the wire.

    a) Calculate the stress on the wire.

    b) Calculate the strain on the wire.

Tip: Don't forget to convert any lengths to m and areas to m² when working out the Young modulus.

Practice Questions — Fact Recall

Q1 What are the units of the Young modulus?

Q2 Name four things you would need to measure when carrying out an experiment to find the Young modulus of a wire.

Q3 What does the gradient of a stress-strain graph tell you?

Q4 What does the area under a straight stress-strain graph tell you?

5. Interpreting Stress-Strain Curves

You've already seen how you can find the Young modulus and the energy stored per unit volume of a stretched material, using its stress-strain graph. Now it's time to look at a few more important features of a stress-strain curve.

Learning Objective:

- Be able to interpret simple stress-strain curves.

Specification Reference 3.2.2

Stress-strain graphs

In the exam you could be given a stress-strain graph and asked to interpret it. Luckily, most stress-strain graphs share three important points — as shown in Figure 1.

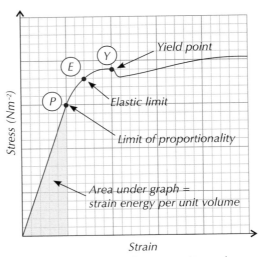

Figure 1: A typical stress-strain graph.

Before point *P*, the graph is a straight line through the origin. This shows that the material is obeying Hooke's law (page 123). The gradient of the line is constant — its the Young modulus (see page 130).

Point *P* is the limit of proportionality — after this, the graph is no longer a straight line but starts to bend. At this point, the material stops obeying Hooke's law, but would still return to its original shape if the stress was removed.

Point *E* is the elastic limit — at this point the material starts to behave plastically. From point E onwards, the material would no longer return to its original shape once the stress was removed.

Point *Y* is the **yield point** — here the material suddenly starts to stretch without any extra load. The yield point (or yield stress) is the stress at which a large amount of plastic deformation takes place with a constant or reduced load.

The area under the first part of the graph gives the energy stored in the material per unit volume (see page 131).

Tip: Plastic deformation is useful if you don't want a material to return to its original shape, e.g. drawing copper into wires or gold into foil (see photo below).

Figure 2: Rolls of gold foil being made at a factory.

Q1   Figure 3 shows a stress-strain graph for a material with three important points marked on it.

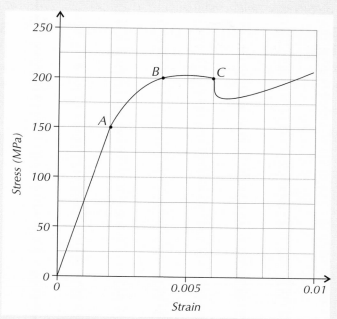

Figure 3: *A stress-strain graph for a material.*

a)   After which point will the material start to deform plastically?

b)   What law does the material obey between the origin and point A?

c)   Which point on the graph marks the yield point of the material?

d)   Find the Young modulus of the material.

e)   Calculate the energy stored per unit volume in the material up to the limit of proportionality.

Practice Questions — Fact Recall

Q1   What is the difference between a material at the elastic limit and the limit of proportionality?

Q2   What is the yield point of a material?

6. Brittle Materials

Some materials don't stretch much when you apply a force and will eventually snap. This can either be useful (such as breaking a chocolate bar), or not so useful (like breaking a bone... ouch).

Stress-strain graphs of brittle materials

The stress-strain graph for a brittle material doesn't curve. The graph shown in Figure 1 below is typical of a **brittle** material.

Learning Objective:

- Describe what is meant by the terms brittleness and brittle fracture.

Specification Reference 3.2.2

Tip: Notice how the straight line just stops. Very dramatic.

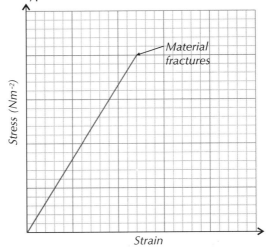

Figure 1: A stress-strain graph for a brittle material.

The graph starts with a straight line through the origin. So brittle materials also obey Hooke's law. However, when the stress reaches a certain point, the material snaps — it doesn't deform plastically.

Examples of brittle materials

As shown in Figure 1, if you apply a force to a brittle material, it won't deform plastically (see p.126), but will suddenly snap when the stress gets to a certain size. Brittle materials can also be quite weak if they have cracks in them.

A chocolate bar is an example of a brittle material — you can break chunks of chocolate off the bar without the whole thing changing shape. Ceramics (e.g. glass and pottery) are brittle too — they tend to shatter.

Figure 2: Ceramics are brittle materials. Which is great, if you're Greek.

The structure of brittle materials

Ceramics are made by melting certain materials, and then letting them cool. The arrangement of atoms in a ceramic can be crystalline or polycrystalline — where there are many regions (or grains) of crystalline structure. The atoms in each grain line up in a different direction.

However they're arranged, the atoms in a ceramic are bonded in a giant rigid structure. The strong bonds between the atoms make them stiff, while the rigid structure means that ceramics are very brittle materials.

When stress is applied to a brittle material any tiny cracks at the material's surface get bigger and bigger until the material breaks completely. This is called **brittle fracture**. The cracks in brittle materials are able to grow because these materials have a rigid structure. Other materials, like most metals, are not brittle because the atoms within them can move to prevent any cracks getting bigger.

Tip: Don't worry if you don't know what crystalline or polycrystalline structures look like — just remember that brittle materials are <u>brittle</u> because they have a <u>rigid structure</u>.

Practice Question — Application

Q1 The graph to the right is a stress-strain graph for two different materials.

Which graph, A or B, shows a brittle material? Explain your answer.

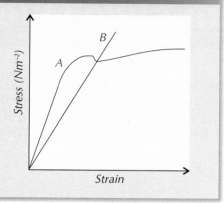

Tip: Think about the features of both graphs.

Practice Questions — Fact Recall

Q1 What is a brittle material?

Q2 Do brittle materials obey Hooke's law? Explain your answer.

Q3 Give an example of a brittle material.

Q4 What is a brittle fracture?

Section Summary

Make sure you know...

- What density is and how to calculate the density of an object, using its mass and volume.
- What Hooke's law is.
- How to calculate the spring constant or stiffness constant for an object.
- What the elastic limit and limit of proportionality of an object are.
- How to use an experiment to investigate the extension of a material.
- What is meant by a material behaving elastically or plastically.
- What tensile stress is and how to calculate it.
- What tensile strain is and how to calculate it.
- What the breaking stress of a material is.
- How to calculate the elastic strain energy stored in a stretched material using a force-extension graph or the equation: energy stored = ½ $F\Delta L$
- How to derive the formula: energy stored = ½ $F\Delta L$.
- How to use the formula for the Young modulus.
- How to carry out an investigation to find the Young modulus of a material.
- How to use the gradient of a stress-strain graph to find the Young modulus of a material.
- That, up to the limit of proportionality, the area under a stress-strain graph is the strain energy per unit volume.
- How to interpret simple stress-strain curves.
- What the yield point of a material is.
- What is meant by brittleness and brittle fracture.
- That brittle materials are brittle because of their rigid structure.

Exam-style Questions

1 A materials scientist carried out an investigation to find how the extension of a rubber cord varied with the forces used to extend it. She measured the extension for an increasing load and then for a decreasing load. The graph below shows her results. Curve A shows loading and curve B shows unloading of the cord.

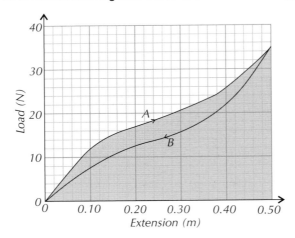

1 (a) State the feature of the graph that shows that the rubber cord is elastic.

(1 mark)

1 (b) Name the physical quantity which is represented by the shaded area on the graph, between the loading curve A and the extension axis.

(1 mark)

1 (c) The rubber cord has a cross-sectional area of 5.0×10^{-6} m^2 and had an initial length of 0.80 m.

Assuming that curve A is linear for an extension of 0.080 m, calculate the Young modulus for the rubber material for small loads. Give your answer in Pa.

(3 marks)

2 A spring is used in a pen as part of the mechanism which opens and closes it. For small loads, the spring obeys Hooke's law.

2 (a) Define Hooke's law.

(2 marks)

2 (b) The spring constant for the spring is 600 Nm^{-1}.

2 (b) (i) Calculate the distance that the spring is compressed when a user pushes it down with a force of 0.90 N.

(2 marks)

2 (b) (ii) The spring must not be compressed more than 0.020 m. Calculate the maximum force that can be applied to the spring.

(2 marks)

3 (a) Describe the experimental method you would use to carry out an investigation to accurately find the Young modulus of a metal wire.

Include a labelled diagram in your answer.

The quality of your written communication will be assessed in this question.

(6 marks)

3 (b) The graph below shows the stress and strain on a metal wire as it was stretched.

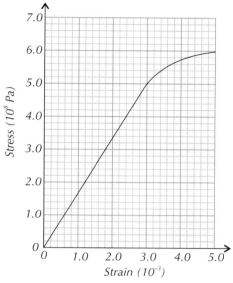

3 (b) Use the graph to calculate the Young modulus of the metal.
Give your answer in an appropriate unit.

(4 marks)

4 A chandelier is used as part of the scenery for a stage show.

4 (a) The chandelier is suspended from the ceiling above the stage by a 2.0 m steel cable. The tension in the cable will be 2.0 kN and it must not extend more than 0.20 mm. The Young modulus for steel is 2.10×10^{11} Pa.

Calculate the minimum cross-sectional area the cable should have, in m^2.

(3 marks)

4 (b) As part of the show, a chandelier falls to the floor and shatters.
The chandelier must be made of a brittle material that will break under a low stress.

4 (b) (i) What is meant by a brittle material?

(1 mark)

4 (b) (ii) State and explain which of the materials, A, B or C, shown by the stress-strain graph below should be chosen to make the chandelier.

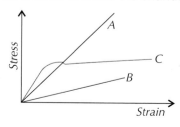

(2 marks)

1. The Nature of Waves

Waves are just vibrations. They transfer energy through a medium, but once they've gone everything goes back to normal... like they were never there.

Wave basics

A **progressive wave** (moving wave) carries energy from one place to another without transferring any material. Imagine a buoy bobbing up and down on a water wave — the buoy doesn't move from its location except to move up and down as the wave passes.

    A wave is caused by something making particles or fields (e.g. electric or magnetic fields) oscillate (or vibrate) at a source. These oscillations pass through the medium as the wave travels. A wave carries energy, and transfers this energy away from its source — so the source of the wave loses energy.

Here are some ways you can tell waves carry energy:

- Electromagnetic waves cause things to heat up.
- X-rays and gamma rays knock electrons out of their orbits, causing ionisation.
- Loud sounds make things vibrate.
- Wave power can be used to generate electricity.

Waves can be reflected, refracted and diffracted.

Reflection — the wave is bounced back when it hits a boundary (see Figure 2). E.g. you can see the reflection of light in mirrors.

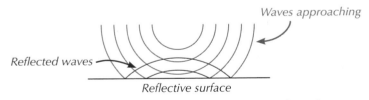

Waves approaching

Reflected waves

Reflective surface

Figure 2: *Waves being reflected as they hit a boundary.*

Refraction — the wave changes direction as it enters a different medium (see Figure 3). The change in direction is a result of the wave slowing down or speeding up.

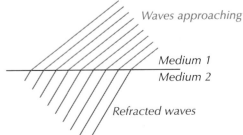

Waves approaching

Medium 1

Medium 2

Refracted waves

Figure 3: *Waves being refracted as they pass from one medium to another.*

Learning Objectives:

- Understand that waves cause the particles of the medium they travel through to oscillate.
- Understand the following characteristics of a wave: amplitude, frequency, wavelength, wave speed and phase difference.
- Know how to calculate wave speed using $c = f\lambda$.

    Specification Reference 3.2.3

Figure 1: *A ripple tank is a shallow tank of water in which waves are created by a vibrating dipper. It is often used to demonstrate wave properties.*

Tip: In Figures 2 and 3, the lines represent the crests of the waves (see page 139).

Tip: There's much more on refraction on pages 148-152.

Diffraction — the wave spreads out as it passes through a gap or round an obstacle (see Figure 4). E.g. you can hear sound from round a corner.

Waves approaching   Diffracted waves

Tip: There's more about diffraction on pages 160-161.

Figure 4: *Waves being diffracted as they pass through a gap.*

Measuring waves

There are lots of measurements that you can use to describe a wave. Make sure you learn what they are, their symbol and the units they're given in. You could be asked to find them from a graph or a diagram of a wave.

- **Displacement**, X, measured in metres
  — how far a point on the wave has moved from its undisturbed position. Going back to the buoy example on page 138, the displacement would be how high the buoy is above sea level, or how low it is below sea level.

- **Amplitude**, a, measured in metres
  — the maximum displacement, i.e. the distance from the undisturbed position to the crest, or trough. The amplitude of a bobbing buoy would be the distance from the undisturbed position (sea level) to the highest point it reaches above sea level, or the lowest point it reaches below sea level.

Tip: Displacement is a vector so it has direction and magnitude (see page 80) — if a point has moved below its undisturbed position, it will have a negative displacement.

Tip: Amplitude can either be measured at a crest or a trough. It doesn't have direction, only magnitude.

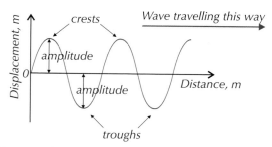

Figure 5: *Diagram showing the displacement and amplitude of a wave.*

Figure 6: *An oscilloscope can be used to measure the different parts of a wave.*

- **Wavelength**, λ, measured in metres
  — the length of one whole wave oscillation or wave cycle, e.g. the distance between two crests (or troughs) of a wave.

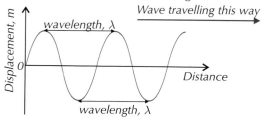

Figure 7: *Diagram to show the wavelength of a wave.*

Tip: One oscillation or wave cycle is a 'section' of a wave from crest to crest, or trough to trough.

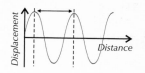

- **Period**, T, measured in seconds
  — the time taken for one whole wave cycle, e.g. the time it takes a buoy to go from its highest point, back to its highest point again.

Tip: Waves with different frequencies and wavelengths can have very different properties (see page 12).

- **Frequency**, f, measured in hertz
  — the number of whole wave cycles (oscillations) per second passing a given point. Or the number of whole wave cycles (oscillations) given out from a source per second. For a buoy, it's the number of times it reaches its highest point per second.

- **Phase difference** (see page 155), measured in degrees or radians.
  — the amount by which one wave lags behind another wave.

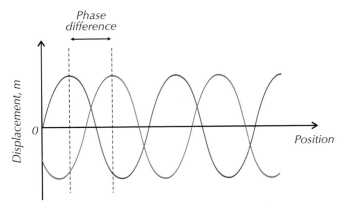

Tip: The phase difference is the difference between two identical points (e.g. the point where the displacement is at a maximum) on two waves.

Figure 8: Diagram to show the phase difference between waves.

Frequency and period

Frequency and period are linked to each other. The number of whole wave cycles (oscillations) per second is 1/(time taken for one oscillation). So the frequency is the inverse of the period:

Tip: You might remember this equation from page 74.

f = Frequency in Hz (= s^{-1})

$$f = \frac{1}{T}$$

T = (Time) period in s

Example

A wave has a period of 0.25 seconds.
How many oscillations will pass a given point each second?

The number of oscillations passing a point per second is the frequency,

so frequency = $\dfrac{1}{\text{time period}}$

$= \dfrac{1}{0.25 \text{ s}}$

$= 4 \text{ Hz}$

So 4 oscillations pass each second.

Exam Tip
If you can remember 1 Hz = 1 s^{-1}, it'll help you get your units right. Don't write s^{-1} in an exam though, Hz is the standard (SI) unit for frequency (see p.186 for more on SI units).

Wave speed

Wave speed can be measured just like the speed of anything else — speed is equal to distance over time (see page 95):

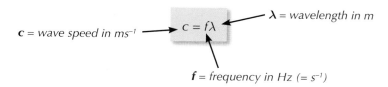

c = wave speed in ms^{-1} $\quad c = \dfrac{d}{t} \quad$ d = distance in m

t = time in s

From this you can get the wave equation (which you've seen before on p.12):

c = wave speed in ms^{-1} $\quad c = f\lambda \quad$ λ = wavelength in m

f = frequency in Hz $(= s^{-1})$

You can derive the wave speed equation by imagining how long it takes for the crest of a wave to move across a distance of one wavelength.

- The distance travelled is the wavelength, λ.
- The time taken to travel one wavelength is the period of the wave, which is equal to $\frac{1}{f}$.

Now substitute these values into the normal speed equation above to get the speed of a wave in terms of wavelength and frequency:

$$speed\ (c) = \frac{distance\ moved\ (\lambda)}{time\ taken\ \left(\frac{1}{f}\right)}$$

Dividing something by $\frac{1}{f}$ is the same as multiplying it by f.
So from this you get the wave speed equation shown above:

$$c = \frac{\lambda}{\left(\frac{1}{f}\right)} = f\lambda$$

Tip: For waves, c is used instead of v, and d is used instead of s — these are different to the symbols used in mechanics. Don't confuse c with the speed of light in a vacuum, 3×10^8 ms^{-1}. That's just the speed of light waves specifically.

Tip: You need to be able to rearrange this equation so you can find c, λ or f.

Tip: Remember, you're not measuring how fast a physical point (like one molecule of rope) moves. You're measuring how fast a point on the wave pattern moves.

Example

Below is a diagram of a water wave.
Calculate the speed of the wave, if the frequency is 5 Hz.

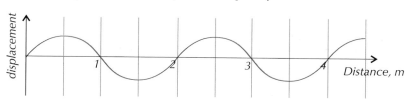

First find λ by calculating the distance, e.g. between two peaks:
$\lambda = 2.5 - 0.5 = 2$ m
Then substitute λ and f into $c = f\lambda$ to find the speed of the wave:
$c = f\lambda = 5 \times 2 = 10$ ms^{-1}

Practice Questions — Application

Q1 For the wave shown below, find:

   a) The displacement at the point A.   b) The amplitude.

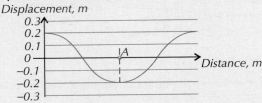

Q2 For the wave shown below:

   a) Find its wavelength.

   b) Find the speed of the wave given that the frequency is 30 Hz.

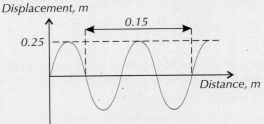

Q3 A wave is travelling at 25.0 ms^{-1} with a frequency of 2.20 Hz. Calculate the wavelength of the wave.

Practice Questions — Fact Recall

Q1 How does a wave transfer energy through a medium?

Q2 What causes a wave to refract?

Q3 Which of the following measurements can take a negative value?

   a) displacement   b) amplitude

Q4 On the diagram below, what's shown by A, B and C?

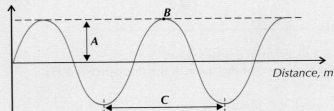

Q5 State what units the following properties of waves are measured in:

   a) displacement,   b) amplitude,   c) frequency.

Q6 How would you calculate the frequency of a wave, given its period?

Q7 What does c stand for in the equation $c = f\lambda$?

Tip: Formula triangles can help you to rearrange equations. Just cross out the thing you need to work out and then carry out the calculation that's left.

2. Transverse and Longitudinal Waves

Learning Objectives:

- Know the characteristics of transverse and longitudinal waves.
- Know that electromagnetic waves are transverse.
- Know that sound waves are longitudinal.
- Understand that transverse waves can be polarised.
- Be able to give applications of polarisation, e.g. sunglasses.

Specification Reference 3.2.3

Waves can exist in two different forms — transverse and longitudinal. Each form has different properties, which is how you can tell them apart.

Transverse waves

In **transverse waves** the vibration is at right angles to the direction of travel. All electromagnetic waves are transverse. Other examples of transverse waves are ripples on water, waves on ropes, and some types of earthquake shock wave (S-waves).

Figure 1 shows how a transverse wave can be demonstrated using a slinky.

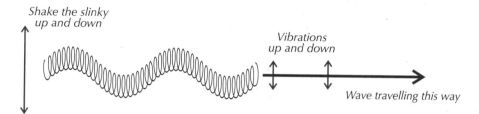

Shake the slinky up and down

Vibrations up and down

Wave travelling this way

Figure 1: *A transverse wave on a slinky.*

Tip: Remember, electromagnetic waves include radio waves, microwaves, infrared, visible light, ultraviolet, X-rays and gamma rays. See p.12 for more on the electromagnetic spectrum.

There are two main ways of drawing transverse waves — see Figure 2. They can be shown as graphs of displacement against distance along the path of the wave (like you've seen on the last few pages). Or they can be shown as graphs of displacement against time for a point as the wave passes. Both sorts of graph often give the same shape, so make sure you check the label on the *x*-axis. Displacements upwards from the centre line are given a + sign. Displacements downwards are given a – sign.

Tip: In displacement-time graphs of waves, the time of one complete wave (e.g. from crest to crest, or trough to trough) is the period of the wave (*T*).

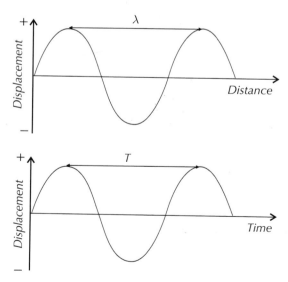

Figure 2: *A displacement-distance graph and a displacement-time graph for a transverse wave.*

Figure 3: *A slinky is shaken from side to side to form a transverse wave.*

Longitudinal waves

In **longitudinal waves** the vibrations are along the direction of travel. The most common example of a longitudinal wave is sound.

A sound wave consists of alternate compressions and rarefactions of the medium it's travelling through. Some types of earthquake shock waves are also longitudinal (P-waves). Figure 4 shows how a longitudinal wave can be demonstrated using a slinky.

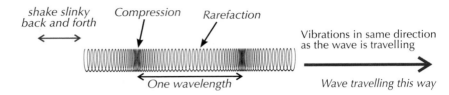

Figure 4: A longitudinal wave on a slinky.

Tip: For a longitudinal wave, the wavelength is the distance between compressions (or rarefactions) instead of between crests or troughs in transverse waves.

It's hard to represent longitudinal waves graphically. You'll usually see them plotted as displacement against time. These can be confusing though, because they look like a transverse wave.

Polarised waves

If you shake a rope to make a wave you can move your hand up and down or side to side or in a mixture of directions — it still makes a transverse wave.

But if you try to pass waves in a rope through a vertical fence, the wave will only get through if the vibrations are vertical. The fence filters out vibrations in other directions. The result is a **polarised wave** — a wave that oscillates in one direction only (see Figure 5).

Tip: Transverse waves drawn on a displacement-time or displacement-distance graph look like they only vibrate in one direction (up and down). But unpolarised transverse waves actually vibrate in all directions on the plane perpendicular to the direction of motion.

Tip: This rope is being twirled, so that it is vibrating in a mixture of vibrations.

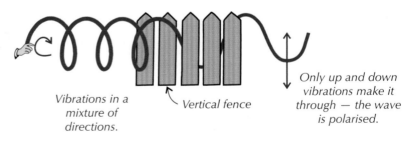

Figure 5: The polarisation of a transverse wave through a fence.

Ordinary light waves are a mixture of different directions of vibration. A **polarising filter** can be used to polarise light and other waves. It only transmits vibrations in one direction. If you have two polarising filters at right angles to each other, then no light will get through — see Figures 6 and 7.

Figure 6: Two polarising filters at right angles to each other block all light.

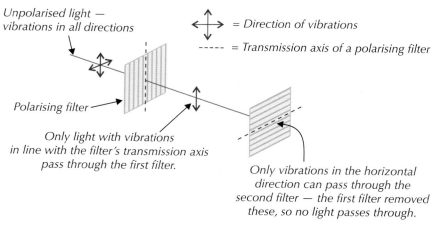

Unpolarised light —
vibrations in all directions

↕ = *Direction of vibrations*

---- = *Transmission axis of a polarising filter*

Polarising filter

Only light with vibrations
in line with the filter's transmission axis
pass through the first filter.

Only vibrations in the horizontal
direction can pass through the
second filter — the first filter removed
these, so no light passes through.

Figure 7: *An unpolarised light wave passing through two*
polarising filters at right angles to each other.

Tip: The transmission
axis of a polarising filter
shows the only direction
of vibrations which can
pass through the filter.

The second filter only blocks out all of the light when the transmission
axis is at right angles to the plane of polarisation. Otherwise, it just reduces
the intensity of the light passing through it (but still allows some light through).

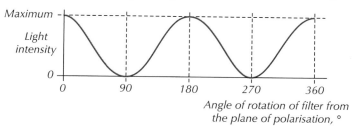

Figure 8: *The effect of rotating a polarising filter on the*
intensity of polarised light passing through it.

Tip: Make sure you
understand why the
graph has peaks and
troughs where it does.
At 90° and 270°, the
transmission axis of
the second filter will
be perpendicular to
the first filter, so no
light will be able to get
through. At 180° and
360° the transmission
axes of both filters will
be aligned, so all of the
light passing through
the first filter will be
able to pass through the
second.

Polarisation can only happen for transverse waves. The fact that you can
polarise light is one proof that it's a transverse wave.

Polarisation in the real world

The polarisation of light and other waves has applications and implications
in everyday life.

Glare reduction

Most light you see is unpolarised — the vibrations are in all possible
directions. But reflected light is partially polarised — most of it vibrates in
the same direction (see Figure 9). When light is reflected by surfaces such as
water, glass and Tarmac, and enters the eye, it can cause glare. The fact that
reflected light is partially polarised allows us to filter it out with polarising filters.

Tip: Glare can be
dangerous when driving
or sailing as it makes it
hard to see.

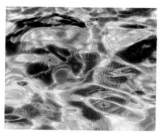

Figure 10: *The light reflecting*
off water is partially polarised,
so a polarising filter can let
you see underwater shapes
more clearly.

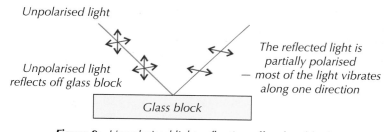

Unpolarised light

Unpolarised light
reflects off glass block

The reflected light is
partially polarised
— most of the light vibrates
along one direction

Glass block

Figure 9: *Unpolarised light reflecting off a glass block.*

If you view partially-polarised reflected light through a polarising filter at the right angle, you can block out most of the reflected light, while still letting through light which vibrates at the angle of the filter. This reduces the intensity of the light entering your eye. This effect is used to reduce unwanted reflections in photography, and in Polaroid sunglasses to reduce glare.

Improving TV and radio signals

TV signals are polarised by the orientation of the rods on the transmitting aerial. To receive a strong signal, you have to line up the rods on the receiving aerial with the rods on the transmitting aerial — if they aren't aligned, the signal strength will be lower, so the rods on TV aerials are all horizontal.

It's the same with radio — if you try tuning a radio and then moving the aerial around, your signal will come and go as the transmitting and receiving aerials go in and out of alignment.

Rotating the plane of polarisation

The plane in which a wave moves and vibrates is called the plane of polarisation, e.g. the rope on page 144 was polarised in the vertical plane by the fence. Some materials (e.g. crystals) rotate the plane of polarised light. Figure 12 shows the effect of putting a material between two polarisation filters at right angles. The material alters the plane of the polarised light and some light passes through the second filter.

Figure 11: The rods on the transmitting aerial (top) and receiving aerial (bottom) are both horizontal.

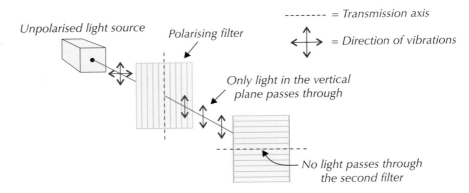

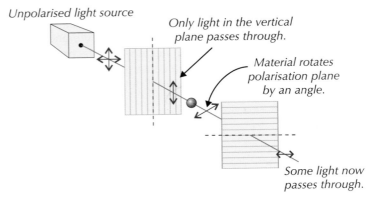

Figure 12: The effect of a material rotating the plane of polarisation of light.

You can measure how much a material rotates the plane of polarised light using two polarising filters like this. Rotate the second filter so that no light passes through — the angle you rotate the filter is the angle that the material rotates the plane of polarisation.

Practice Questions — Application

Q1 The diagram below shows an unpolarised wave passing through two polarising filters.

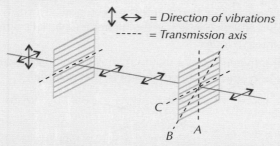

$\updownarrow$ $\leftrightarrow$ = Direction of vibrations
----- = Transmission axis

a) Is this wave transverse or longitudinal? Explain your answer.

b) Which line, A, B or C, represents the transmission axis of the second polarising filter? Explain your answer.

c) Explain what would happen if the second polarising filter was rotated 90°.

Q2 Bruno is watching TV when the signal suddenly disappears. When he goes outside to investigate he finds a fat seagull sat on his TV aerial, causing it to droop. Why would this cause a loss in signal?

Practice Questions — Fact Recall

Q1 What is the difference between transverse and longitudinal waves?

Q2 What does A represent on the graph of a transverse wave below?

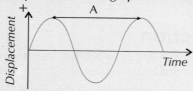

Q3 Give an example of a transverse wave and a longitudinal wave.

Q4 What happens when you put two polarising filters at right angles in front of a beam of light?

Q5 What happens to unpolarised light when it is reflected?

Q6 Explain how Polaroid sunglasses reduce glare.

Q7 Other than polarising sunglasses, give one example of how polarised waves are relevant to everyday life.

3. Refractive Index

You came across refraction on p.138 — light changes speed and direction if it passes into a material with a different density. You can work out the new direction if you know the refractive index of the material.

The refractive index of a material

Light goes fastest in a vacuum. It slows down in other materials, because it interacts with the particles in them. The more **optically dense** a material is, the more light slows down when it enters it. The optical density of a material is measured by its refractive index — the higher a material's optical density is, the higher its refractive index.

The **refractive index** of a material, n, is the ratio between the speed of light in a vacuum, c, and the speed of light in that material, c_s.

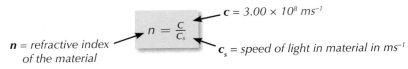

$$n = \frac{c}{c_s}$$

$c = 3.00 \times 10^8 \ ms^{-1}$

n = refractive index of the material

c_s = speed of light in material in ms^{-1}

The refractive index of a material is a property of that material only. The speed of light in air is only a tiny bit smaller than c. So you can assume the refractive index of air, $n_{air} = 1$.

Example

The refractive index of a plastic block is 1.47. What's the speed of light in the plastic?

First rearrange the refractive index equation to make c_s the subject:

$$n = \frac{c}{c_s} \Rightarrow c_s = \frac{c}{n}$$

Then just put in the numbers:

$$c_s = \frac{c}{n} = \frac{3.00 \times 10^8}{1.47} = 2.04 \times 10^8 \ ms^{-1} \ \text{(to 3 s.f.)}$$

The law of refraction

If light is passing through a boundary between two materials, you can use the law of refraction to calculate unknown angles or refractive indices.

The angle that incoming light makes to the normal, θ_1, is called the **angle of incidence**. The angle the refracted ray makes with the normal, θ_2, is the **angle of refraction**.

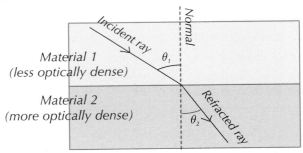

Figure 1: Refraction of light passing into a more optically dense material.

Sidebar

Learning Objectives:

- Understand what the refractive index of a substance is, and how to calculate it using the formula $n = \frac{c}{c_s}$.
- Be able to use the law of refraction for a boundary of two substances, $n_1 \sin\theta_1 = n_2 \sin\theta_2$.

Specification Reference 3.2.3

Tip: When a wave is refracted, its speed and wavelength change but its frequency remains constant.

Tip: The refractive index has no units — it's just a ratio.

Tip: The normal is the straight line drawn at a right angle to the boundary between the two materials at the point the incident ray hits.

Figure 2: The refraction of light waves causes objects to look distorted underwater.

The law of refraction for a boundary between two materials is given by:

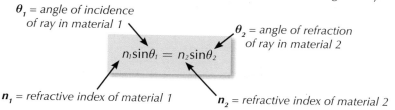

θ_1 = angle of incidence of ray in material 1

θ_2 = angle of refraction of ray in material 2

$$n_1\sin\theta_1 = n_2\sin\theta_2$$

n_1 = refractive index of material 1

n_2 = refractive index of material 2

Tip: You might have learnt the angle of incidence as i and the angle of refraction as r. This equation just uses the symbols θ_1 and θ_2 for them instead.

As light moves across a boundary between two materials of different optical densities, its direction changes because of its change in speed.
The direction can change in two ways:

- Towards the normal, if it passes from a less optically dense material into a more optically dense material. E.g. if $n_1 < n_2$ then $\theta_1 > \theta_2$.
- Away from the normal, if it passes from a more optically dense material into a less optically dense material. E.g. if $n_1 > n_2$ then $\theta_1 < \theta_2$.

Looking back at Figure 2, the green material is more optically dense, so $\theta_1 > \theta_2$.

Exam Tip
You're given the law of refraction and the equation for finding the refractive index in the data and formulae booklet.

Examples

Calculate the refractive index of material 2 in the diagram, given that material 1 has a refractive index of 1.1.

First look at what information you've been given:

$n_1 = 1.1$, $n_2 = ?$, $\theta_1 = 39.5°$, $\theta_2 = 29°$

You can use the law of refraction to find the missing value, but you'll have to rearrange the equation first to find n_2:

$$n_1\sin\theta_1 = n_2\sin\theta_2 \Rightarrow n_2 = \frac{n_1\sin\theta_1}{\sin\theta_2}$$

$$\Rightarrow n_2 = \frac{1.1\sin 39.5°}{\sin 29°} = 1.4 \text{ (to 2 s.f.)}$$

39.5°

Material 1

Material 2

29°

You can check your answer seems right by looking at how the direction changes. Here $\theta_1 > \theta_2$ so $n_1 < n_2$, which your answer shows.

Tip: It's easy to remember which way the ray bends if you picture a car (representing light rays) driving from the road (representing a less optically dense material) into sand (representing a more optically dense material) at an angle. When a tyre goes from road to sand, that side of the car will slow down and the car will turn into the sand.

Tip: Make sure your calculator is set to degrees for these examples.

Calculate the angle of incidence of the light ray in the diagram to the right.

Start again by looking at what you know already:

$n_1 = 1.00$, $n_2 = 1.50$, $\theta_1 = ?$, $\theta_2 = 36.5°$

θ_1

Refractive index : 1.00
Refractive index : 1.50

36.5°

Then rearrange the law of refraction equation to find θ_1:

$$n_1\sin\theta_1 = n_2\sin\theta_2 \Rightarrow \theta_1 = \sin^{-1}\left(\frac{n_2\sin\theta_2}{n_1}\right)$$

$$\Rightarrow \theta_1 = \sin^{-1}\left(\frac{1.50\sin 36.5°}{1.00}\right) = 63.2° \text{ (to 3 s.f.)}$$

Tip: Remember to be consistent with your significant figures — you should try to give your answer to the same s.f. as any numbers given in the question. If there's a mixture in the question, give it to the lowest number of s.f., or one more.

Exam Tip
The speed of light in a vacuum (c) is 3.00×10^8 ms^{-1} — it's in the data and formulae book if you can't remember it.

Q1 The speed of light in a material is 1.94×10^8 ms^{-1}.

 a) Calculate the refractive index of the material.

 b) Light travels from air ($n = 1$) into the material. Will the light bend towards or away from the normal as it enters the material? Explain your answer.

Q2 A fisherman sees a lobster cage on the sea floor and tries to retrieve it by lowering a winch directly over where the cage appears to be. The winch lands behind the cage.

 a) Explain why the cage isn't exactly where he thought it was.

 b) The fisherman uses an underwater camera to get a better view. Light travels from the lobster cage and hits the camera lens at an angle of 37.2° to the normal. If water has a refractive index of 1.40 and the lens has a refractive index of 1.49, at what angle to the normal will the refracted ray in the camera lens be?

Exam Tip
You'll be given the formula for calculating the refractive index in the exam, but you need to know how and when to use it.

Q1 What is the refractive index of a material?

Q2 Write down the formula for calculating the refractive index of a material and say what each part of the equation represents.

Q3 Light travels from one material to another and refracts at the boundary. If you know the angle of incidence, the angle of refraction and the refractive index of the first material, how would you find the refractive index of the second material?

Q4 In what way will light bend if it passes at an angle into a medium with a higher refractive index than the material it just left?

4. Critical Angle and TIR

Learning Objectives:
- Understand what the critical angle is and how to calculate it using $\sin \theta_c = \frac{n_2}{n_1}$.
- Understand what total internal reflection is.
- Know that light which has an angle of incidence greater than the critical angle will undergo total internal reflection.
- Understand how fibre optic cables work, and how they are used in communications.

Specification Reference 3.2.3

When light goes from a more optically dense material into a less optically dense material (e.g. glass to air), interesting things can happen.

The critical angle of a boundary

Shine a ray of light at a glass to air boundary, then gradually increase the angle of incidence. As you increase the angle of incidence (θ_1), the angle of refraction (θ_2) gets closer and closer to 90°. Eventually θ_1 reaches a **critical angle** (θ_c) for which $\theta_2 = 90°$. The light is refracted along the boundary — see Figure 1.

This can happen for any boundary where the light is passing from a more optically dense material (n_1, higher refractive index) into a less optically dense material (n_2, lower refractive index).

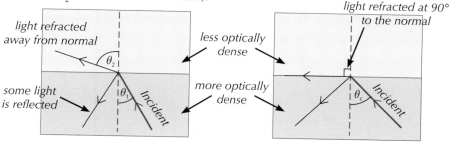

Figure 1: Refraction of light near to and along a boundary, when incident below and at the critical angle.

You can work out the critical angle for a certain boundary with the equation:

θ_c = critical angle ⟶ $\sin \theta_c = \frac{n_2}{n_1}$ ⟵ n_2 = refractive index of less optically dense material

n_1 = refractive index of more optically dense material

Figure 2: Light enters the prism from underneath and then strikes the prism-air boundary at the critical angle. Some light is reflected (left) and some continues parallel to the prism surface (top).

You can derive this formula by rearranging the law of refraction:

$$n_1 \sin \theta_1 = n_2 \sin \theta_2$$

First, rearrange it to get the angles on the same side:

$$\frac{\sin \theta_1}{\sin \theta_2} = \frac{n_2}{n_1}$$

The angle of incidence is equal to the critical angle when the angle of refraction is 90°, so put these values in:

$\sin 90° = 1$ ⟶ $\frac{\sin \theta_c}{\sin 90°} = \frac{n_2}{n_1}$

$\sin 90° = 1$, so the formula becomes:

$$\sin \theta_c = \frac{n_2}{n_1}$$

The refractive index of air is 1, so this can be simplified for a material to air boundary by letting $n_2 = 1$:

Refractive index of material ⟶ $n_1 = \frac{1}{\sin \theta_c}$ ⟵ critical angle for material to air boundary

Exam Tip
The formula for finding the critical angle is given in the data and formulae booklet in the exam, so you don't need to remember it. Just make sure you know what the symbols mean, and when and how to use it.

Tip: The assumption here is that air is the _less optically dense_ material — this is usually the case, because light travels almost as fast in air as it does in a vacuum.

Examples

Find the critical angle of a glass to air boundary if the glass has a refractive index of 1.5.

You've been asked to find the critical angle for a boundary with air, and you know the refractive index of the other material. So you can use the formula for the critical angle of a material to air boundary on the previous page. But you need to rearrange it for θ_c first:

$$n_1 = \frac{1}{\sin\theta_c} \Rightarrow \sin\theta_c = \frac{1}{n_1}, \text{ which gives:}$$

$$\theta_c = \sin^{-1}\left(\frac{1}{n_1}\right) = \sin^{-1}\left(\frac{1}{1.5}\right) = 42° \text{ (to 2 s.f.)}$$

A plastic block is immersed in a liquid. If the refractive index of the liquid is 1.40 and the critical angle for light travelling from the plastic to the liquid is 79.1°, find the refractive index of the plastic.

Write down what you know: $\theta_c = 79.1°$, $n_1 = ?$, $n_2 = 1.40$

Then rearrange the critical angle formula on the previous page to find n_1:

$$\sin\theta_c = \frac{n_2}{n_1} \Rightarrow n_1 = \frac{n_2}{\sin\theta_c} = \frac{1.40}{\sin 79.1°} = 1.43 \text{ (to 3 s.f.)}$$

Tip: Make sure your calculator is set to degrees mode to work out the inverse sin ($\sin^{-1}$) of this angle.

Total internal reflection

At angles of incidence greater than the critical angle, refraction can't happen. That means all the light is reflected back into the material. This effect is called **total internal reflection** (**TIR**) — see Figures 3 and 4.

Figure 3: Total internal reflection of a laser beam inside an optical fibre (light travelling from right to left).

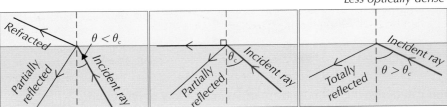

Figure 4: Light hitting a boundary with a less optically dense material at different angles of incidence.

Optical fibres

An **optical fibre** is a very thin flexible tube of glass or plastic fibre that can carry light signals over long distances and round corners using TIR. The core of an optical fibre has a high refractive index (it is optically dense) but is surrounded by cladding with a lower refractive index (less optically dense).

Tip: You might hear optical fibres called 'step-index optical fibres'. This just refers to the 'step down' of the refractive index from the core to the cladding.

Tip: The science and use of optical fibres is known as fibre optics.

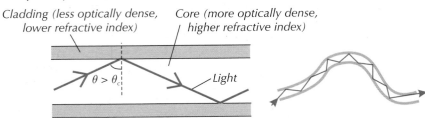

Figure 5: An optical fibre.

Light is shone in at one end of the fibre. The fibre is so narrow that the light always hits the boundary between the fibre and cladding at an angle greater than the critical angle. So all the light is totally internally reflected from boundary to boundary until it reaches the other end. It doesn't matter what shape the fibre is in either — TIR always occurs until light comes out of the other end.

Light running through optical fibres is used to transmit phone and cable TV signals. It has many advantages over the old system of using electricity flowing through copper cables (although this is still used in places):

- The signal can carry more information because light has a high frequency.
- The light doesn't heat up the fibre — so almost no energy is lost as heat.
- There is no electrical interference.
- They are much cheaper to produce.
- The signal can travel a long way, very quickly and with minimal signal loss (although some does occur — see below).

Tip: Electrical interference is usually the result of electromagnetic radiation from external sources or electromagnetic induction (this is covered at A2 level).

Signal degradation in optical fibres

Information is sent down optical fibres as pulses of light that carry a digital signal. A digital signal either has a value of 1 or 0, and looks like the diagram on the right. In this form, signal degradation is minimal, but it does occur:

- As the signal travels, some of its energy is lost through absorption and scattering by the material the optical fibre is made from. Energy is also lost if any light escapes the fibre. This energy loss results in the amplitude of the signal being reduced. A signal booster can be used along the fibre to reverse this effect.
- A signal that travels straight down the middle of a fibre will take less time than one which bounces off the sides. This means parts of the signal will arrive at the end of the fibre before the rest, and so the signal is broadened.

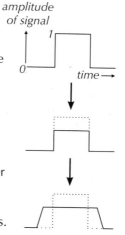

Figure 7: The degradation of a digital signal.

Tip: A light ray that travels straight down the middle of a fibre is called an axial ray. Those that bounce around the sides are called non-axial rays.

Tip: The signal is broadened because it stretches over a longer time. This could cause a loss in quality if separate signals broaden and start to merge together.

Practice Questions — Application

Q1 a) An optical fibre has a core and cladding with refractive indices of 1.52 and 1.40 respectively.
Find the critical angle for the boundary.

b) What angle of incidence would light need to be at for total internal reflection to happen at this boundary?

Q2 If total internal reflection happens where light travelling through material 1 meets a boundary with material 2, what can you say about the refractive index of these materials? How do you know this?

Q3 Show that, if the cladding of an optical fibre was more optically dense than the core ($n_1 < n_2$), there would be no critical angle (and so total internal reflection would be impossible).

Tip: For Q3, try finding the critical angle for any values where $n_1 < n_2$ and see what happens.

Practice Questions — Fact Recall

Q1 What do we mean by the critical angle of a boundary of two materials?

Q2 Give three advantages of using optical fibres for communication.

5. Superposition and Interference

Learning Objectives:

- Understand the principle of superposition of waves.

- Understand what interference is, and know when it is constructive, destructive and totally destructive.

- Understand what it means for two particles on a wave to be in phase.

- Understand what it means for two waves to be in phase.

Specification Reference 3.2.3

When waves pass through each other, they combine their displacements — they can make a bigger wave, a smaller wave, or destroy each other...

Superposition of waves

Superposition happens when two or more waves pass through each other. At the instant that waves cross, the displacements due to each wave combine. Then each wave continues on its way. You can see this if two pulses are sent simultaneously from each end of a rope, as in Figure 1.

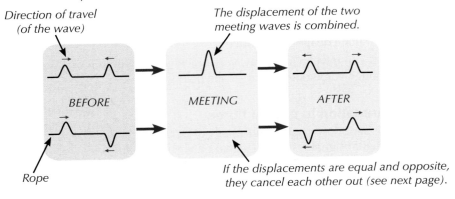

Direction of travel (of the wave)

The displacement of the two meeting waves is combined.

BEFORE *MEETING* *AFTER*

Rope

If the displacements are equal and opposite, they cancel each other out (see next page).

Figure 1: *Superposition of waves.*

The principle of **superposition** says that when two or more waves cross, the resultant displacement equals the vector sum of the individual displacements.

"Superposition" means "one thing on top of another thing". You can use the same idea in reverse — a complex wave can be separated out mathematically into several simple sine waves of various sizes.

Tip: Remember... The vector sum is just the sum of the two displacements taking into account <u>both</u> magnitude and direction (see page 80).

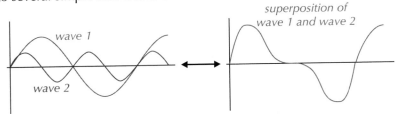

wave 1

wave 2

superposition of wave 1 and wave 2

Figure 2: *Two sine waves shown as separate waves and as a superposition.*

Constructive and destructive interference

The superposition of two or more waves can result in **interference**. Interference can either be constructive or destructive.

- When two waves meet, if their displacements are in the same direction, the displacements combine to give a bigger displacement. A crest plus a crest gives a big crest. A trough plus a trough gives a big trough. This is known as **constructive interference**.

- If a wave with a positive displacement (crest) meets a wave with a negative displacement (trough), they will undergo **destructive interference** and cancel each other out. The displacement of the combined wave is found by adding the displacements of the two waves (see Figure 3).

Tip: Remember, amplitude only has magnitude, but displacement has direction and magnitude. See page 139 for more.

Tip: A trough and a crest won't cancel each other out completely unless they have the same magnitude.

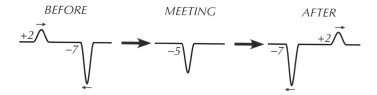

Figure 3: *Destructive interference.*

> **Tip:** Graphically, you can superimpose waves by adding the individual displacements at each point along the *x*-axis, and then plot them.

- If two waves with equal and opposite displacements meet (i.e. a crest and a trough with equal magnitudes), they cancel each other out completely. This is called **total destructive interference** (see Figure 1).

Figure 4: *Constructive and destructive interference can be shown by water waves in a ripple tank.*

Phase difference

Two points on a wave are in phase if they are both at the same point in the wave cycle. Two points in phase interfere constructively with each other. Points in phase have the same displacement and velocity.
In Figure 5, points A and B are in phase; points A and C are out of phase; and points A and D are exactly out of phase.

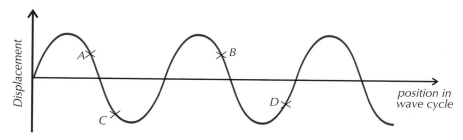

Figure 5: *Points in and out of phase on a wave pattern.*

> **Tip:** If two points are exactly out of phase, they're an odd integer of half-cycles apart (1 half-cycle, 3 half-cycles, etc.).

> **Tip:** The position on the *x*-axis tells you at what point in the wave cycle you are. It's usually measured in degrees (see below).

It's mathematically handy to show one complete cycle of a wave as an angle of 360° (2π radians) — see Figure 6. The phase difference of two points on a wave is the difference in their positions in a wave's cycle, measured in degrees or radians. Two points with a phase difference of zero or a multiple of 360° (2π radians) are in phase. Points with a phase difference of odd-number multiples of 180° (π radians) are exactly out of phase.

> **Tip:** Radians are just a different unit for angle measurement. There are 2π radians in 360°, and π radians in 180°.

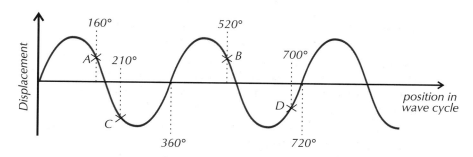

Figure 6: *The points from Figure 5 shown as angles.*

> **Tip:** Points A and B are a full cycle apart (360°), while points A and D are three half-cycles apart (180° × 3 = 540°).

The phase difference between two waves (rather than two points on one wave) is the amount by which one wave lags behind the other. So you can also talk about two different waves being in or out of phase. Two waves are in phase if their phase difference is 0 or a multiple of 360° — see Figure 7. In practice this is usually because both waves come from the same oscillator. In other situations there will nearly always be a phase difference between two waves.

Tip: Waves don't need to have the same amplitude to be in phase, but they do need to have the same frequency and wavelength.

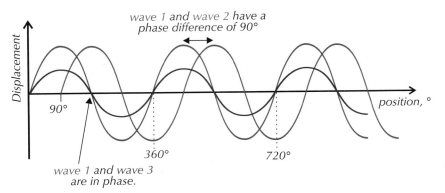

Figure 7: Two waves in phase and a third wave out of phase by 90°.

Tip: Compare the position of two equivalent points on two waves (e.g. the top of two crests) to find the phase difference between them.

Practice Questions — Application

Q1 Draw the superposition of the following waves:

a)

b)

Q2 a) In the diagram below, which point (if any) is in phase with
 i) point A   ii) point B   iii) point C
 b) How many points are exactly out of phase with point G?

Displacement

Position, °

Practice Questions — Fact Recall

Q1 What does the principle of superposition say?
Q2 Describe constructive interference.
Q3 What is total destructive interference?
Q4 What is the phase difference of two points on a wave?
Q5 When are two points on a wave exactly out of phase?
Q6 What does it mean for two waves to be in phase?

6. Stationary Waves

So far you've been looking at progressive waves — waves that move. Now it's time for stationary waves — waves that stay where they are. They don't really do anything but bob up and down.

What is a stationary wave?

A **stationary wave** is the superposition of two progressive waves with the same frequency (or wavelength) and amplitude, moving in opposite directions. Unlike progressive waves, no energy is transmitted by a stationary wave.

You can demonstrate stationary waves by setting up a driving oscillator at one end of a stretched string with the other end fixed.

Learning Objectives:
- Understand that stationary waves are formed by two waves of the same frequency travelling in opposite directions.
- Understand graphical representations of stationary waves, and their nodes and antinodes on a string.

Specification Reference 3.2.3

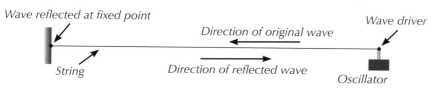

Figure 1: Set-up for demonstrating a stationary wave.

The wave generated by the oscillator is reflected back and forth. For most frequencies the resultant pattern is a jumble. However, if the oscillator happens to produce an exact number of waves in the time it takes for a wave to get to the end and back again, then the original and reflected waves reinforce each other.

The frequencies at which this happens are called **resonant frequencies** and it causes a stationary wave where the overall pattern doesn't move along — it just vibrates up and down, so the string forms oscillating 'loops' (Figure 3).

Figure 2: A stationary wave being demonstrated using the same apparatus as in Figures 1 and 3.

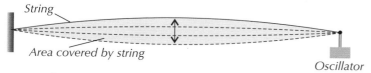

Figure 3: A string oscillating at a resonant frequency.

These stationary waves are transverse, so each particle vibrates at right angles to the string. Nodes are points on the wave where the amplitude of the vibration is zero — they just stay perfectly still (see Figure 4). Antinodes are points of maximum amplitude. At resonant frequencies, an exact number of half wavelengths fits onto the string.

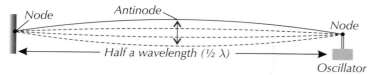

Figure 4: A stationary wave with two nodes and an antinode.

A stationary wave is the superposition of two progressive waves, so it's just two waves interfering (page 154):

- At a node, there is total destructive interference — the displacement of the two waves always cancel each other out.
- At an antinode, there is constructive interference — the displacement of the two waves combine to make a bigger displacement.

Exam Tip
If you're asked to sketch a standing wave, make sure you make it clear where the nodes and antinodes are. You don't need to draw loads of dotted lines like in Figure 4, as long as you show what shape the string is vibrating in.

Resonant frequencies

A stationary wave is only formed at a resonant frequency (when an exact number of half wavelengths fits on the string). There are some special names for each resonant frequency.

Fundamental Frequency

This stationary wave is vibrating at its lowest possible resonant frequency, called the **fundamental frequency** — see Figures 2-5. It has one "loop" with a node at each end. One half wavelength fits onto a string, and so the wavelength is double the length of the string.

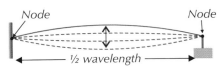

Figure 5: A stationary wave vibrating at its fundamental frequency.

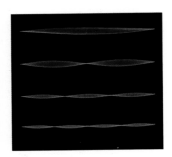

Figure 6: A stationary wave vibrating at its fundamental frequency, and second, third and fourth harmonics (going from top to bottom).

Second Harmonic

Figure 7 (and 6) shows the **second harmonic**, or **first overtone**. It has twice the fundamental frequency. There are two "loops" with a node in the middle and one at each end. Two half wavelengths fit on the string, so the wavelength is the length of the string.

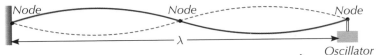

Figure 7: A stationary wave vibrating at its second harmonic.

> **Tip:** At the ath harmonic, the number of antinodes is equal to a, and the number of nodes is equal to $a + 1$.

Third Harmonic

The **third harmonic** (or second overtone) is three times the fundamental frequency — see Figure 8 (and 6). $1\frac{1}{2}$ wavelengths fit on the string.

Figure 8: A stationary wave vibrating at its third harmonic.

You can have as many harmonics as you like — an extra loop and an extra node are just added with each one, the number of λ that fit goes up by $\frac{1}{2}$, and the frequency increases by one fundamental frequency. For example, Figure 6 shows the fourth harmonic of a stationary wave.

The fundamental frequency depends on the length, mass and tension of the string.

- The longer the string, the lower the fundamental frequency because the half-wavelength is longer ($c = f\lambda$, so if λ increases, f decreases for fixed c).
- The heavier (i.e. the more mass per unit length) the string, the lower the fundamental frequency — because waves travel more slowly down the string. For a given length a lower velocity, c, makes a lower frequency, f.
- The looser the string the lower the fundamental frequency — again because waves travel more slowly down a loose string.

> **Tip:** At the ath harmonic, $\frac{a}{2}$ wavelengths will fit on the string.

> **Tip:** $c = f\lambda$ was covered on page 141.

> **Exam Tip**
> If you're given the fundamental frequency, you can work out the resonant frequency f at the ath harmonic with $f = a \times$ fundamental frequency.

Example

A banjo string vibrates with a fundamental frequency of 290 Hz. Find the frequency of vibration of the string at the third harmonic.

The third harmonic is three times the fundamental frequency, so:
$f = 290 \times 3 = 870$ Hz

Other demonstrations of stationary waves

Stationary microwaves

You can set up a stationary wave by reflecting a microwave beam at a metal plate (see Figure 9). The superposition of the wave and its reflection produces a stationary wave. You can find the nodes and antinodes by moving the probe between the transmitter and reflecting plate. The meter or loudspeaker receives no signal at the nodes and maximum signal at the antinodes.

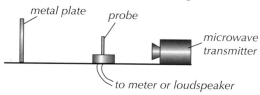

metal plate *probe*
microwave transmitter
to meter or loudspeaker

Figure 9: *Apparatus for demonstrating stationary microwaves.*

Stationary sound waves

Powder in a tube of air can show stationary sound waves — see Figure 11. A loudspeaker produces stationary sound waves in the glass tube. The powder laid along the bottom of the tube is shaken away from the antinodes but left undisturbed at the nodes.

Figure 10: *A thermogram showing the surface heat of an object in a microwave. Some bits are hot (red) and some bits are cold (green). This is partly because interfering microwaves form nodes (cold areas) and antinodes (warm areas).*

loudspeaker *glass tube*
to signal generator
powder is left undisturbed at the nodes

Figure 11: *Apparatus for demonstrating stationary sound waves.*

Practice Questions — Application

Q1 For the stationary wave in the diagram below, find the wavelength.

6 m
Fixed   *Fixed*

Q2 The diagram below represents a stationary wave on a string which is fixed at A and driven by an oscillator at B.

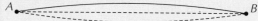

A   *B*

a) The length of the string AB is 2.5 m and the frequency of the wave is 100 Hz.
Calculate the speed of the waves forming the stationary wave.

b) If the wave is now vibrating at a frequency of 200 Hz, how many wavelengths would fit on the string? What is the name for this resonant frequency?

Practice Questions — Fact Recall

Q1 How is a stationary wave formed?

Q2 Does a stationary wave transfer energy?

Q3 Describe what a resonant frequency of a string is.

Q4 Describe a string vibrating at its second harmonic.

7. Diffraction

Diffraction is the reason you can hear sound when you're round a corner from the source — it's just waves spreading out through gaps or around obstacles.

Diffraction through gaps

The way that waves spread out as they come through a narrow gap or go round obstacles is called **diffraction**. The amount of diffraction depends on the wavelength of the wave compared with the size of the gap:

- When the gap is a lot bigger than the wavelength, diffraction is unnoticeable — see Figure 1, left-hand diagram.
- You get noticeable diffraction through a gap several wavelengths wide (Figure 1, middle diagram).
- The most diffraction is when the gap is the same size as the wavelength (Figure 1, right-hand diagram).
- If the gap is smaller than the wavelength, the waves are mostly just reflected back.

You can see diffraction patterns in ripple tanks:

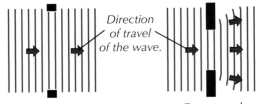

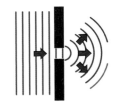

Gap much bigger than wavelength — no diffraction.   *Gap several wavelengths wide — some diffraction.*   *Gap the same size as the wavelength — maximum diffraction.*

Figure 1: *The diffraction of water waves in a ripple tank.*

When sound passes through a doorway, the size of the gap and the wavelength are usually roughly equal, so a lot of diffraction occurs. That's why you have no trouble hearing someone through an open door to the next room, even if the other person is out of your line of sight. The reason that you can't see him or her is that when light passes through the doorway, it is passing through a gap around a few million times bigger than its wavelength — the amount of diffraction is tiny.

Diffraction around obstacles

When a wave meets an obstacle, you get diffraction around the edges. Behind the obstacle is a 'shadow', where the wave is blocked. The wider the obstacle compared with the wavelength of the wave, the less diffraction you get, and so the longer the shadow.

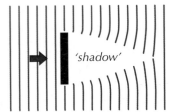

Figure 3: *The diffraction of waves around an obstacle.*

Learning Objectives:

- Understand the diffraction patterns that are made by waves passing through a single slit.
- Understand that the amount of diffraction depends on the wavelength compared with the size of the gap.

Specification Reference 3.2.3

Tip: Remember... a ripple tank is just a shallow tank of water with a dipper oscillating in it — generating water waves.

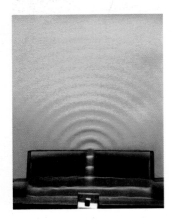

Figure 2: *Diffraction in a ripple tank.*

Tip: Houses in valleys or next to mountains sometimes struggle to get good TV and radio signals because the shorter wavelength waves don't diffract much around the wide obstacles.

The diffraction of light

Light shone through a narrow slit will diffract and sometimes produce a diffraction pattern. To observe a light diffraction pattern, you need to use a light source that is **monochromatic**. Monochromatic light is light of a single wavelength (and so a single colour). If you use light that isn't monochromatic, different wavelengths will diffract by different amounts and the pattern produced won't be very clear.

White light is made up of a continuous range of wavelengths across the visible light spectrum. You can put a colour filter in front of white light to make it a single wavelength, but you get clearer diffraction patterns if you use a laser.

Laser light is monochromatic — it has a single wavelength (and frequency) and a single colour, so it's really useful for looking at the diffraction of light. But you need to be careful using lasers. Laser beams are very powerful and could damage your eyesight, so you should always make sure you don't look directly at the beam (see page 164).

The diffraction of light is shown by shining a laser beam through a very narrow slit onto a screen — see Figure 4. You can alter the amount of diffraction by changing the width of the slit. If the wavelength of a light wave is roughly similar to the size of the aperture (slit), you get a diffraction pattern of light and dark fringes.

Tip: Laser light is also coherent — you'll learn what that means on the next page.

Tip: This is often called the single-slit experiment — you'll come across the double-slit experiment on page 164.

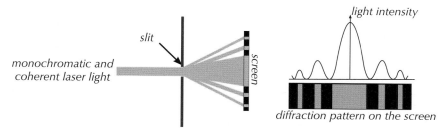

Figure 4: *Light diffraction pattern from a single slit.*

The pattern has a bright central fringe with alternating dark and bright fringes on either side of it. The narrower the slit, the wider and less intense the diffraction pattern. The fringe pattern is due to interference.

- The bright fringes are due to constructive interference, where waves from across the width of the slit arrive at the screen in phase.
- The dark fringes are due to total destructive interference, where waves from across the width of the slit arrive at the screen completely out of phase.

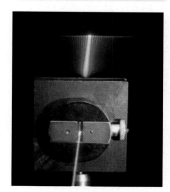

Figure 5: *Diffraction of a laser beam through a single slit.*

Tip: Interference was explained on page 154, if you need a refresher.

Practice Questions — Fact Recall

Q1 What sort of waves diffract?

Q2 What size of gap would you expect to produce the most diffraction?

Q3 What is monochromatic light?

Q4 What property of laser light means that it will produce a clearer diffraction pattern than white light.

Q5 What sort of interference is responsible for the bright fringes on a diffraction pattern produced by laser light passing through a single slit?

8. Interference

When two wave sources interfere, they can make pretty interference patterns. You need both sources to be pretty much identical...

Two-source interference

Two-source interference is when the waves from two sources interfere to produce a pattern. In order to get clear interference patterns, the waves from the two sources must be monochromatic and **coherent**. Two waves are coherent if they have the same wavelength and frequency and a fixed phase difference between them. If a light source is coherent, the troughs and crests line up — this causes constructive interference and a very intense beam.

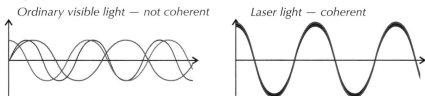

Ordinary visible light — not coherent   *Laser light — coherent*

Figure 1: *Coherent and non-coherent light sources.*

Interference still happens when you're observing waves of different wavelength and frequency — but it happens in a jumble. If the sources are coherent, clear patterns of constructive and destructive interference are seen (see next page). Whether you get constructive or destructive interference at a point depends on how much further one wave has travelled than the other wave to get to that point. The amount by which the path travelled by one wave is longer than the path travelled by the other wave is called the **path difference**.

At any point an equal distance from two sources in phase you will get constructive interference (see Figure 2). These points are known as **maxima**. You also get constructive interference at any point where the path difference is a whole number of wavelengths. At these points the two waves are in phase and reinforce each other, which is why you get constructive interference.

At points where the path difference is half a wavelength, one and a half wavelengths, two and a half wavelengths etc., the waves arrive out of phase and you get total destructive interference. These points are known as **minima**.

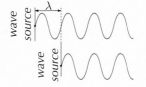

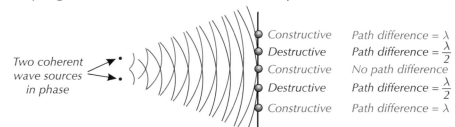

Constructive	Path difference $= \lambda$
Destructive	Path difference $= \frac{\lambda}{2}$
Constructive	No path difference
Destructive	Path difference $= \frac{\lambda}{2}$
Constructive	Path difference $= \lambda$

Figure 2: *Two-source interference.*

Constructive interference occurs when:

$$\text{path difference } = n\lambda \ (\text{where } n = 0, 1, 2, ...)$$

Destructive interference occurs when:

$$\text{path difference } = \frac{(2n + 1)\lambda}{2} = \left(n + \frac{1}{2}\right)\lambda$$

Two coherent sources of sound waves each with a wavelength of 1.5 m are set up so that they produce interference fringes. When the path difference is 3.75 m, would you expect constructive or destructive interference?

- Path difference (p.d.) is found by: $p.d. = x\lambda$, where $x = n$ for constructive interference and $x = n + \frac{1}{2}$ for destructive interference (n is an integer).

- So $p.d. = x\lambda \Rightarrow x = \dfrac{p.d.}{\lambda} = \dfrac{3.75}{1.5} = 2.5$. This is in the form $n + \frac{1}{2}$ ($n = 2$), so this is destructive interference.

Two-source interference patterns

It's easy to demonstrate two-source interference for either sound or water because they've got wavelengths of a handy size that you can measure. The trick is to use the same oscillator to drive both sources. For water, one vibrator drives two dippers (see Figure 3). For sound, one oscillator is connected to two loudspeakers (see Figure 4).

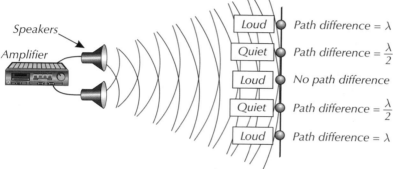

Speakers

Amplifier

Loud	Path difference = λ
Quiet	Path difference = $\frac{\lambda}{2}$
Loud	No path difference
Quiet	Path difference = $\frac{\lambda}{2}$
Loud	Path difference = λ

Figure 4: *Two-source interference of sound waves.*

Figure 3: *Two-source interference of water waves demonstrated by two dippers vibrating at the same frequency in a ripple tank.*

In Figure 4, an interference pattern is produced at the black line. Constructive interference (at $p.d. = n\lambda$) causes the sound to increase in volume, so you get a loud area. Destructive interference causes the sound to decrease in volume, so you get a quiet area.

To see interference patterns with microwaves, you can use two microwave transmitter cones attached to the same signal generator (see Figure 5). You also need a microwave receiver probe (like the one used in the stationary waves experiment on page 159). If you move the probe along the path of the orange arrow, you'll get an alternating pattern of strong and weak signals.

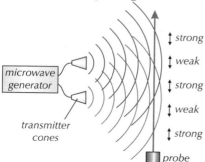

microwave generator

↕ strong
↕ weak
↕ strong
↕ weak
↕ strong

transmitter cones

probe

Figure 5: *Two-source interference with microwaves*

Demonstrating two-source interference of light is much more tricky though.

Double-slit interference of light

You can't arrange two separate coherent light sources because they might not be coherent with each other. Remember, a laser is a source of monochromatic and coherent light. You can effectively create two coherent light sources by shining a single laser through two slits (known as a single-source double-slit set-up).

The slits have to be about the same size as the wavelength of the laser light so that it is diffracted (see page 160). This makes the light from the slits act like two coherent point sources. You get a pattern of light and dark fringes, depending on whether constructive or destructive interference is taking place — see Figure 7.

You might see this experiment referred to as "Young's double-slit experiment" — Thomas Young was the first person to carry it out, although he used a source of white light instead of a laser.

Figure 6: *A laser beam passing through a double slit and forming a diffraction pattern on a screen.*

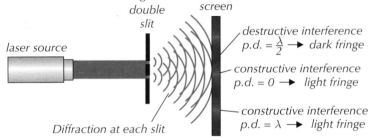

Figure 7: *Two-source interference of light*

If you were to use a non-coherent light source such as white light instead of a coherent monochromatic laser, the diffraction pattern would be less intense, with wider maxima. The pattern would also contain different colours with a central white fringe, because white light is made up of a continuous range of frequencies (see page 12).

Tip: Remember, light that isn't monochromatic is made up of different wavelengths of light, which will diffract by different amounts and makes the fringes much less clear.

Laser safety precautions

Working with lasers is very dangerous because laser light is focused into a very direct, powerful beam of monochromatic light. If you looked at a laser beam directly, your eye's lens would focus it onto your retina, which would be permanently damaged. To make sure you don't cause damage while using lasers, make sure you:

- Never shine the laser towards a person.
- Are wearing laser safety goggles.
- Avoid shining the laser beam at a reflective surface.
- Have a warning sign on display (see Figure 8).
- Turn the laser off when it's not needed.

Figure 8: *Laser warning signs should be used to alert people of the danger of laser beams.*

The double-slit formula

Thomas Young came up with an equation to work out the wavelength of the light from the experiment above.

The fringe spacing (w), wavelength (λ), spacing between slits (s) and the distance from the slits to the screen (D) (see Figure 9) are all related by Young's double-slit formula, which works for all waves.

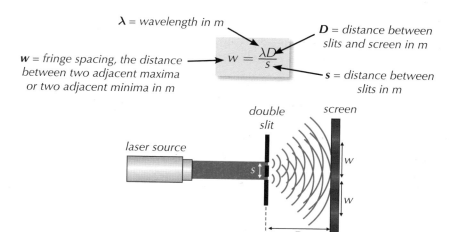

λ = wavelength in m

D = distance between slits and screen in m

w = fringe spacing, the distance between two adjacent maxima or two adjacent minima in m

$$w = \frac{\lambda D}{s}$$

s = distance between slits in m

laser source

double slit

screen

Figure 9: *A diagram to show s, w and D from the double-slit formula.*

Exam Tip
You need to be able to use and rearrange this formula, but you don't need to memorise it or know how to derive it.

Since the wavelength of light is so small you can see from the formula that a high ratio of D/s is needed to make the fringe spacing big enough to see. Rearranging, you can use $\lambda = \frac{ws}{D}$ to calculate the wavelength of light.

The fringes are usually so tiny that it's very hard to get an accurate value of w. It's easier to measure across several fringes then divide by the number of fringe widths between them.

Tip: Measuring across several fringes will reduce the error in your measurement (p.179).

Examples

The maxima of an interference pattern produced by shining a laser light through a double slit onto a screen is shown in Figure 10. The slits were 0.20 mm apart and the distance between the slits and the screen was 15.0 m.

a) Find the wavelength of the laser light.

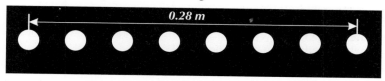

0.28 m

Figure 10: *A double-slit interference pattern.*

Tip: Don't get confused here. There are 8 bright spots (maxima), but only 7 gaps (fringe widths) between them. So you need to divide the total width by 7 and not 8.

You can rearrange Young's double-slit formula to find the wavelength (λ). But first you need to find the fringe spacing of one fringe (w). Seven fringe widths in figure 10 have a spacing of 0.28 m, so one fringe width has a spacing of $\frac{0.28}{7} = 0.04$ m.

Rearrange the formula and substitute in the information you know $w = 0.04$ m, $s = 0.00020$ m and $D = 15.0$ m.

$$w = \frac{\lambda D}{s} \Rightarrow \lambda = \frac{ws}{D} = \frac{0.04 \times 0.00020}{15} = 5.3 \times 10^{-7} \text{ m} \quad \text{(to 2 s.f.)}$$

b) Find the fringe spacing if a laser with a wavelength of 7.2×10^{-7} m is used instead.

You don't need to rearrange this time — just plug in the numbers:

$$w = \frac{\lambda D}{s} \Rightarrow \frac{(7.2 \times 10^{-7}) \times 15}{0.00020} = 0.054 \text{ m}$$

Evidence for the wave nature of light

Tip: It was later discovered that light has properties of both waves and particles. See pages 41-43 for more on wave-particle duality.

Towards the end of the 17th century, two important theories of light were published — one by Isaac Newton and the other by a chap called Huygens. Newton's theory suggested that light was made up of tiny particles, which he called "corpuscles". And Huygens put forward a theory using waves.

The corpuscular theory could explain reflection and refraction, but diffraction and interference are both uniquely wave properties. If it could be shown that light showed interference patterns, that would help settle the argument once and for all.

Young's double-slit experiment (over 100 years later) provided the necessary evidence. It showed that light could both diffract (through the two narrow slits) and interfere (to form the interference pattern on the screen).

Practice Questions — Application

Q1 A blue-violet laser with a wavelength of 450 nm is shone through a double-slit system to produce an interference pattern on a screen, as shown in Figure 11. The screen is 12.0 m from the slits and the slits are 0.30 mm apart.

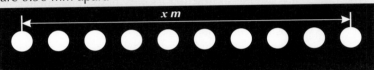

Figure 11: A double-slit interference pattern.

a) Give one reason why a laser is used instead of white light.

b) Explain why the pattern shown is formed.

c) Find the fringe spacing, w.

d) Find the value of x.

e) Give two examples of safety precautions that should be taken whilst performing this experiment.

Q2 A laser with $\lambda = 615$ nm is shone through a double slit to produce a diffraction pattern on a screen with fringes 1.29 cm apart. If the slits are 0.11 mm apart, find the distance, D, between the slits and the screen.

Tip: A nanometre (nm) is equal to 1×10^{-9} m.

Practice Questions — Fact Recall

Q1 What does it mean for two wave sources to be coherent?

Q2 What is meant by the path difference of two waves?

Q3 At what path differences will you see constructive interference?

Q4 What must be true of two wave sources if they produce a clear, standard two-source interference pattern?

Q5 a) How can you create two coherent sources of sound waves?

   b) How can you create two coherent sources of light waves?

Q6 Write down Young's double-slit formula which links fringe spacing (w), wavelength (λ), distance between slits (s) and distance between slits and screen (D).

Exam Tip
You'll be given Young's double-slit formula in the exam, but it might help you answer questions quicker if you know it off by heart.

9. Diffraction Gratings

If you shine light through loads of slits, the interference patterns produced are much sharper. This means they can be measured a lot more accurately — which is handy when analysing light from stars.

Diffraction with a diffraction grating

You can carry out single-source, double-slit type experiments (see p.164) using more than two equally spaced slits. You get basically the same shaped pattern as for two slits — but the bright bands are brighter and narrower and the dark areas between are darker, so the interference pattern produced is sharper.

A **diffraction grating** contains lots of equally spaced slits very close together and so can be used to do this (see Figure 1). When monochromatic light (all of the same wavelength) is passed through a diffraction grating with hundreds of slits per millimetre at normal incidence (right angles to the grating), the interference pattern is really sharp because there are so many beams reinforcing the pattern. Sharper fringes make for more accurate measurements.

Learning Objectives:

- Understand how a diffraction grating works.

- Be able to derive and use $d\sin\theta = n\lambda$, where n is the order number.

- Understand how diffraction can be used to look at line spectra, and the applications of this.

Specification Reference 3.2.3

Tip: The pattern is different for white light — see page 169.

Tip: You might see this type of grating called a plane diffraction grating.

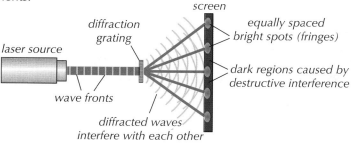

Figure 1: Laser light passing through a diffraction grating.

For monochromatic light, all the maxima in the diffraction pattern formed are sharp lines. There's a line of maximum brightness at the centre called the **zero order line** — which is in the same direction as the beam incident on the grating (see Figure 3). The lines just either side of the central one are called **first order lines**. The next pair out are called **second order lines** and so on.

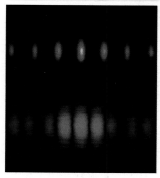

Figure 2: Interference patterns produced by a laser going through a diffraction grating (top) and a double-slit set-up (bottom).

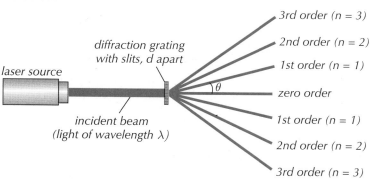

Figure 3: The order of maxima for light passing through a diffraction grating.

Tip: Be careful here — the space between slits is d, but for double-slit experiments it was s.

For a grating with slits a distance d (m) apart, the angle between the incident beam and the nth order maximum is given by an equation which you'll need to be able to derive (see next page).

Derivation of the diffraction grating equation

You can calculate the wavelength of light being used in a diffraction grating experiment using the diffraction grating equation:

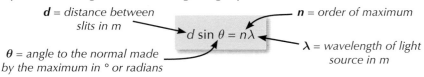

d = distance between slits in m

n = order of maximum

$$d \sin \theta = n\lambda$$

θ = angle to the normal made by the maximum in ° or radians

λ = wavelength of light source in m

Tip: Remember **SOH** CAH TOA (see page 81):

$$\sin \theta = \frac{\text{opposite}}{\text{hypotenuse}}$$

Consider the first order maximum (where n = 1 on the previous page). This happens at the angle where the waves from one slit line up with waves from the next slit that are exactly one wavelength behind — see Figure 4.

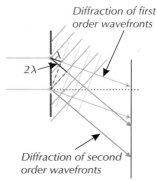

Diffraction of first order wavefronts

2λ

Diffraction of second order wavefronts

Figure 5: The path difference of second order wavefronts is 2λ.

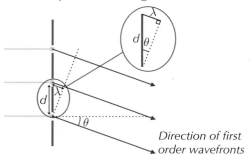

Direction of first order wavefronts

Figure 4: Diffraction of first order waves at an angle of θ.

- Call the angle between the first order maximum (blue line) and the incoming light (yellow line) θ.

- Now look at the triangle highlighted in the diagram. The angle is θ (using basic geometry), d is the slit spacing, and the path difference is λ.

Tip: The angle θ is found by looking at angles in a right angle:

$\theta°$

$90 - \theta°$

$\theta°$

- So for the first maximum, using trigonometry, $\sin \theta = \dfrac{\text{opposite}}{\text{hypotenuse}} = \dfrac{\lambda}{d}$, so:

$$d \sin \theta = \lambda$$

- The other maxima occur when the path difference is 2λ, 3λ, 4λ, etc. (see Figure 5), so the nth order maximum occurs when the path difference is $n\lambda$. So to make the equation general, just replace λ with $n\lambda$, where n is an integer — the order of the maximum (the order number).

$$d \sin \theta = n\lambda$$

Tip: If the grating has N slits per metre, then the slit spacing, d, is just $1/N$ metres.

Tip: Make sure that your calculator is working in the correct mode, depending on whether you want degrees or radians.

Example

Green laser light of wavelength 500 nm is transmitted through a perpendicular diffraction grating with 3.00×10^5 slits per metre. At what angle to the normal are the second order maxima seen?

There are 3.00×10^5 slits per metre, so the slit spacing is:

$$d = \frac{1}{3.00 \times 10^5} = 3.33... \times 10^{-6} \text{m}$$

Rearrange the diffraction grating equation, $d \sin \theta = n\lambda$, for θ, and remember n = 2, as it's the second order we're after. So:

$$\theta = \sin^{-1}\left(\frac{n\lambda}{d}\right) = \sin^{-1}\left(\frac{2 \times (5 \times 10^{-7})}{3.33... \times 10^{-6}}\right) = 17.5° \text{ (to 3 s.f.)}$$

From this equation you can draw a few conclusions:

- If λ is bigger, sin θ is bigger, and so θ is bigger. This means that the larger the wavelength, the more the pattern will spread out.

- If d is bigger, sin θ is smaller. This means that the coarser the grating, the less the pattern will spread out.

- Values of sin θ greater than 1 are impossible. So if for a certain n you get a result of more than 1 for sin θ you know that that order doesn't exist.

Tip: Coarser just means fewer slits in a given width.

White light spectra

White light is really a mixture of colours. If you diffract white light through a diffraction grating then the patterns due to different wavelengths within the white light are spread out by different amounts.

Tip: Spectra is the plural of spectrum.

Each order in the pattern becomes a spectrum, with red on the outside and violet on the inside. The zero order maximum stays white because all the wavelengths just pass straight through.

Tip: If spectra sound familiar, it's because they were covered in Unit 1 — see page 39.

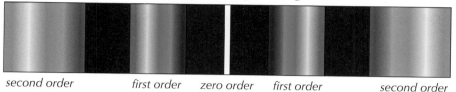

| second order | first order | zero order (white) | first order | second order |

Figure 6: *The interference pattern produced when white light passes through a diffraction grating.*

When you split up light from a star using a diffraction grating, you can see **line absorption spectra** — spectra with dark lines corresponding to different wavelengths of light (see Figure 7) that have been absorbed. Each element in the star's atmosphere absorbs light of a different wavelength. So you can compare an absorption line spectrum from an object with spectra from different elements, or different objects made up of known elements, to see what elements the object contains (see Figure 7).

Astronomers analyse the spectra of stars and chemists analyse the spectra of certain materials to see what elements are present. They use diffraction gratings rather than prisms because they're more accurate.

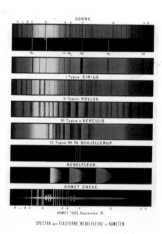

Figure 7: *The absorption line spectra of various astronomical objects.*

Example

Figure 8 shows the absorption spectra of star X's atmosphere, hydrogen, helium and sodium. Which of the elements are present in the atmosphere?

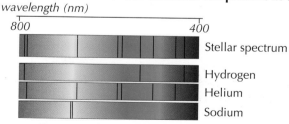

wavelength (nm)

Figure 8: *The absorption spectra of star X's atmosphere, hydrogen, helium and sodium.*

If the spectrum of Star X contains all of the lines in the spectrum of an element, then that element is present. Tracing up from the spectrum of each element you can see that all of the lines from hydrogen and helium can be found in the stellar spectrum, but not those from sodium. So only hydrogen and helium are present in the star's atmosphere.

Exam Tip
If this comes up on the exam, it's easy marks. Use a ruler to trace up from the elements to make it easier.

Practice Questions — Application

Q1 Figure 9 shows the spectra of a material X and elements A, B and C. Which of the three elements are present in material X?

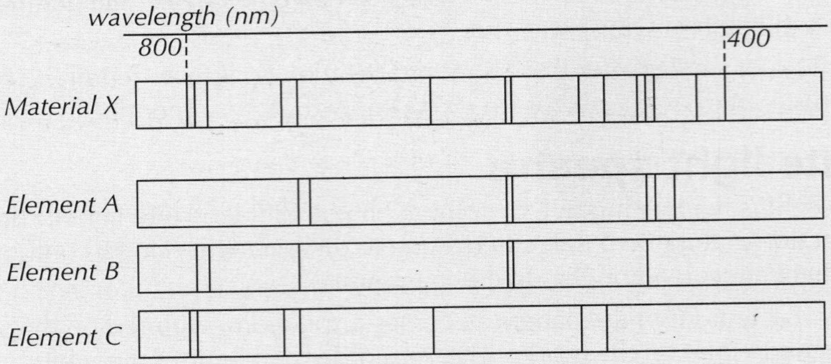

Figure 9: The emission spectra of material X and elements A, B and C.

Q2 An orange laser beam with a wavelength of 590 nm is transmitted through a perpendicular diffraction grating with 4.5×10^5 slits per metre.

a) At what angle to the normal is the third order maximum seen?

b) Use the diffraction grating formula to show whether there will be a fourth order maximum.

c) A red laser beam is used instead with a wavelength of 700 nm. Describe what will happen to the interference pattern, and explain why.

Practice Questions — Fact Recall

Q1 What's a diffraction grating?

Q2 Why is it often better to use a diffraction grating instead of a double-slit set-up?

Q3 What's the zero order line of a diffraction grating experiment?

Q4 Write down the diffraction grating equation.

Q5 What would happen to the interference pattern produced if you increased the wavelength of light transmitted through a diffraction grating?

Q6 Why is a spectrum formed when white light passes through a diffraction grating?

Q7 Give one use for line spectra in science.

Tip: You don't need to know the diffraction grating equation, but you do need to know how to derive it — knowing it off by heart will definitely help.

Section Summary

Make sure you know...

- Waves carry energy, without transferring any material, by making particles or fields vibrate (oscillate).
- That a wave which carries energy is called a progressive wave.
- That waves can be reflected, refracted and diffracted (and can show interference).
- What displacement, amplitude, wavelength, period, frequency and phase difference mean for waves.
- How to use the formula $c = f\lambda$ to find the value of c, f or λ.
- The characteristics of transverse and longitudinal waves, and some examples of each.
- How to draw a transverse wave on a displacement-distance graph or a displacement-time graph.
- A polarised wave only vibrates in one direction, and only transverse waves can be polarised.
- How a polarising filter works, including what the transmission axis of a polarising filter is.
- Reflected waves are partially polarised and cause glare, which can be reduced by Polaroid material.
- The role of polarisation in transmitting and receiving TV and radio signals.
- Certain materials can rotate the plane of polarisation.
- How to find the refractive index of a material using $n = \frac{c}{c_s}$, and know that it is a measure of how optically dense it is.
- How to use the law of refraction, $n_1 \sin \theta_1 = n_2 \sin \theta_2$.
- Light bends towards the normal if it passes into a more optically dense material, and away from the normal if it passes into a less optically dense material.
- That when light passes into a less optically dense material, there is a critical angle of incidence (θ_c) at which the angle of refraction is 90°.
- How to calculate the critical angle of a boundary using $\sin \theta_c = \frac{n_2}{n_1}$.
- That when the angle of incidence is greater than the critical angle, you get total internal reflection.
- How optical fibres work, including the function of the cladding.
- Why optical fibres are used in communications, and their advantages over other methods.
- That when two waves cross, they experience superposition and their displacements combine.
- That superposition causes interference, which can be constructive, destructive or totally destructive.
- What the phase difference of two points on a wave is, and when two points on a wave are in phase.
- What the phase difference of two waves is, and when two waves are in phase.
- That a stationary wave transfers no energy, and is formed by two progressive waves of the same frequency travelling in opposite directions.
- What nodes and antinodes are, and understand graphical representations of stationary waves.
- The characteristics of the different resonant frequencies of a stationary wave.
- What is meant by coherent and monochromatic.
- That laser light (a coherent and monochromatic source) shone through a narrow, single slit can demonstrate light diffraction and interference.
- That two coherent wave sources can be used to produce two-source interference patterns.
- What is meant by path difference.
- Laser light shone through a double-slit system acts as two coherent light sources, producing interference patterns (and fringes).
- How to use Young's double-slit formula, $w = \frac{\lambda D}{s}$.
- How diffraction gratings work, and how to use the diffraction grating formula, $d \sin \theta = n\lambda$.
- That spectra can be produced using diffraction gratings and can be used to analyse light from stars.

Exam-style Questions

1   A photographer uses a polarising lens filter for water scenes to reduce glare.

1 (a) (i)   Explain why light that has been reflected causes glare.

(1 mark)

1 (a) (ii) Explain how a polarising filter helps to reduce glare.

(2 marks)

1 (b)   Only transverse waves can be polarised. Name the other type of progressive wave, and give an example of that type of wave.

(2 marks)

1 (c)   A light wave has a wavelength of 650 nm. Calculate its frequency.

(2 marks)

2   The figure below shows two rays of light entering a step-index optical fibre used for communications.

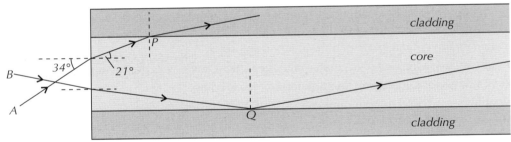

not drawn to scale

Figure 1: *Two rays entering a step index optical fibre.*

2 (a) (i)   Light travels at 2.03×10^8 ms^{-1} in the cladding. Calculate the refractive index of the cladding to an appropriate number of significant figures.

(2 marks)

2 (a) (ii) Find the refractive index of the core of the optical fibre.

(3 marks)

2 (b) (i)   Calculate the critical angle of the core-cladding boundary.

(2 marks)

2 (b) (ii) Explain why light ray A enters the cladding of the optical fibre.

(2 marks)

2 (b) (iii) Describe what has happened to ray B, and explain why.

(2 marks)

2 (c)   State **two** advantages of using optical fibres instead of electrical wires for communications.

(2 marks)

3 A student is investigating diffraction patterns. He directs the laser beam through a double-slit system, where the slits are 0.15 mm apart and the screen is 7.5 m from the slits.
The interference pattern produced is shown below.

Figure 2: *Maxima of a double-slit interference pattern.*

3 (a) (i) Find the wavelength of the laser beam.

(4 marks)

3 (a) (ii) Explain why the student used a laser and not a standard light source.

(2 marks)

3 (b) (i) Describe the difference you would expect to see in the interference pattern if a diffraction grating was used instead of the double slit in this experiment.

(1 mark)

3 (b) (ii) Calculate the angle of the first order maxima if the same laser is shone through a diffraction grating with 2.55×10^5 slits per metre.

(4 marks)

4 Two students form a stationary wave with a rope. One student holds one end of the rope still while the other oscillates the other end up and down at a constant frequency, as shown in Figure 3.

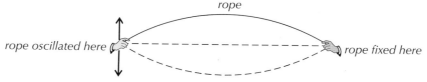

Figure 3: *A stationary wave formed by a rope.*

4 (a) Explain how a stationary wave is formed on the rope.

(3 marks)

4 (b) (i) The rope has a length of 1.5 m and the stationary wave has a frequency of 2.5 Hz. What is the fundamental frequency of the rope?

(1 mark)

4 (b) (ii) If the frequency of oscillations on the rope were increased to 7.5 Hz, how many nodes would there be on the rope?

(2 marks)

4 (b) (iii) Calculate the wave speed of a progressive wave on the rope by using the frequency of 7.5 Hz.

(2 marks)

1. Variables and Data

When you're planning an experiment you need to think carefully about what things you're going to change, what things you're going to measure and how you're going to record your results.

Variables

You probably know this all off by heart but it's easy to get mixed up sometimes. So here's a quick recap. A **variable** is a quantity that has the potential to change, e.g. mass. There are two types of variable commonly referred to in experiments:

Independent variable — the thing that you change in an experiment.

Dependent variable — the thing that you measure in an experiment.

Tip: When drawing graphs, the dependent variable should go on the *y*-axis, the independent variable on the *x*-axis. The only exceptions to this at AS-level are load-extension (or force-extension) and stress-strain graphs.

Tip: For more on potentiometers see page 71.

--- **Example** ---

You could investigate the effect of varying the voltage across a filament lamp on the current flowing through it using the circuit shown in Figure 1 below:

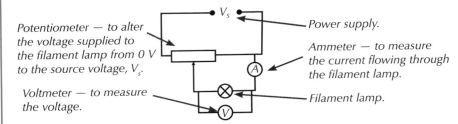

Potentiometer — to alter the voltage supplied to the filament lamp from 0 V to the source voltage, V_s.

Power supply.

Ammeter — to measure the current flowing through the filament lamp.

Voltmeter — to measure the voltage.

Filament lamp.

Figure 1: *Circuit diagram for measuring the current flowing through a filament lamp.*

- The independent variable will be the voltage supplied to the lamp.
- The dependent variable will be the current flowing through the lamp.
- All the other variables must be kept the same. These include the length of the connecting leads and the filament bulb used.

Types of data

Experiments always involve some sort of measurement to provide data. There are different types of data — and you need to know what they are.

1. Discrete data

You get discrete data by counting. E.g. the number of weights added to the end of a spring would be discrete (see Figure 2). You can't have 1.25 weights. That'd be daft. Shoe size is another good example of a discrete variable.

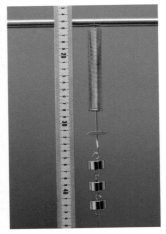

Figure 2: *An experiment to find the stiffness constant of a spring. The number of weights added to the spring is discrete data, but the extension of the spring is continuous data (p.175).*

2. Continuous data

A continuous variable can have any value on a scale. For example, the extension of a spring or the current through a circuit. You can never measure the exact value of a continuous variable.

3. Categoric data

A categoric variable has values that can be sorted into categories. For example, types of material might be brass, wood, glass, steel.

4. Ordered (ordinal) data

Ordered data is similar to categoric, but the categories can be put in order. For example, if you classify frequencies of light as 'low', 'fairly high' and 'very high' you'd have ordered data.

Figure 3: *Different types of materials. Material is a type of categoric data.*

Tables of data

Before you start your experiment, make a table to write your results in. You'll need to repeat each test at least three times to check your results are reliable (see page 182 for more on reliable results). Figure 4 (below) is the sort of table you might end up with when you investigate the effect of voltage on current.

Voltage (V)	Current (A) Run 1	Current (A) Run 2	Current (A) Run 3	Average current (A) (to 3 s.f.)
0.0	0.000	0.000	0.000	**0.000**
1.0	0.104	0.105	0.102	**0.104**
2.0	0.150	0.151	0.149	**0.150**
3.0	0.188	0.187	0.187	**0.187**
4.0	0.219	0.220	0.218	**0.219**
5.0	0.248	0.249	0.222	**0.249**

Figure 4: *Table of results showing the effect of voltage on current through a filament lamp.*

Tip: To find the average of each set of repeated measurements you need to add them all up and divide by how many there are (see page 180 for more on averaging).

For example, the average current at a voltage of 2.0 V is:

$$\frac{(0.150 + 0.151 + 0.149)}{3}$$

$$= 0.150 \text{ A}$$

Watch out for **anomalous results**. These are ones that don't fit in with the other values and are likely to be wrong. They're usually due to experimental errors, such as making a mistake when measuring. You should ignore anomalous results when you calculate averages.

Tip: Just because you ignore anomalous results in your calculations you shouldn't ignore them in your write-up. Try to find an explanation for what went wrong so that it can be avoided in future experiments.

┌ **Example** ─────────────────────────

Look at the table in Figure 4 again — the current at 5.0 V in Run 3 looks like it might be an anomalous result. It's much lower than the values in the other two runs. It could have been caused by the filament lamp being hotter by the end of Run 3.

The anomalous result has been ignored when the average was calculated — that's why the average current at 5.0 V is 0.249 A ((0.248 + 0.249) ÷ 2 = 0.249 (to 3 s.f.)), rather than 0.240 A ((0.248 + 0.249 + 0.222) ÷ 3 = 0.240 (to 3 s.f.)).

2. Graphs and Charts

You'll usually be expected to make a graph of your results. Graphs make your data easier to understand — so long as you choose the right type.

Types of graphs and charts

Tip: Use simple scales when you draw graphs — this'll make it easier to plot points.

Tip: Whatever type of graph you make, you'll only get full marks if you:

1. Choose a sensible scale — don't do a tiny graph in the corner of the paper.

2. Label both axes — including units.

3. Plot your points accurately — using a sharp pencil.

Bar charts

You should use a bar chart when one of your data sets is categoric or ordered data, like in Figure 1.

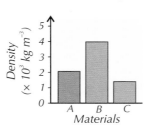

Figure 1: Bar chart to show density of three materials.

Pie charts

Pie charts are normally used to display categoric data, like in Figure 2.

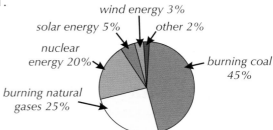

Figure 2: Pie chart to show the different types of energy production in a particular country.

Line Graphs

Line graphs are best when you have two sets of continuous data, like in Figure 3. Current and voltage are both continuous variables — you could get any value on the *x* or *y*-axis.

Tip: A line of best fit should have about half of the points above it and half of the points below. You can ignore any anomalous points like the one circled in Figure 4.

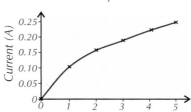

Figure 3: Line graph to show current against voltage.

Scatter graphs

Scatter graphs, like Figure 4, are great for showing how two sets of data are related (or correlated — see below for more on correlation). Don't try to join all the points — draw a line of best fit to show the trend.

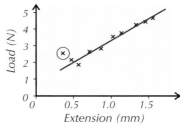

Figure 4: Scatter graph showing the relationship between load and extension of a material.

Scatter graphs and correlation

Correlation describes the relationship between two variables — usually the independent one and the dependent one. Data can show positive correlation, negative correlation or no correlation (see Figure 5).

Tip: Computers can make it a lot quicker to collect, record and analyse big sets of data from experiments — but you've still got to understand what all the numbers and graphs they churn out mean.

Positive correlation
As one variable increases the other also increases.

Negative correlation
As one variable increases the other decreases.

No correlation
There is no relationship between the variables.

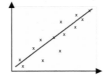

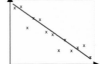

Figure 5: Scatter graphs showing positive, negative and no correlation.

Correlation and cause

Ideally, only two quantities would ever change in any experiment — everything else would remain constant. But in experiments or studies outside the lab, you can't usually control all the variables. So even if two variables are correlated, the change in one may not be causing the change in the other. Both changes might be caused by a third variable.

Tip: If an experiment really does confirm that changing one variable causes another to change, we say there's a <u>causal link</u> between them.

Example

Some studies have found a correlation between exposure to the electromagnetic fields created by power lines and certain ill health effects. So some people argue that this means we shouldn't live close to power lines, or build power lines close to homes. But it's hard to control all the variables between people who live near power lines and people who don't. Ill health in people living near power lines could be affected by many lifestyle factors or even genetics. Also, people living close to power lines may be more likely to believe that any ill health they suffer is due to the EM fields from the power lines if they are aware of the studies.

Tip: Watch out for bias too — for instance, a neighbourhood campaigning against unsightly power lines being built nearby may want to show that they are a health danger.

Straight-line graphs

If you plot two variables that have a linear relationship, you'll get a straight-line graph. Using the fact that the equation of a straight line is $y = mx + c$, (where m = gradient and c = y-intercept) you can use your graph to work out certain values, and the relationship between your variables.

Tip: x and y have a linear relationship if $y = mx + c$, where m and c are constants.

Proportionality

If you plot two variables against each other and get a straight line that goes through the origin, the two variables are **directly proportional**. The y-intercept, c, is 0, so the equation of the straight line is $y = mx$ where m is a constant. The constant of proportionality, m, is the gradient of the graph.

Tip: Two variables are directly proportional if one variable = constant × other variable.

Tip: Remember the gradient is the slope of the line.

Example

Current and potential difference are directly proportional for ohmic conductors. You can see this by using the circuit in Figure 6. Use the variable resistor to decrease (or increase) the resistance in small equal steps. This changes the amount of current flowing through the ohmic conductor. Take readings of current through it and potential difference across it at each step. Once you have all the data, plot a graph of I against V (Figure 7). The graph you'll get is a straight line going through the origin — so current and potential difference are directly proportional.

Tip: For more on this experiment — see p.52.

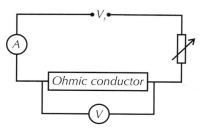

Figure 6: Circuit for showing the proportional relationship between I and V for an ohmic conductor.

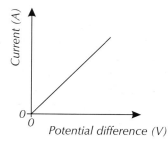

Figure 7: An I-V graph for a component.

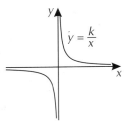

Figure 8: An inverse proportionality relationship between x and y.

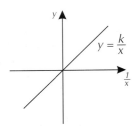

Figure 9: If $y = \frac{k}{x}$, plotting y against $\frac{1}{x}$ gives a straight line through the origin.

Tip: To find R, just calculate the inverse of $\frac{1}{R}$ found from the graph.

Tip: For more on work functions, see page 35.

Tip: If you were to calculate the gradient, you should get h, Planck's constant.

Tip: Here, $y = E_{K(max)}$, $m = h$, $x =$ frequency and $c = -\phi$.

Non-linear relationships

Straight line graphs are really easy to work with, but some variables won't produce a straight-line graph if you plot them against each other. You can sometimes change what you plot on the axes so that you get one though.

For example, say two variables are inversely proportional then $y = \frac{k}{x}$, where k is a constant. If you plot y against x, you'll get a curved graph which shoots off to infinity (Figure 8). It's not very easy to work out the value of k from this graph, but if you plot y against $\frac{1}{x}$ you'll get a lovely straight-line graph (Figure 9) with a constant gradient of k that goes through the origin. This is because the graph plotted is $y = k\left(\frac{1}{x}\right)$, which is just the equation of a straight line in form $y = mx + c$, where $m = k$ and $x = \frac{1}{x}$.

Finding the gradient and y-intercept

If you've plotted a straight-line graph, you can read the gradient and y-intercept straight off it. This means you can work out certain quantities from your graph.

┌─ **Example** ─────────────────

Returning to the example of the ohmic conductor from page 177, you can use the I-V graph to calculate the resistance of the component.

I and V are directly proportional, so $I = kV$. You know from $V = IR$ that $I = \frac{1}{R}V$, so the gradient $= \frac{1}{R}$. $I = \frac{1}{R}V$ is just the equation of a straight line where $y = I$, $x = V$, $m = \frac{1}{R}$ and $c = 0$. You can work out $\frac{1}{R}$ from the graph — it's the gradient. You can find the gradient of the straight-line graph by dividing the change in y (Δy) by the change in x (Δx).

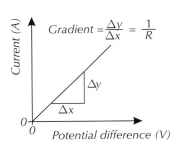

Figure 10: Using an I-V graph to work out the resistance of a component.

┌─ **Example** ─────────────────

The solid line in the graph in Figure 11 shows how the maximum kinetic energy of the electrons on a metal surface varies with the frequency of the light shining on it. You can use a graph like this to find the value of the work function of the metal (ϕ) by extending the graph back to the y-axis.

Rearranging the equation $hf = \phi + E_{K(max)}$ gives $E_{K(max)} = hf - \phi$. Since h and ϕ are constants, $E_{K(max)} = hf - \phi$ is just the equation of a straight line (in the form: $y = mx + c$). You can just read ϕ from the graph — it's the intercept on the vertical axis. You'll just need to continue the line back to the y-axis to find the intercept, then the value of the y-intercept will be $-\phi$.

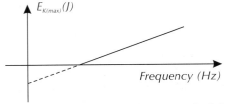

Figure 11: You can extend the line on a graph to find the y-intercept.

3. Error Analysis

Scientists always have to include the uncertainty of a result, so you can see the range the actual value probably lies within. Dealing with error and uncertainty is an important skill — you need to make sure that you know and try to minimise the uncertainty of your results and can evaluate how convincing they are.

Types of error

Every measurement you take has an experimental uncertainty. Say you've done something outrageous like measure the length of a piece of wire with a centimetre ruler. You might think you've measured its length as 30 cm, but at best you've probably measured it to be 30 ± 0.5 cm. And that's without taking into account any other errors that might be in your measurement.

The ± bit gives you the range in which the true length (the one you'd really like to know) probably lies — 30 ± 0.5 cm tells you the true length is very likely to lie in the range of 29.5 to 30.5 cm. The smaller the uncertainty, the nearer your value must be to the true value, so the more accurate your result. There are two types of error that cause experimental uncertainty:

Random errors

No matter how hard you try, you can't get rid of random errors. They can just be down to noise, or that you're measuring a random process such as nuclear radiation emission. You get random error in any measurement.

If you measured the length of a wire 20 times, the chances are you'd get a slightly different value each time, e.g. due to your head being in a slightly different position when reading the scale. It could be that you just can't keep controlled variables exactly the same throughout the experiment. Or it could just be the wind was blowing in the wrong direction at the time.

Systematic errors

You get systematic errors not because you've made a mistake in a measurement — but because of the apparatus you're using or your experimental method, e.g. using an inaccurate clock. The problem is often that you don't know they're there. You've got to spot them first to have any chance of correcting for them. Systematic errors usually shift all of your results to be too high or too low by the same amount. They're annoying, but there are things you can do to reduce them if you manage to spot them (see next page).

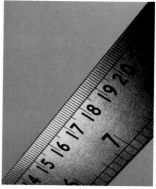

Figure 1: This ruler measures to the nearest millimetre. Any measurement you take using it will have an uncertainty of ± 0.5 mm.

Tip: To get the lowest possible value, subtract the value after the ± sign, and to get the highest possible value, add it.

Tip: A newton meter that always measures values 1 N greater than they should be will shift all your results up by 1 N — this would introduce a systematic error due to the apparatus used.

Example

You could investigate the stiffness constant (see page 123) of a particular rubber band using the apparatus in Figure 2.

- The stiffness constant of the rubber band increases with temperature. If the surrounding temperature changes, it could introduce a random error.

- If the ruler is not correctly lined up to the top of the piece of rubber, all the extension measurements would be shifted by the same amount. This would introduce a systematic error due to your experimental method.

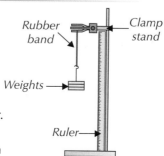

Figure 2: An experiment to find the stiffness constant of a rubber band.

Tip: All sorts of things are affected by temperature, from the properties of a material to the current flowing in a circuit.

Reducing uncertainty

There are a few different ways you can reduce the uncertainty in your results:

- Use higher precision apparatus:
  The more precisely you can measure something, the less random error (see page 179) there is in the measurement. So if you use more precise equipment you can instantly cut down the random error in your experiment. Using apparatus with a higher sensitivity will give you a higher precision (e.g. swapping a millimetre ruler for a micrometer to measure the diameter of a wire).

- Calibration:
  You can calibrate your apparatus by measuring a known value. If there's a difference between the measured and known value, you can use this to correct the inaccuracy of the apparatus, and so reduce your systematic error.

- Repeating measurements:
  By repeating a measurement several times and averaging, you reduce the random uncertainty in your result. The more measurements you average over, the less error you're likely to have.

Figure 3: *A micrometer is very precise, it gives readings to within 0.01 mm.*

Tip: To calibrate a set of scales you could weigh a 10 g mass and check that it reads 10 g. If these scales are precise to the nearest 0.1 g, then you can only calibrate to within 0.05 g. Any measurements taken will have an uncertainty of ± 0.05 g.

Averaging

In the exam, you might be given a graph or table of information showing the results for many repetitions of the same experiment, and asked to estimate the true value and give an uncertainty in that value. Here's how to go about it:

1. Estimate the true value by averaging the results you've been given — just like in the example on page 175. (Make sure you state whatever average it is you take, e.g. mean, mode etc., otherwise you might not get the mark.)

2. To get the uncertainty, you just need to look how far away from your average value the maximum and minimum values in the graph or table you've been given are.

Example

A class measure the resistance of a component to 1 d.p. and record their results on the bar chart shown below. Estimate the resistance of the component, giving a suitable range of uncertainty in your answer.

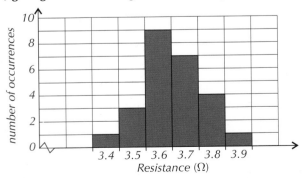

There were 25 measurements, so taking the mean:

$$\frac{(3.4 + (3.5 \times 3) + (3.6 \times 9) + (3.7 \times 7) + (3.8 \times 4) + 3.9)}{25} = 3.65 \,(\text{to 3 s.f.})$$

The maximum value found was 3.9 Ω, the minimum value was 3.4 Ω. Both values are both about 0.25 Ω from the average value, so the answer is 3.65 ± 0.25 Ω.

Tip: Just add up the heights of all the bars to find the total number of measurements.

Tip: If the maximum and minimum are different distances from the average, use the largest value after the ±.

Percentage uncertainty

You might get asked to work out the percentage uncertainty in a measurement. If you know the uncertainty of the measurement, just divide this by the measurement taken and multiply by 100, as shown below.

Examples

- The resistance of a filament lamp is given as $5.0 \pm 0.4\ \Omega$.

  The percentage uncertainty in the resistance measured is:

  Uncertainty $\longrightarrow \dfrac{0.4}{5.0} \times 100 = 8\%$
  Measurement $\longrightarrow$

- A balance is calibrated to within 0.1 g, and you measure a mass as 4.0 g.

  Saying that it's calibrated to 0.1 g means that the uncertainty in any measurement is $\pm\ 0.1$ g.

  The percentage uncertainty is: $(0.1 \div 4.0) \times 100 = 2.5\%$.

  Measuring a larger quantity reduces the percentage uncertainty in the measurement — a mass of 40.0 g has a percentage uncertainty of: $(0.1 \div 40.0) \times 100 = 0.25\%$.

Tip: See page 180 if you need a reminder of what calibrated means.

Most measuring equipment has the precision it's calibrated to written on it. Where it doesn't, you can usually use the scale as a guide (e.g. if a ruler has a 1 mm scale, it is probably calibrated to within 0.5 mm).

Tip: You should always choose appropriate measuring equipment for the precision you need to work with.

Error bars

Most of the time in science, you work out the uncertainty in your final result using the uncertainty in each measurement you make. When you're plotting a graph, you show the uncertainty in each measurement by using error bars to show the range the point is likely to lie in. You probably won't get asked to plot any error bars — but you might need to read off a graph that has them.

Example

The error in measuring the extension of material X can be found using the error bars in the graph below.

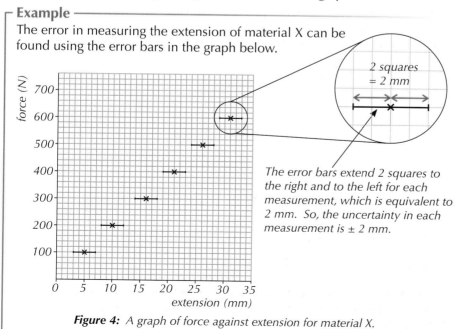

The error bars extend 2 squares to the right and to the left for each measurement, which is equivalent to 2 mm. So, the uncertainty in each measurement is $\pm\ 2$ mm.

Tip: Be careful — sometimes error bars are calculated using a set percentage of uncertainty for each measurement, and so will change depending on the measurement.

Figure 4: A graph of force against extension for material X.

Measuring uncertainty of final results

Normally when you draw a graph you'll want to find the gradient or intercept. E.g. for a force-extension graph, the gradient's k, the stiffness constant of the object being tested. To find the value of k, you draw a nice line of best fit on the graph and calculate your answer from that.

You can then draw the maximum and minimum slopes possible for the data through all of the error bars. By calculating the value of the gradient (or intercept) for these slopes, you can find maximum and minimum values the true answer is likely to lie between. And that's the uncertainty in your answer.

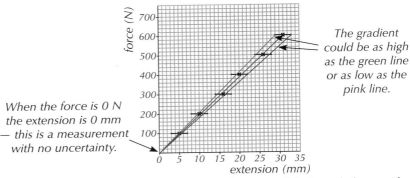

The gradient could be as high as the green line or as low as the pink line.

When the force is 0 N the extension is 0 mm — this is a measurement with no uncertainty.

Figure 5: *The maximum and minimum slopes possible through the error bars.*

Evaluations

Now that you can measure uncertainty, you'll need to evaluate your results to see how convincing they are. You need to be careful about what words you use — valid, accurate, precise and reliable may all sound similar, but they all say different things about your results.

1. Valid results

A valid result answers the original question, using reliable data. For example, if you haven't controlled all the variables your results won't be valid, because you won't be testing just the thing you wanted to.

2. Accurate results

An accurate result is one that is really close to the true answer. You can only say your results are accurate if you know the true value of what you're measuring.

3. Precise results

A precise result is one taken using sensitive instruments that measure in small increments.

4. Reliable results

Reliable means the results can be consistently reproduced in independent experiments. And if the results are reproducible they're more likely to be true. If the data isn't reliable for whatever reason you can't draw a valid conclusion.

For experiments, the more repeats you do, the more reliable the data. If you get the same result twice, it could be the correct answer. But if you get the same result 20 times, it'd be much more reliable. And it'd be even more reliable if everyone in the class got about the same results using different apparatus.

If you have a large percentage uncertainty, your results won't be very reliable. A small percentage uncertainty means your results are more reliable.

Tip: When there is an error in the y-intercept, you can find it with the same method. Just draw the minimum and maximum lines of best fit and see where they cross the y-axis.

Tip: It's possible for results to be precise but not accurate, e.g. a balance that weighs to 1/1000th of a gram will give precise results, but if it's not calibrated properly the results won't be accurate.

Tip: Part of the scientific process (see page 2) involves other scientists repeating your experiment too — then if they get the same results you can be more certain they're reliable.

Tip: A large percentage uncertainty means a large error in comparison to the size of the result.

4. Conclusions and Safety

Once you've got results, you can use them to form a conclusion. But be careful... your conclusion must be supported by your results, and you should keep in mind how much you can believe your results (see evaluations on the previous page). You'll also need to consider any risks that were involved and discuss the safety precautions used.

Drawing conclusions

The data should always support the conclusion. This may sound obvious but it's easy to jump to conclusions. Conclusions have to be specific — not make sweeping generalisations.

┌─ **Example** ─────────────────────────────────

The stress of a material X was measured at strains of 0.002, 0.004, 0.006, 0.008 and 0.010. Each strain reading had an error of 0.001. All other variables were kept constant, and the results are shown in Figure 1.

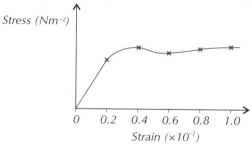

Stress (Nm⁻²)

0   0.2   0.4   0.6   0.8   1.0

Strain (×10⁻²)

Figure 1: *Graph to show the effect of strain on the stress of a material.*

A science magazine concluded from this data that material X's yield point is at a strain of 0.005. This could be true — but the data doesn't support this. Because strain increases of 0.002 at a time were used and the stress at in-between strains wasn't measured, you can't tell where the yield point is from the data. All you know is that the yield point is somewhere between 0.004 and 0.006, as the stress drops between these values.

Also, the graph only gives information about this particular experiment. You can't conclude that the yield point would be in this range for all experiments — only this one. And you can't say for sure that doing the experiment at, say, a different constant temperature, wouldn't give a different yield point.

You must also consider the error in the strain readings. The error in each reading is 0.001, which gives a percentage uncertainty of 50% for the lowest strain reading. This means the results could be unreliable.

└──

Tip: For more on interpreting stress-strain graphs see page 132.

Tip: Taking more readings in an experiment can allow you to make stronger conclusions. If a measurement had been taken at a strain of 0.005 here, you'd have been able to say more about where the yield point was. It's also good to do a practice experiment to get an idea of roughly where the yield point is before you start.

Tip: Whoever funded the research (e.g. an engineering company) may have some influence on what conclusions are drawn from the results, but scientists have a responsibility to make sure that the conclusions they draw are supported by the data.

Risks, hazards and ethical considerations

In any experiment you'll be expected to show that you've thought about the risks and hazards. You'll need to take appropriate safety measures depending on the experiment. For example, anything involving lasers will usually need special laser goggles and to work with radioactive substances you'll probably need to wear gloves.

You need to make sure you're working ethically too. This is most important if there are other people or animals involved. You have to consider their welfare first.

Figure 2: *A scientist wearing laser goggles while working with lasers.*

Exam Help

1. Exam Structure and Technique

Passing exams isn't all about revision — it really helps if you know how the exam is structured and have got your exam technique nailed so that you pick up every mark you can.

Exam structure

For AQA AS-Level Physics you're gonna have to sit through two exams (Unit 1 and Unit 2) and complete a practical assessment (Unit 3).

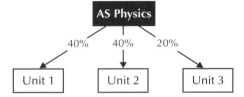

Unit 1 — Particles, quantum phenomena and electricity

This paper will be 1 hour 15 minutes long and have 70 marks up for grabs. It's worth 40% of your total AS-Level and is made up of 6-7 structured questions.

Unit 2 — Mechanics, materials and waves

This paper will be 1 hour 15 minutes long and have 70 marks up for grabs. It's worth 40% of your total AS-Level and is also made up of 6-7 structured questions.

Unit 3 — Investigative and practical skills in AS Physics

You'll do this unit in school with your teacher. It'll test your understanding of physics and your ability to collect and process data and use it to answer questions. It's worth 20% of your total AS-Level.

There are two different ways in which you can complete Unit 3. You only need to do one of them — your school will decide which one you'll do:

- **Teacher assessed** — You'll do practical work throughout the year which your teacher will use to assess your practical skills. You'll also have to collect and process some data and use it to answer questions in a written test to assess your investigative skills. This will be marked by your teacher too.

- **Externally marked** — You'll complete five short practical exercises which aren't marked (but you still have to do), as well as a longer practical activity set by AQA. In the long practical you'll collect and process data and then use it to answer questions in a written test, marked externally.

Figure 1: Physics lesson — a newtonmeter being used to measure the weight of an object.

The assessments in Unit 3 test that you can use standard laboratory equipment, demonstrate safe and skilful practical techniques, take measurements with precision and accuracy, correctly record data and analyse and evaluate your experiment. This may sound a bit menacing but there's some stuff on pages 174-183 to help you out.

Quality of written communication (QWC)

Units 1 and 2 in AS-Level Physics will have a quality of written communication element — this just means that the examiner will assess your ability to write properly. In each of these units, there will be at least one part of a question where your written communication will be assessed. In these parts, you'll be awarded a mark between 0 and 6 which is based on the written quality and scientific accuracy of your answer. To get top marks, you need to make sure that:

- your scribble, sorry, writing is legible,
- your spelling, punctuation and grammar are accurate,
- your writing style is appropriate,
- you organise your answer clearly and coherently,
- you use specialist scientific vocabulary where it's appropriate.

The examiner will only give (or deduct) marks for QWC when the question tells you that it will be assessed, but you should make sure all your answers are clear and easy to read throughout the exam to avoid losing marks.

Exam Tip
You'll need to use black ink or a black ball-point pen to write your answers, so make sure that you've got a couple ready for the exam.

Exam Tip
You may be asked to draw and label a diagram for extra marks in QWC questions.

Time management

This is one of the most important exam skills to have. How long you spend on each question is really important in an exam — it could make all the difference to your grade. Check out the exam timings given by AQA that can be found on the previous page and on the front of your exam paper. These timings give you about 1 minute per mark — try to stick to this to give yourself the best chance to pick up as many marks as possible.

Some questions will require lots of work for only a few marks but other questions will be much quicker. Don't spend ages struggling with questions that are only worth a couple of marks — move on. You can come back to them later when you've bagged loads of other marks elsewhere.

Exam Tip
Everyone has their own method of getting through the exam. Some people find it easier to go through the paper question by question and some people like to do the questions they find easiest first. The most important thing is to find out the way that suits you best before the exam — that means doing all the practice exams you can before the big day.

Examples

The questions below are both worth the same number of marks but require different amounts of work.

1 **(a)** Define the term 'isotope'.

(2 marks)

2 **(a)** Draw a labelled diagram of a circuit that would be suitable for a student to measure the resistance of component A.

(2 marks)

Question 1 (a) only requires you to write down a definition — if you can remember it this shouldn't take you too long.

Question 2 (a) requires you to draw a diagram including a number of components — this may take you a lot longer than writing down a definition, especially if you have to add quite a few components and work out whether they should be in parallel or series.

So, if you're running out of time it makes sense to do questions like 1 (a) first and come back to 2 (a) if you've got time at the end.

Exam Tip
Don't forget to go back and do any questions that you left the first time round — you don't want to miss out on marks because you forgot to do the question.

Calculations

There's no getting away from those pesky calculation questions — they come up a lot in AS-Level Physics. The most important thing to remember is to show your working. You've probably heard it a million times before but it makes perfect sense. It only takes a few seconds more to write down what's in your head and it'll stop you from making silly errors and losing out on easy marks. You won't get a mark for a wrong answer but you could get marks for the method you used to work out the answer.

Units
Make sure you always give the correct units for your answer.

Example

Here's an example of a question where you need to change the units so they match the answer the examiner wants.

1   Find the energy of a photon with wavelength 3.2×10^{-9} m.
     Give your answer in kJ.

(2 marks)

$E = \dfrac{hc}{\lambda}$ gives the energy of a photon in joules.
Make sure you convert the units to kilojoules by dividing by 1000.

You might need to convert quantities into the right units before using a formula. Most formulas need quantities to be in something called SI units — the International System of Units. Here's a list of some of the common quantities you need to know and their SI units.

Quantity name	Unit name	Unit symbol
Length	metres	m
Mass	kilograms	kg
Time	seconds	s
Energy, work, heat	joules	J
Current	amperes	A
Resistance	ohms	Ω
Potential difference, e.m.f.	volts	V
Charge	coulombs	C
Force, weight	newtons	N
Power	watts	W
Pressure, stress	pascals	Pa
Frequency	hertz	Hz

Figure 2: Quantities and their SI units.

Significant figures
Use the number of significant figures given in the question as a guide for how many to give in the answer. You should always give your answer to the lowest number of significant figures (s.f.) given in the question, or one higher — it's always good to write down the full unrounded answer, followed by your rounded answer. You should write down the number of significant figures you've rounded to after your answer too — it shows the examiner you really know what you're talking about.

Examples

In this question the data given to you is a good indication of how many significant figures you should give your answer to.

1 (b) Calculate the extension measured by the student in m. (The stiffness constant of the metal is 1.24×10^3 Nm^{-1}.)

(2 marks)

The data in the question is given to 3 s.f. so it makes sense to give your answer to 3 s.f. too. But sometimes it isn't as clear as that.

3 (b) A force of 50 N is applied to a steel girder with a cross-sectional area of 0.519 m^2. Calculate the tensile stress in the cable.

(2 marks)

There are two types of data in this question, force data and cross-sectional area data. The force data is given to 2 s.f. and the cross-sectional area data is given to 3 s.f.. You should give your answer to the lowest number of significant figures given — in this case that's to 2 s.f.. The answer is 96.339... Nm^{-2} so the answer rounded correctly would be 96 Nm^{-2} (to 2 s.f.).

Figure 3: *A calculator. In an exam your brain can turn to mush and you can forget how to do the most simple maths. Don't be afraid to put every calculation into your calculator (even if it's just 2×10). If it stops you making mistakes then it's worth it.*

Standard form

Sometimes it's easier to give your answer in standard form, or you might be given values in standard form. Standard form is used for writing very big or very small numbers in a more convenient way. Standard form must always look like this:

This number must always be between 1 and 10. ⟶ $A \times 10^n$ ← 'n' is the number of places the decimal point moves.

Examples

Here's how to write 3 500 000 in standard form.

▪ First remove zeros from the right or left until you get to a non-zero number on both sides. Write the rest down with a decimal point after the first digit and a '× 10' after the number:

$$3.5 \times 10$$

▪ Then count how many places the decimal point has moved to the left. This number sits to the top right of the 10.

$$3\,500\,000 = 3.5 \times 10^6$$

▪ Et voilà... that's 3 500 000 written in standard form.

Here are some more examples.

▪ You can write 450 000 as 4.5×10^5.

▪ The number 0.000056 is 5.6×10^{-5} in standard form — the n is negative because the decimal point has moved to the right instead of the left.

▪ You can write 0.003456 as 3.456×10^{-3}.

Tip: So if the number had been 3 050 000, you'd start by writing 3.05×10.

Tip: Your calculator might give you your answer in standard form already — result.

Answers

Unit 1

Section 1 — Particles and Radiation

1. Atomic Structure

Page 8 — Application Questions
Q1 a) 8
    b) $8 + 8 = 16$
    c) $^{16}_{8}O$
Q2 a) $^{45}_{21}X$ (the nucleon number is $21 + 24 = 45$)
    b) E.g. $^{46}_{21}X$
    Isotopes have the same number of protons but a different
    number of neutrons. So the proton number must be the same
    as element X but the nucleon number must be different.
Q3 a) 2
    b) 2
    Isotopes have the same proton number.
    c) Mass = $3 \times$ (nucleon mass) = $3 \times (1.67 \times 10^{-27})$
              = **5.01×10^{-27} kg**
      Charge = $2 \times$ (proton charge) = $2 \times (1.60 \times 10^{-19})$
              = **3.20×10^{-19} C**
      Specific charge = $(3.20 \times 10^{-19}) \div (5.01 \times 10^{-27})$
                 = **6.39×10^{7} C kg^{-1}**
    Remember you're after the specific charge of the nucleus
    (not the whole atom). The nucleus contains 2 protons so the
    relative charge is +2. Multiply this by the charge of a proton
    to get the charge of the nucleus.

Page 8 — Fact Recall Questions
Q1 Inside an atom there is a nucleus which contains neutrons and protons. Electrons orbit the nucleus. Most of the atom is empty space as the electrons orbit at relatively large distances.
Q2 The relative charge of a proton is +1,
    the relative charge of a neutron is 0 and
    the relative charge of an electron is –1.
Q3 The relative mass of protons and neutrons is 1 and the relative mass of an electron is 0.0005.
Q4 The number of protons in the nucleus of an atom.
Q5 The number of protons and neutrons in the nucleus of an atom.
Q6 The relative mass of an atom is the same as the nucleon number.
    Remember... electrons have virtually no mass and nucleons
    have a relative mass of 1.
Q7 The charge of a particle divided by its mass. It is measured in C kg^{-1}.
Q8 Atoms with the same number of protons but different numbers of neutrons.

2. Stable and Unstable Nuclei

Page 11 — Application Questions
Q1 The proton number has gone up by 1 and the nucleon number has stayed the same so it is beta-minus decay.
Q2 Beta-minus decay, because the nucleus is neutron-rich.
    It couldn't be alpha decay because the proton number is not
    large enough.
Q3 a) For separations less than around 0.5 fm the strong nuclear force is repulsive. So at 0.4 fm it would be repulsive.
    b) For separations between about 0.5 fm and 3 fm the strong nuclear force is attractive. So at 1.5 fm it would be attractive.
    c) For separations bigger than about 3 fm the strong nuclear force has no effect. So at 4.2 fm there would be no strong interaction.
Q4 a) $^{222}_{87}Y$
    b) $^{226}_{90}Y$
Q5 $^{238}_{94}Pu \rightarrow {}^{234}_{92}U + {}^{4}_{2}\alpha$
Q6 $^{14}_{6}C \rightarrow {}^{14}_{7}N + {}^{0}_{-1}\beta + \overline{\nu}$

Page 11 — Fact Recall Questions
Q1 The electromagnetic force (between protons) and the strong nuclear force.
Q2 Between 0 and about 0.5 fm.
Q3 Between about 0.5 and 3 fm.
Q4 The electrostatic repulsion is much greater than the gravitational attraction. Without another force, the strong nuclear force, the nucleus would fly apart.
Q5

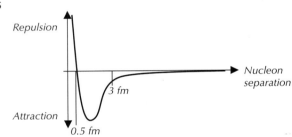

Q6 An electron
Q7 Because the forces in the nucleus cannot hold it together, making it unstable.
Q8 The nucleon number decreases by 4 and the proton number decreases by 2.
Q9 a) An electron and an antineutrino particle.
    b) Neutron-rich nuclei, i.e. ones with many more neutrons than protons.
    c) A neutron turns into a proton, so the nucleon number stays the same and the proton number increases by 1.

3. Antiparticles and Photons

Page 15 — Application Questions
Q1 $E = hf = (6.63 \times 10^{-34}) \times (6.0 \times 10^{13}) = $ **4.0×10^{-20} J (to 2 s.f.)**
Q2 $E = \dfrac{hc}{\lambda} = ((6.63 \times 10^{-34}) \times (3.00 \times 10^{8})) \div (2.4 \times 10^{-6})$
        = **8.3×10^{-20} J (to 2 s.f.)**
    Don't forget to change the units of λ from km to m.
Q3 $E_{min} = 2E_0 = 2 \times$ (proton rest energy) = 2×938.257
           = **1876.514 MeV**
Q4 $E_{min} = E_0 = $ **0.510999 MeV**

Page 15 — Fact Recall Questions
Q1 A photon is a 'packet' of EM radiation.
Q2 $E = \dfrac{hc}{\lambda}$
Q3 a) An antiparticle has the opposite charge to its corresponding particle.
    b) An antiparticle has the same mass and rest energy as its corresponding particle.
Q4 A positron

Q5 a) −1
    b) 0
    c) 0
Q6 Energy can be converted into mass and produce particles, if there is enough energy. The mass is always produced in a particle antiparticle pair.
Q7 Two gamma ray photons.

4. Classification of Particles

Page 19 — Application Questions
Q1 +4
Remember, it's the total number of baryons in the helium nucleus. Nucleons are baryons and the nucleon number is 4, so there are 4 baryons in the nucleus.

Q2 a) The equation is: $n \rightarrow p + e^- + \overline{\nu}_e$
       Electron lepton number: $0 : 0 + 1 + (-1)$
       So L_e is 0 on both sides.
    b) Charge: $0 : 1 + (-1) + 0$
       So charge is 0 on both sides.
Q3 The equation is: $K^- \rightarrow \mu^- + \nu_\mu$
    Muon lepton number: $0 : 1 + 1$
    So L_μ is 0 on the left hand side and 2 on the right hand side.

Page 19 — Fact Recall Questions
Q1 Hadrons
Q2 Proton
Q3 a) 0
    b) −1
    c) 0
Q4 An electron and an electron antineutrino.
Q5 π^0
Q6 A fundamental particle that does not feel the strong nuclear force.
Q7 +1
Q8 Electron lepton number, muon lepton number and baryon number.

5. Quarks and Antiquarks

Page 24 — Application Questions
Q1 It must have 3 quarks, 0 charge and strangeness −1. The quark composition is uds.
Q2 a) This interaction can happen — charge, baryon number, lepton number and strangeness are all conserved.
    b) This interaction can happen — charge, baryon number, lepton number are all conserved.
       K^- *is* $s\overline{u}$ *and* π^0 *is* $u\overline{u}$, $d\overline{d}$ *or* $s\overline{s}$, *so a quark changes character in this interaction which means it must use the weak interaction — strangeness doesn't need to be conserved.*
    c) This interaction cannot happen as muon lepton number is not conserved.
Q3 The strangeness on the left is 0 and the strangeness on the right is $-1 + (+1) = 0$

Page 24 — Fact Recall Questions
Q1 up, down and strange
Q2 $+\frac{1}{3}$
Q3 −1
Q4 a) uud
    b) udd
    c) $\overline{udd}$
Q5 1 quark and 1 antiquark.
Q6 The energy used to remove a quark from a hadron creates a quark-antiquark pair. It's called quark confinement.
Q7 The weak interaction. In β^- decay, a neutron decays to a proton, so a down quark changes to an up quark.
Q8 Charge, baryon number, lepton numbers.
    Energy, mass and momentum are also conserved.

6. Particle Interactions

Page 29 — Application Questions
Q1 a) Beta-plus decay
    b)

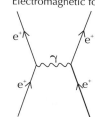

Q2

Q3 a) Electromagnetic force and the virtual photon.
    b)

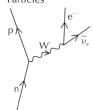

Page 29 — Fact Recall Questions
Q1 A virtual particle that lets a force act between two particles in an interaction.
Q2 Virtual photons
Q3 W^+ boson and W^- boson
Q4 Particles
Q5

Q6 Because it is proton rich.
Q7 In electron capture, a proton captures an electron from the atom, turning into a neutron and emitting a neutrino.
    In an electron-proton collision, an electron collides with a proton, producing a neutron and a neutrino.
Q8 Electron-proton collision
Q9 The W^+ boson is the exchange particle and a neutron and an electron neutrino are produced.

Exam-style Questions — Pages 31-32
1   (a) (i)   Three *(1 mark)*
        (ii) Two *(1 mark)*
        (iii) uss *(1 mark)*
    The particle has a charge of 0 so you need an up quark to cancel the charge of the two strange quarks.

(b) (i) Any two from: charge, baryon number, mass, electron lepton number, muon lepton number.
(1 mark for each correct answer, up to two marks)

(ii) Strangeness *(1 mark)*

(iii) The weak interaction is responsible for this decay, and strangeness is not always conserved by the weak interaction *(1 mark)*.

(c) (i) Proton *(1 mark)*

(ii)

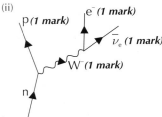

p *(1 mark)* e⁻ *(1 mark)* $\bar{\nu}_e$ *(1 mark)* W⁻ *(1 mark)* n

(iii) β⁻ decay *(1 mark)*

(iv) The weak interaction *(1 mark)* and exchange particle W⁻ boson *(1 mark)*.

2 (a) (i) There are 94 protons *(1 mark)*
There are 240 – 94 = 146 neutrons *(1 mark)*

(ii) The specific charge is charge ÷ mass
The charge of a proton is 1.60×10^{-19} C
The mass of a nucleon is 1.67×10^{-27} kg
There are 94 protons, so the charge of the nucleus is $94 \times (1.60 \times 10^{-19}) = 1.504 \times 10^{-17}$ C *(1 mark)*.
There are 240 nucleons so the mass of the nucleus is $240 \times (1.67 \times 10^{-27}) = 4.008 \times 10^{-25}$ kg *(1 mark)*.
So specific charge is $(1.504 \times 10^{-17}) \div (4.008 \times 10^{-25})$
$= 3.752... \times 10^7$ C kg⁻¹
$= \mathbf{3.8 \times 10^7}$ **C kg⁻¹ (to 2 s.f.)** *(1 mark)*.

(iii) The strong nuclear force *(1 mark)*.

(iv) $^{240}_{94}\text{Pu} \rightarrow {}^{236}_{92}\text{U} + {}^{4}_{2}\alpha$
(3 marks — 1 mark for each component correct)

(b) (i) Isotopes have the same proton number so the proton number is 94.
So the nuclide notation is $^{241}_{94}\text{Pu}$
(2 marks available, one for using nuclide notation correctly and one for correct numbers)

(ii) With nine α decays, the proton number will decrease from 94 by 18 to 76. The proton number of Tl is 81 so you need five β⁻ decays.
(3 marks for correct answer — 1 mark if correct proton number given after nine α decays)

3 (a) (i) The electromagnetic force *(1 mark)* with the exchange particle being virtual photons *(1 mark)*.

(ii)

p p γ p p

(3 marks — 1 mark for two protons in, 1 mark for 2 protons out and 1 mark for the virtual photon)

(b) (i) Pair production *(1 mark)*.

(ii) Certain properties, such as baryon number and charge must be conserved in particle interactions, so a particle-antiparticle pair must always be produced *(1 mark)*.

(iii) $E_{min} = 2E_0 = 2 \times (938.257)$ *(1 mark)*
$= 1876.514$ MeV
$= \mathbf{1880}$ **MeV (to 3 s.f.)** *(1 mark)*.

(iv) The process is called annihilation *(1 mark)*.
Two gamma ray photons are produced *(1 mark)*.

Section 2 — Electromagnetic Radiation and Quantum Phenomena

1. The Photoelectric Effect

Page 36 — Application Questions

Q1 $E = hf$, so $f = E \div h$.
$h = 6.63 \times 10^{-34}$ Js, $E = 4.3 \times 10^{-20}$ J,
so $f = 4.3 \times 10^{-20} \div 6.63 \times 10^{-34} = \mathbf{6.5 \times 10^{13}}$ **Hz (to 2 s.f.)**
Always round your answers to the same number of significant figures as the data you're given in the question.

Q2 The work function is the minimum amount of energy required for an electron to be emitted from the zinc's surface. The energy of each photon is greater than this value, and so they will be able to transfer enough energy to release electrons from the zinc sheet.

Q3 a) The maximum kinetic energy of the electrons increases as the frequency of the incident light increases. Increasing the frequency of the light increases the energy of each photon ($E = hf$), and so more energy can be transferred to the free electrons in the metal. The maximum kinetic energy of the photoelectrons emitted is the energy transferred by a photon minus the work function energy. The work function energy remains the same, so as the energy of the incident photons increases, the kinetic energy of the emitted electrons also increases.

b) $E = hf$, $h = 6.63 \times 10^{-34}$ Js, $f = 1.20 \times 10^{16}$ Hz,
so $E = (6.63 \times 10^{-34}) \times (1.20 \times 10^{16})$
$= 7.956 \times 10^{-18} = \mathbf{7.96 \times 10^{-18}}$ **J (to 3 s.f.)**

c) $hf = \phi + E_k$, $E_k = 7.26 \times 10^{-18}$ J,
$hf = 7.956 \times 10^{-18}$ J,
so the work function of the metal (ϕ) is
$\phi = hf - E_k = 7.956 \times 10^{-18} - 7.26 \times 10^{-18}$
$= \mathbf{6.96 \times 10^{-19}}$ **J**

Page 36 — Fact Recall Questions

Q1 The photoelectric effect is when electrons are emitted from the surface of a metal when light of a high enough frequency (usually ultraviolet light) is shone on it.

Q2 More electrons will be emitted, but their maximum kinetic energy will remain the same.

Q3 a) A photon is a discrete wave-packet of EM radiation.
b) $E = hf$ (where E = energy in J, h = 6.63×10^{-34} Js, f = frequency in Hz)

Q4 Before an electron can be emitted by a metal, it needs enough energy to break the bonds holding it there. This means there is a minimum amount of energy an electron needs before it can escape the metal surface. The threshold frequency is the frequency of light that has photons with this energy.

Q5 The maximum amount of energy that can be transferred to an electron is the energy of one photon. There is a minimum amount of energy needed to free the electron from the metal (the work function energy). Therefore the maximum amount of kinetic energy an electron can have is the energy of one photon minus the work function energy.

Q6 $hf = \phi + E_k$
h = the Planck constant = 6.63×10^{-34} Js,
f = frequency of the incident light (in Hz),
ϕ = work function of the metal (in J),
E_k = kinetic energy of the emitted electron (in J).

2. Energy Levels in Atoms

Page 40 — Application Question

Q1　a) An atom which has one or more of its electrons in an energy level higher than the ground state.

　　b) 3.40 eV

　　The energy of each level in an atom shows how much energy is needed for an electron in that level to be removed from the atom. The electron is in the n = 2 energy level, and so needs 3.40 eV.

　　c) $\Delta E = E_1 - E_2 = 13.6 - 3.4 = 10.2$ eV.

　　　10.2 eV = $10.2 \times 1.6 \times 10^{-19}$ J = 1.632×10^{-18} J

　　　$E = hf$, so $f = E \div h = 1.632 \times 10^{-18} \div 6.63 \times 10^{-34}$

　　　= **2.46×10^{15} Hz (to 3 s.f.)**

Page 40 — Fact Recall Questions

Q1　An electronvolt is the kinetic energy carried by an electron after it's been accelerated through a potential difference of 1 volt. 1 eV = 1.6×10^{-19} J.

Q2　The transitions between energy levels that the electrons make are between definite energy levels, so the energy of each photon emitted can only take a certain allowed value.

Q3　The energy needed to remove an electron from the ground state of an atom.

Q4　Fast-moving free electrons that are accelerated by the voltage across the tube collide with the electrons of the mercury atoms. These collisions transfer energy to the electrons and excite them to a higher energy level. When these excited electrons return to their ground states, they lose energy by emitting photons of ultraviolet light. A phosphorus coating on the inside of the tube absorbs these photons, exciting electrons in the coating to much higher levels. These electrons then fall down the energy levels and lose energy by emitting many lower energy photons of visible light.

Q5　Photons of particular frequencies being absorbed or emitted by atoms. The frequencies correspond to the differences in energy between the discrete energy levels in atoms.

3. Wave-Particle Duality

Page 43 — Application Questions

Q1　$\lambda = \frac{h}{mv}$, so the de Broglie wavelength is inversely proportional to the velocity of the electron. Therefore increasing the velocity will decrease the de Broglie wavelength of the electrons.

Q2　a) $\lambda = \frac{h}{mv}$, so momentum = $mv = h \div \lambda$.

　　　$h = 6.63 \times 10^{-34}$ Js, $\lambda = 1.62 \times 10^{-10}$ m,

　　　$mv = 6.63 \times 10^{-34} \div 1.62 \times 10^{-10}$

　　　$= 4.09259... \times 10^{-24}$ kg ms^{-1}

　　　= **4.09×10^{-24} kg ms^{-1} (to 3 s.f.)**

　　　Make sure you always include units with your answer — it could get you some precious extra marks in the exam.

　　b) $m_e = 9.11 \times 10^{-31}$ kg,

　　　$v = mv \div m_e$

　　　$= 4.09259... \times 10^{-24} \div 9.11 \times 10^{-31}$

　　　$= 4.4924... \times 10^{6}$ ms^{-1}

　　　$= 4.49 \times 10^{6}$ ms^{-1} (to 3 s.f.)

　　　$E_k = \frac{1}{2}mv^2 = \frac{1}{2} \times 9.11 \times 10^{-31} \times (4.4924... \times 10^6)^2$

　　　= **9.19×10^{-18} J (to 3 s.f.)**

Q3　a) $\lambda = \frac{h}{mv} = \frac{6.63 \times 10^{-34}}{6.64 \times 10^{-27} \times 60}$

　　　$= 1.664... \times 10^{-9}$ m

　　　= **1.67×10^{-9} m (to 3 s.f.)**

　　b) $\lambda = \frac{h}{mv}$

　　　$1.664 \times 10^{-9} = \frac{6.63 \times 10^{-34}}{9.11 \times 10^{-31} \times v}$

　　　$v = \frac{6.63 \times 10^{-34}}{9.11 \times 10^{-31} \times 1.664 \times 10^{-9}}$

　　　= **4.37×10^{5} ms^{-1} (to 3.s.f.)**

Page 43 — Fact Recall Questions

Q1　All particles can be shown to have both particle and wave properties. Waves can also show particle properties.

Q2　Diffraction shows light has wave properties, and the photoelectric effect shows light has particle properties.

Q3　Electron diffraction

Exam-style Questions — Pages 45-46

1　(a) (i)　The work function of a metal is the minimum energy an electron needs to escape the surface of a metal *(1 mark)*.

　　　(ii)　The energy of photons depends on the frequency of the light *(1 mark)*. Below a certain frequency (the threshold frequency), the photons don't have enough energy to release an electron from the metal's surface *(1 mark)*.

　　　(iii)　If light acted only as a wave, the electrons in a metal would slowly absorb the energy of incident light waves until they had enough energy to escape the metal *(1 mark)* no matter how the frequency of the light varied — there would be no threshold frequency observed *(1 mark)*.

　　(b) (i)　$\phi = hf_o$,

　　　　$f_o = 1.03 \times 10^{15}$ Hz, $h = 6.63 \times 10^{-34}$ Js,

　　　　so $\phi = hf_o = 6.63 \times 10^{-34} \times 1.03 \times 10^{15}$

　　　　= **6.83×10^{-19} J (to 3 s.f.)**

　　　　(2 marks for correct answer, 1 mark for correct working if answer incorrect)

　　　(ii)　$hf = \phi + E_k$

　　　　$hf = 3.0 \times 10^{-18}$ J, $\phi = 6.83 \times 10^{-19}$ J (to 3 s.f.),

　　　　substituting into $hf = \phi + E_k$ gives:

　　　　$3.0 \times 10^{-18} = 6.83 \times 10^{-19} + E_k$

　　　　$E_k = 3.0 \times 10^{-18} - 6.83 \times 10^{-19} = $ **2.3×10^{-18} J (to 2 s.f.)**

　　　　(2 marks for correct answer, 1 mark for correct working if answer incorrect)

2　(a)　An atom which has an electron (or electrons) that have absorbed energy and jumped to a higher energy level/state than the ground state *(1 mark)*.

　　(b)　A coating on the inside of the tube absorbs the photons emitted by the mercury atoms *(1 mark)*. This excites the electrons in the atoms of the coating into higher energy levels. These electrons lose this energy and fall into lower energy levels by emitting photons of visible light *(1 mark)*.

　　(c) (i)　Energy transferred = 8.0 − 1.80 = 6.20 eV.

　　　　1 eV = 1.6×10^{-19} J,

　　　　so 6.20 eV = $6.20 \times 1.6 \times 10^{-19}$ J = **9.92×10^{-19} J.**

　　　　(2 marks for correct answer, 1 mark for attempting to multiply by 1.6×10^{-19} if answer incorrect)

　　　(ii)　$E = \frac{hc}{\lambda}$,

　　　　$\lambda = \frac{hc}{E} = \frac{6.63 \times 10^{-34} \times 3.00 \times 10^{8}}{9.92 \times 10^{-19}}$

　　　　= **2.00×10^{-7} m (to 3 s.f.)**

　　　　(2 marks for correct answer, 1 mark for correct working if answer incorrect)

　　(d)　10.4 eV *(1 mark)*

3 (a) All particles can be shown to have both particle and wave properties. Waves can also show particle properties *(1 mark)*.
(b) Electron diffraction *(1 mark)*.
(c) (i) $m_e = 9.11 \times 10^{-31}$ kg, $E_k = 1.02 \times 10^{-26}$ J

Rearrange $E_k = \frac{1}{2}mv^2$ to give $v = \sqrt{\frac{2E_k}{m}}$

$v = \sqrt{\frac{2 \times 1.02 \times 10^{-26}}{9.11 \times 10^{-31}}}$

$= 149.64...\ \text{ms}^{-1}$

$= \mathbf{150\ ms^{-1}}$ **(to 3 s.f.)**

(2 marks in total — 2 marks for correct answer, otherwise 1 mark for correct working if answer is incorrect.)

If a question asks you to give your answer to an appropriate number of significant figures, it probably means you'll get a mark for doing it. Always round your answer to the same number of significant figures as the data you're given in the question.

(ii) $\lambda = \frac{h}{mv} = \frac{6.63 \times 10^{-34}}{9.11 \times 10^{-31} \times 149.64...}$

$= 4.863...\times 10^{-6}\ \text{m}$

$= \mathbf{4.86 \times 10^{-6}\ m}$ **(to 3 s.f.)**

(3 marks in total — 2 marks for correct answer, 1 mark for correct working if answer incorrect)

4 (a) Atoms can only absorb and emit photons *(1 mark)* with energies equal to differences between the electron energy levels *(1 mark)*. The lines visible in a line spectrum correspond to photons with these allowed certain energies *(1 mark)*.
(b) (i) 434 nm $= 4.34 \times 10^{-7}$ m

$E = \frac{hc}{\lambda} = \frac{6.63 \times 10^{-34} \times 3.00 \times 10^8}{4.34 \times 10^{-7}}$ *(1 mark)*

$= 4.5829...\times 10^{-19}$ J *(1 mark)*

$1\ \text{eV} = 1.6 \times 10^{-19}$ J,

so $E = 4.5829...\times 10^{-19}$ J $\div 1.6 \times 10^{-19}$

$= \mathbf{2.86\ eV}$ **(to 3 s.f.)** *(1 mark)*

The energy difference between n = 5 and n = 2 energy levels is $3.40 - 0.54 = 2.86$ eV *(1 mark)*. This is the same as the photons producing the 434 nm line in the spectrum, and so this line must caused by electrons falling between these two levels *(1 mark)*.
(ii) E.g. n = 2 to n = 1 *(1 mark)*.

Section 3 — Current Electricity

2. Current and Potential Difference
Page 49 — Application Questions
Q1 $I = \Delta Q \div \Delta t = 91 \div 30 = \mathbf{3.0\ A}$ **(to 2 s.f.)**
Q2 $V = W \div Q = 114 \div 56.0 = \mathbf{2.04\ V}$ **(to 3 s.f.)**
Q3 a) 5 minutes = 300 seconds
       $\Delta Q = I \times \Delta t = 1.30 \times 300 = \mathbf{390\ C}$
    b) $W = V \times Q = 24.0 \times 390\ C = \mathbf{9360\ J}$ (or 9.36 kJ)

Page 49 — Fact Recall Questions
Q1 Current is the rate of flow of charge in a circuit.
Q2 in series
Q3 The potential difference between two points is the work done in moving a unit charge between the points.

3. Resistance
Page 51 — Application Questions
Q1 $V = I \times R = 2.10 \times 8.62 = \mathbf{18.1\ V}$ **(to 3 s.f.)**
Q2 $R = V \div I = 13.4 \div 1.21 = \mathbf{11.1\ \Omega}$ **(to 3 s.f.)**
Q3 The resistance of the component must be decreasing, if the current is increasing.
    $V = I \times R$. So if the current is increasing, to get the same voltage as before, the resistance must be decreasing.
Q4 $R = V \div I = 15.6 \div 3.20 = 4.875\ \Omega$
    $V = I \times R = 4.10 \times 4.875 = \mathbf{20.0\ V}$ **(to 3 s.f.)**
    You know the resistance of the wire will stay constant because it is an ohmic conductor.

Page 51 — Fact Recall Questions
Q1 The resistance of something is a measure of how difficult it is to get a current to flow through it.
    It is defined as $R = V \div I$.
Q2 temperature
Q3 Nothing — the resistance of an ohmic conductor is constant (if temperature is constant).

4. I-V Characteristics
Page 55 — Application Questions
Q1 a) E.g.

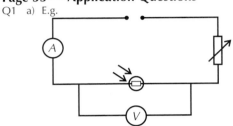

    b) E.g. use the variable resistor to decrease (or increase) the resistance of the circuit in small, equal steps. For each change in resistance, take a reading from the ammeter to find the current through the component, and a reading from the voltmeter to find the voltage across it. Reverse the direction of electricity flow by switching the wires connected to the power pack. Then repeat the same method to collect data for negative values of V and I. The student would need to keep the light intensity constant because the resistance of LDRs changes with light intensity.
Q2 a) a diode
    b) The diode requires a voltage of about 0.6 V in the forward direction before it will conduct, so there is no current flow until 0.6 V on the diagram. After 0.6 V, the current is allowed to flow, and increases (exponentially) with an increase in potential difference.
    c) In reverse bias, the resistance of the diode is very high.

Page 55 — Fact Recall Questions
Q1 a) *Current / A*

P.d. / V

b)

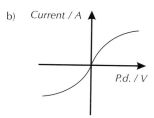

Q2 A filament lamp is not an ohmic conductor. It's characteristic I-V graph is not a straight line — so voltage is not proportional to current.

Q3 It increases. When the temperature increases, the particles in the conductor vibrate more. The vibrations make it more difficult for the charge-carrying electrons to get through the metal — the current can't flow as easily and the resistance increases.

Q4 Warming a thermistor gives more electrons enough energy to escape from their atoms. This means that there are more charge carriers available, so the resistance is lower.

Q5 E.g. temperature sensor

5. Resistivity & Superconductors

Page 57 — Application Questions

Q1 Convert 6 mm^2 into m^2: $6 \times 1 \times 10^{-6} = 6 \times 10^{-6}$ m^2
$\rho = (R \times A) \div L = (200 \times 6 \times 10^{-6}) \div 3.0 \times 10^{-3}$
$= \textbf{0.4 } \boldsymbol{\Omega}\textbf{m}$

Q2 Assuming the wire has a circular cross-section:
cross-sectional area $= \pi r^2 = \pi \times (2.34 \times 10^{-3})^2$
$= 1.72... \times 10^{-5}$ m^2
$R = (\rho \times L) \div A = (5.6 \times 10^{-8} \times 0.141) \div (1.72... \times 10^{-5})$
$= \textbf{4.59} \times \textbf{10}^{-4} \ \boldsymbol{\Omega}$ **(to 3 s.f.)**

Q3 $A = (\rho \times L) \div R = (1.68 \times 10^{-8} \times 0.0100$ m$) \div 0.000457$
$= 3.676... \times 10^{-7}$ m^2
Assuming the wire has a circular cross-section:
$A = \pi r^2$, $r = \sqrt{(A \div \pi)} = \sqrt{(3.676... \times 10^{-7} \div \pi)}$
$r = \textbf{3.42} \times \textbf{10}^{-4}$ **m (to 3 s.f.)**

Page 57 — Fact Recall Questions

Q1 Length, area and resistivity.

Q2 The resistivity of a material is the resistance of a 1 m length with a 1 m^2 cross-sectional area. It is measured in ohm-metres (Ωm).

Q3 A material that has zero resistivity when cooled below a 'transition temperature'.

Q4 E.g. it is very difficult to cool a material to below its transition temperature. / It is very expensive to keep a material cooled to below its transition temperature.

Q5 Any two of: e.g. power cables / strong electromagnets / fast electronic circuits.

6. Power and Electrical Energy

Page 60 — Application Questions

Q1 **3400 W (3.4 kW)**
Power is defined as the energy transfer per second. It's measured in watts, where 1 watt is equal to 1 joule per second.

Q2 a) $P = E \div t = 12\,500 \div 2.00 = \textbf{6250 W}$
b) $I = P \div V = 6250 \div 8.00 = \textbf{781 A (to 3 s.f.)}$

Q3 $P = V \times I$, so rearranging: $I = P \div V$
$I = 5200 \div 230 = \textbf{23 A (to 2 s.f.)}$

Q4 $E = VIt = 230 \times 1.2 \times 45 = \textbf{12 400 J (to 3 s.f.)}$

Q5 $P = 1250$ W
$P = I^2R$, so rearranging: $I = \sqrt{(P \div R)}$
$I = \sqrt{(1250 \div 54.2)} = \textbf{4.80 A (to 3 s.f.)}$

Page 60 — Fact Recall Questions

Q1 Power (P) is the rate of transfer of energy. It's measured in watts (W), where 1 watt is equivalent to 1 joule per second.

Q2 E.g. $P = VI$, $P = V^2/R$, $P = I^2R$

Q3 The voltage across the starter motor is low and the motor needs a high power to start the engine. As $P = VI$, this means the current flowing through the motor has to be very high to provide the large power needed.

7. E.m.f. and Internal Resistance

Page 64 — Application Questions

Q1 $\varepsilon = V + v$, so $v = \varepsilon - V = 2.50 - 2.24 = \textbf{0.26 V}$

Q2 $V = \varepsilon - Ir$,
so $\varepsilon = V + Ir = 4.68 + (0.63 \times 0.89) = \textbf{5.2 V (to 2 s.f.)}$

Q3 $\varepsilon = I(R + r)$, so $\varepsilon \div I = R + r$ and so $R = (\varepsilon \div I) - r$
$R = (15.0 \div 26.1) - 8.28 \times 10^{-3} = \textbf{0.566 } \boldsymbol{\Omega}\textbf{ (to 3 s.f.)}$

Q4 $P = I^2R = (1.2)^2 \times 0.50 = 0.72$ W
So **0.72 J** is dissipated each second.

Q5 a) $\varepsilon = \textbf{5 V}$
The e.m.f. is the intercept on the vertical axis.
b) internal resistance $= -$gradient of the graph
$= \Delta y \div \Delta x = $ e.g. $5 \div 0.6 = \textbf{8.3 } \boldsymbol{\Omega}\textbf{ (to 2 s.f.)}$
c) The straight line would still have the same y-intercept at 5 V. The gradient $= -r$, so the gradient would be half as steep as that for the original power supply, so it would intercept the x-axis at 1.2 A.

Page 64 — Fact Recall Questions

Q1 In a battery, chemical energy is used to make electrons move. As they move, they collide with atoms inside the battery and lose energy — this is the internal resistance.

Q2 The load resistance is the total resistance of all the components in the external part of the circuit.
The load resistance doesn't include the internal resistance of the power source.

Q3 Volts (V)

Q4 The energy wasted per coulomb overcoming an internal resistance.

Q5 Car batteries have to deliver a high current to start an engine, so they need a low internal resistance to supply this — since the voltage supplied by the battery is constant and relatively low and $V = IR$.

Q6 The gradient is $-r$ (where r is the internal resistance) and the y-intercept is ε (the electromotive force).

8. Conservation of Energy and Charge in Circuits

Page 69 — Application Questions

Q1 a) $R_{total} = R_1 + R_2 + R_3$
$40 \ \Omega = R_1 + 20 \ \Omega + 10 \ \Omega$
$R_1 = 40 - 20 - 10 = \textbf{10 } \boldsymbol{\Omega}$
b) 0.4 A
The current flowing through a series circuit is the same at all points of the circuit.

Q2 a) A and B are in parallel, so:
Total e.m.f. of A and $B = A = B = 3$ V
Then find total e.m.f by adding e.m.f.s in series:
Total e.m.f. of cells $=$ (total of A and B) $+ C$
$= 3$ V $+ 3$ V $= \textbf{6 V}$
b) The p.d. across the load will be 6 V, because when there is no internal resistance in the cells, the terminal p.d. will match their combined e.m.f.
c) First calculate the total resistance of the 15 Ω and 10 Ω resistors in parallel, using $1/R = 1/R_1 + 1/R_2$
$1/R = 1/15 + 1/10 = 1/6$
$R = 6 \ \Omega$
Then add the resistance in series:
$R_{total} = R_1 + R_2 = 6 + 10 = \textbf{16 } \boldsymbol{\Omega}$

Q3 In parallel, the current flowing through the circuit will be split equally at the junction of the three cells. In series, the current flowing through each cell will be exactly the same as the current flowing through the circuit. So in series, the cells will have a bigger current flowing through them than in the parallel circuit.

Q4 a) First calculate the total resistance of the 3 Ω and 6 Ω resistors in parallel, using $1/R = 1/R_1 + 1/R_2$
$1/R = 1/3 + 1/6 = 1/2$
$R = 2\ \Omega$
Resistors in series add up and the total resistance is 10 Ω, so the total resistance of the 12 Ω and R_1 resistors in parallel is equal to:
$10\ \Omega - 2\ \Omega - 5\ \Omega = 3\ \Omega$
The 5 Ω here is the resistance of the resistor in between the two sets of parallel resistors.
So for the R_1 resistor and the 12 Ω resistor in parallel, the total resistance is 3 Ω. So:
$1/3 = 1/R_1 + 1/4$
$1/R_1 = 1/3 - 1/4 = 1/12$
$R_1 = \mathbf{12\ \Omega}$

b) $I = V_{total} \div R_{total}$
$I = 12 \div 10 = 1.2\ A$
$V = I \times R = 1.2 \times 5 = \mathbf{6\ V}$

c) The p.d. across the resistors in parallel (3 Ω and 6 Ω) is:
$V = I \times R = 1.2 \times 2 = 2.4\ V$
So the current through the 6 Ω is:
$I = V \div R = 2.4 \div 6 = \mathbf{0.4\ A}$
Remember, current splits depending on the resistance — it doesn't just split equally between resistors (unless the resistors have equal resistance).

Page 69 — Fact Recall Questions

Q1 The total current entering a junction = the total current leaving it.

Q2 The total e.m.f. around a series circuit = the sum of the p.d.s across each component.

Q3 They are in series.

Q4 parallel

9. The Potential Divider

Page 72 — Application Questions

Q1 a) $V_{out} = \dfrac{R_2}{R_1 + R_2} V_S = \dfrac{3.0}{12 + 3.0} \times 16 = \mathbf{3.2\ V}$

b) $V_{out} = \dfrac{R_2}{R_1 + R_2} V_S$, so $5 = \dfrac{R_2}{12 + R_2} \times 16$
$5(12 + R_2) = 16R_2 \Rightarrow 60 + 5R_2 = 16R_2 \Rightarrow 60 = 11R_2$
$R_2 = \dfrac{60}{11} = \mathbf{5.5\ \Omega}$ (to 2 s.f.)

Q2 $V_{out} = \dfrac{R_2}{R_1 + R_2} V_S$ so, $\dfrac{V_{out}}{V_S} = \dfrac{R_2}{R_1 + R_2} = \dfrac{4}{16} = \dfrac{1}{4}$
$4R_2 = R_1 + R_2$
$3R_2 = R_1$
So, for example, you could have $R_1 = 9\ \Omega$ and $R_2 = 3\ \Omega$.
Here, you can have any values that $3R_2 = R_1$ is true for.

Q3 a) $V_{out} = \dfrac{R_2}{R_1 + R_2} V_S$ so, $V_{out} = \dfrac{1.5}{3 + 1.5} \times 1.5$
$V_{out} = \mathbf{0.5\ V}$

b) $V_{out} = \dfrac{R_2}{R_1 + R_2} V_S$ so, $0.3 = \dfrac{R_2}{3 + R_2} \times 1.5$
$0.3(3 + R_2) = 1.5R_2 \Rightarrow 0.9 + 0.3R_2 = 1.5R_2$
$0.9 = 1.2R_2$
$R_2 = \mathbf{0.75\ \Omega}$

Page 72 — Fact Recall Questions

Q1 A potential divider is a circuit containing a voltage source and a couple of resistors in series. The voltage across one of the resistors is used as an output voltage. If the resistors aren't fixed, the circuit will be capable of producing a variable output voltage.

Q2 $V_{out} = \dfrac{R_2}{R_1 + R_2} V_S$

Q3 You can make a light sensor using a potential divider by using an LDR as one of the resistors.

Q4 A potential divider containing a variable resistor.

Q5 E.g. a volume control on a stereo, dimmer switch.

10. Alternating Current

Page 76 — Application Questions

Q1 a) $I_{rms} = \dfrac{I_0}{\sqrt{2}} = \dfrac{8.2}{\sqrt{2}} = 5.798... = \mathbf{5.8\ A}$ (to 2 s.f.)

b) $R = \dfrac{V_0}{I_0} = \dfrac{9.0}{8.2} = \mathbf{1.1\ \Omega}$ (to 2 s.f.)

Q2 a) $V_{rms} = \dfrac{V_0}{\sqrt{2}}$, so $V_0 = \sqrt{2}\ V_{rms}$
$V_0 = \sqrt{2} \times 120 = \mathbf{170\ V}$ (to 3 s.f.)

b) $P = V_{rms} \times I_{rms} = 120 \times 20.0 = \mathbf{2400\ W}$

Q3 a) $20\ ms\,cm^{-1} = 0.02\ s\,cm^{-1}$
Wave spans 8 cm, so:
Time period = $0.02 \times 8 = 0.16\ s$
Frequency = $1 \div T = 1 \div 0.16 = \mathbf{6.25\ Hz}$

b) From the graph, peak voltage = $3 \times 0.5\ V = 1.5\ V$
$V_{rms} = \dfrac{V_0}{\sqrt{2}} = \dfrac{1.5}{\sqrt{2}} = \mathbf{1.1\ V}$ (to 2 s.f.)

Page 76 — Fact Recall Questions

Q1 An electron beam moving across the screen.

Q2 There would be a straight vertical line on the voltage axis.

Q3 The voltage of an a.c. supply will be below the peak voltage most of the time. That means it won't have as high a power output as a d.c. supply with the same peak voltage. To compare them properly, you need to average the a.c. voltage somehow. A normal average won't work, because the positive and negative bits cancel out.

Q4 $I_{rms} = \dfrac{I_0}{\sqrt{2}}$

Exam Questions — Pages 78-79

1 (a) (i) $P = IV = 0.724 \times 3.00 = \mathbf{2.17\ W}$ (to 3 s.f.)
(2 marks for correct answer, 1 mark for correct working if answer incorrect)

(ii) 5 minutes = 300 seconds
$\Delta Q = I \times \Delta t = 0.724 \times 300 = \mathbf{217\ C}$ (to 3 s.f.)
(2 marks for correct answer, 1 mark for correct working if answer incorrect)

(iii) $V = W \div Q = 56.5 \div 217.2 = \mathbf{0.26\ V}$ (to 2 s.f.)
(2 marks for correct answer, 1 mark for correct working if answer incorrect)

(iv) p.d. across the filament lamp = $I \times R$
$= 0.724 \times 2.00$
$= 1.448\ V$ *(1 mark)*

$V_{total} = V_1 + V_2 + V_{bulb}$
$3.00 = 0.260 + V_2 + 1.448$
$V_2 = \mathbf{1.29\ V}$ (to 3 s.f.)
(2 marks for correct answer, 1 mark for correct working if answer incorrect)

(b) (i) No, the filament lamp is not an ohmic conductor as V is not directly proportional to I at all points on the graph *(1 mark)*.

(ii) Current flowing through the lamp increases its temperature and the resistance of the metal filament increases as the temperature increases — this gives the graph a curved shape ***(1 mark)***. There is a limit to the amount of current that can flow through the filament bulb: more current means an increase in temperature, which means an increase in resistance, which means the current decreases again — this is why the I-V graph for the filament lamp levels off at high currents ***(1 mark)***.

2 (a) As the electrons move through the battery, they collide with atoms inside the battery and transfer some of their energy ***(1 mark)***. (The small amount of resistance that causes this energy loss inside the battery is called internal resistance).

(b) E.g.

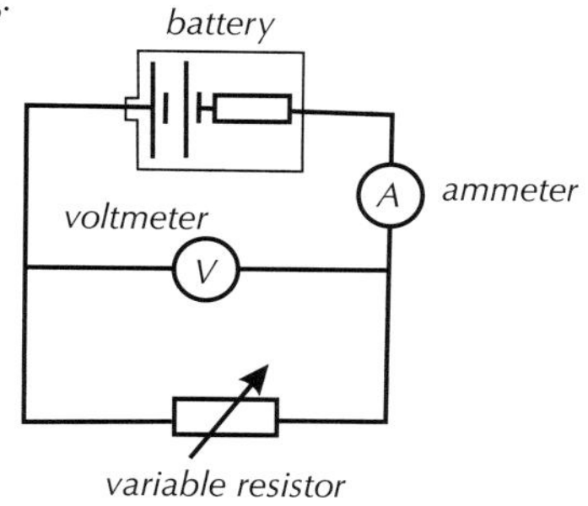

(1 mark for working circuit containing a battery and a resistor or variable resistor, 1 mark for ammeter and voltmeter or ohm meter correctly placed in circuit)

(c) (i)

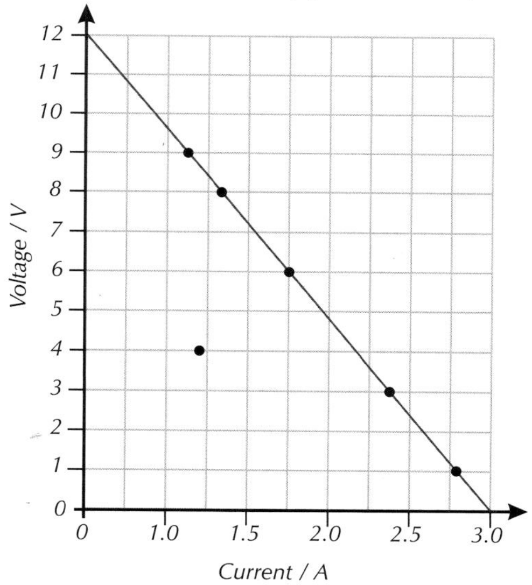

(1 mark for all points correctly plotted, 1 mark for line of best fit drawn)

(ii) e.m.f. = y-intercept = **12 V** ***(1 mark)***

(iii) internal resistance = –gradient = $-\Delta y \div \Delta x$ ***(1 mark)***
(E.g. = 12 ÷ 3) = **4 Ω**
(2 marks for correct answer, 1 mark for correct working if answer incorrect)

3 (a) (i) Its resistance will decrease. ***(1 mark)***.

(ii) E.g. Power cables that transmit electricity without any loss of power. / Really strong electromagnets. / Electronic circuits that work really fast, because there's no resistance to slow them down. ***(1 mark)***

(b) (i) $1/R = 1/R_1 + 1/R_2$
$1/R = 1/10 + 1/10$
$1/R = 1/5$
$R = 5\ \Omega$
$R_{total} = 10 + 5 =$ **15 Ω**
(2 marks for the correct answer, 1 mark for correct working if answer incorrect)

(ii) $I = V_{total} \div R_{total}$
$I = 12 \div 15 =$ **0.8 A**
(2 marks for the correct answer, 1 mark for correct working if answer incorrect)

(c) (i) $R_{total} = 3.21 \times 10^{-3} + 5 = 5.00...\ \Omega$
$I = V_{total} \div R_{total}$
$I = 12 \div 5.00... =$ **2.4 A (to 2 s.f.)**
(2 marks for the correct answer, 1 mark for correct working if answer incorrect)

(ii) $\rho = (R \times A) \div L = (3.21 \times 10^{-3} \times 3.05 \times 10^{-6}) \div 0.0300$
$=$ **3.26×10^{-7} Ωm (to 3 s.f.)**
(2 marks for the correct answer, 1 mark for correct working if answer incorrect, 1 mark for appropriate number of significant figures — also accept 4 s.f.)

Whenever you're asked in a question to give your answer to an appropriate number of significant figures, there is a mark up for grabs for doing so.

(iii) E.g. when the superconducting wire reaches its transition temperature its resistivity (and resistance) will become zero ***(1 mark)***. As there is another resistor in the circuit the current flowing through the superconductor will then only be resisted by this resistor and so the current flowing through the superconductor will have reached its maximum value (its resistance can't decrease any more). ***(1 mark)***

Unit 2

Section 1 — Mechanics

1. Scalars and Vectors

Page 83 — Application Questions

Q1 $v = \sqrt{2.0^2 + 0.75^2} = 2.1\ \text{ms}^{-1}$ (to 2 s.f.)
$\theta = \tan^{-1}\frac{0.75}{2} = 21°$ (to 2 s.f.)
So the resultant velocity is **2.1 ms⁻¹ at 21° down from the horizontal.**
Once you've found the magnitude of the vector you could use sin or cos to find the angle θ too, but it's safer to use tan as you know the values of the opposite and adjacent sides are correct.

Q2 Horizontal component $F_h = F\cos\theta = 12\cos 56°$
$=$ **6.7 N (to 2 s.f.)**
Vertical component $F_v = F\sin\theta = 12\sin 56° =$ **9.9 N (to 2 s.f.)**

Q3 Start by drawing a scale diagram with an appropriate scale (e.g. 3 cm = 1 N). Then measure the side and angle:
The resultant force is 5.0 N on a bearing of 055°.

Q4 Start by drawing a diagram to show the forces on the brick:

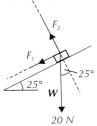

Then use trigonometry to find the size of F_1 and F_2:
a) $F_1 = \sin 25° \times 20 = $ **8.5 N (to 2 s.f.)**
b) $F_2 = \cos 25° \times 20 = $ **18 N (to 2 s.f.)**

Page 83 — Fact Recall Questions
Q1 A scalar quantity has only size, while a vector quantity has size and direction.
Q2 The resultant (vector).

2. Forces in Equilibrium
Page 86 — Application Questions
Q1 Draw a scale diagram of the forces (e.g. using a scale of 1 cm = 1 N), joined up tip-to tail:

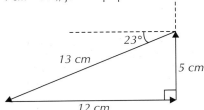

They form a closed triangle, so the object's in equilibrium.
Q2 Either:
Start by drawing the forces in a closed triangle:

$F = \sqrt{7.1^2 + 14.6^2} = $ **16.2 N (to 3 s.f.)**
Or:
Resolve the forces horizontally:
$(\cos 64° \times F) - 7.1 = 0 \Rightarrow F = \dfrac{7.1}{\cos 64°} = 16.2\,\text{N (to 3 s.f.)}$

You could have also resolved the forces vertically, in which case you'd use F sin 64° and 14.6 N instead.

Page 86 — Fact Recall Question
Q1 The sum of all forces acting on a body in equilibrium is 0.

3. Moments
Page 89 — Application Questions
Q1 $M = F \times d = 73.1 \times 0.25 = $ **18.3 Nm (to 3 s.f.)**
Q2 Anticlockwise moment applied by child on left:
$M = F \times d = 450 \times 1.5 = 675$ Nm
So clockwise moment applied by child on right = 675 Nm
$M = F \times d \Rightarrow d = \dfrac{M}{F} = \dfrac{675}{500} = $ **1.35 m**
Q3 $T = F \times d \Rightarrow F = \dfrac{T}{d} = \dfrac{50}{0.35} = $ **140 N (to 2 s.f.)**

Page 89 — Fact Recall Questions
Q1 A moment is the turning effect of a force around a turning point. It's the force × the perpendicular distance from the pivot to the line of action of the force.
Q2 The moment applied by a couple is called torque.

4. Centre of Mass and Stability
Page 91 — Fact Recall Questions
Q1 The centre of mass of an object is the single point that you can consider its whole weight to act through.
Q2 For an object not to topple, its centre of mass needs to stay within the object's base.

5. Uniform Acceleration
Page 93 — Application Questions
Q1 $u = 0$ ms^{-1} $v = 10$ ms^{-1} $t = 20$ s $a = ?$ $s = ?$
so use $s = \dfrac{(u+v)}{2}t \Rightarrow s = \dfrac{(0+10)}{2} \times 20 = $ **100 m**
Q2 $u = 25$ ms^{-1} $v = 0$ ms^{-1} $t = 20$ s $a = ?$ $s = ?$
$v = u + at \Rightarrow a = \dfrac{v-u}{t} = \dfrac{0-25}{20} = -1.25\,\text{ms}^{-2}$
So the deceleration is **1.25 ms^{-2}**.
Q3 $s = 100$ m $u = 0$ ms^{-1} $t = 9.8$ s $v = ?$ $a = ?$
$s = ut + \tfrac{1}{2}at^2 \Rightarrow a = \dfrac{s - ut}{\frac{1}{2}t^2}$
$= \dfrac{100 - (0 \times 9.8)}{\frac{1}{2} \times 9.8^2} = $ **2.08 ms^{-2} (to 3 s.f.)**

Page 93 — Fact Recall Questions
Q1 The velocity of an object is its rate of change of displacement.
Q2 The acceleration of an object is its rate of change of velocity.
Q3 The equations are:
$v = u + at$
$s = \dfrac{(u+v)}{2} \times t$
$s = ut + \tfrac{1}{2}at^2$
$v^2 = u^2 + 2as$

6. Displacement-Time graphs
Page 97 — Application Questions
Q1

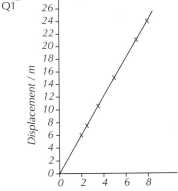

Q2 a) The cyclist is moving forwards at a constant velocity.
b) The cyclist is moving forwards but decelerating.
c) The cyclist isn't moving.
d) The cyclist is moving back towards the starting point at a constant velocity.
Q3 First find the rocket's acceleration:
$v = u + at \Rightarrow a = \dfrac{v-u}{t} = \dfrac{100-0}{5} = 20\,\text{ms}^{-2}$
Then work out the rocket's displacement at intervals with $s = ut + \tfrac{1}{2}at^2$:

t (s)	s (m)
0	0
1	10
2	40
3	90
4	160
5	250

Then plot the graph:

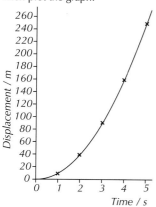

Q4 a)

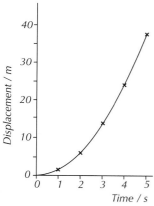

b) Draw a tangent at $t = 3$ and measure its gradient:

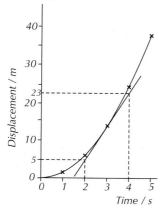

$$v = \frac{\Delta y}{\Delta x} = \frac{23 - 5}{4 - 2} = \frac{18}{2} = \textbf{9 ms}^{-1}$$

Page 97 — Fact Recall Questions

Q1 A curved line on a displacement-time graph shows acceleration (or deceleration).

Q2 A straight line on a displacement-time graph shows constant velocity.

Q3 The velocity is given by the gradient of the displacement-time graph.

7. Velocity-Time graphs
Page 101 — Application Questions

Q1

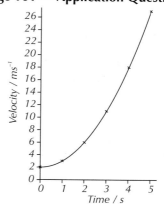

Q2 Find the displacement by finding the area under the graph. To do this, split it into a triangle and a rectangle:

You could also treat it as a trapezium and work out the area directly using the formula for the area of a trapezium.

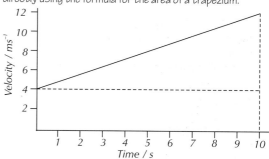

Area of triangle = ½ × base × height = ½ × 10 × 8 = 40
Area of rectangle = base × height = 10 × 4 = 40
So displacement = 40 + 40 = **80 m**

Q3 a)

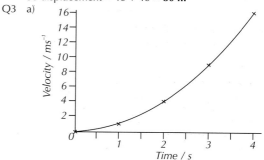

b) To find the acceleration, draw a tangent at $t = 2$ and find its gradient:

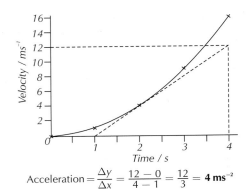

$$\text{Acceleration} = \frac{\Delta y}{\Delta x} = \frac{12 - 0}{4 - 1} = \frac{12}{3} = \mathbf{4\ ms^{-2}}$$

Page 101 — Fact Recall Questions
Q1 The gradient of a velocity-time graph tells you the acceleration.
Q2 Uniform acceleration on a velocity-time graph is shown by a straight line.
Q3 The area under a velocity-time graph tells you the displacement.
Q4 Non-uniform acceleration is shown on a velocity-time graph by a curved line.

8. Newton's Laws of Motion
Page 103 — Application Questions
Q1
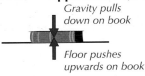
Gravity pulls down on book

Floor pushes upwards on book

Q2 When a bird flaps its wings it pushes down on the air. The air then pushes back up on the bird's wings with the same force, which causes it to lift.
Q3 $F = m \times a \Rightarrow F = 24.1 \times 3.5 = \mathbf{84.4\ N\ (to\ 3\ s.f.)}$
Q4 $F = m \times a \Rightarrow a = \frac{F}{m} = \frac{18}{0.61} = \mathbf{30\ ms^{-2}\ (to\ 2\ s.f.)}$
Q5 First find the force they push each other with:
$F = m \times a = 60 \times 2.3 = 138\ N$
Then find the acceleration of the other skater:
$F = m \times a \Rightarrow a = \frac{F}{m} = \frac{138}{55} = \mathbf{2.5\ ms^{-2}\ (to\ 2\ s.f.)}$

Page 103 — Fact Recall Question
Q1 Newton's 1st law: The velocity of an object won't change unless a resultant force acts on it. This means a body will stay still or move in a straight line at a constant speed unless there's a resultant force acting on it.
Newton's 2nd law: Resultant force = mass × acceleration. This means a larger force acting on an object causes a larger acceleration, and a larger mass means a smaller acceleration for a given force.
Newton's 3rd law: If an object A exerts a force on object B, then object B exerts an equal but opposite force on object A. This means every action has an equal and opposite reaction.

9. Free Fall and Projectile Motion
Page 107 — Application questions
Q1 $s = \frac{1}{2}gt^2 = \frac{1}{2} \times -9.81 \times 6.19^2 = -187.9...\,m$

So height = **188 m (to 3 s.f.)**
Height is a scalar quantity so you don't need to worry about the minus signs here.

Q2 $v^2 = u^2 + 2as \Rightarrow v = \sqrt{0^2 + (2 \times -9.81 \times -6.83)}$
$= (-)11.57...\,ms^{-1}$
So it's travelling at **11.6 ms⁻¹ (to 3 s.f.)**.
Q3 First find how long it's in the air by considering only the vertical velocity:
$s = \frac{1}{2}gt^2 \Rightarrow t = \sqrt{\frac{2s}{g}} = \sqrt{\frac{2 \times -1.61}{-9.81}} = 0.5729...\,s$
Then find out how far it travels in this time:
$s = ut = 502 \times 0.5729... = \mathbf{288\ m\ (to\ 3\ s.f.)}$
Remember there's no acceleration in the horizontal direction.
Q4 a) Consider only the vertical velocity:
$u = \sin 60° \times 25 = 21.65...\,ms^{-1}$
$v^2 = u^2 + 2gs$
$\Rightarrow v = \sqrt{21.65...^2 + 2 \times (-9.81) \times (0)} = -21.65...\,ms^{-1}$
The rock will be moving towards the ground, so it will have a negative final velocity.
$v = u + at \Rightarrow t = \frac{v - u}{a} = \frac{-21.65... - 21.65...)}{-9.81}$
$= 4.413... = \mathbf{4.41\ s\ (to\ 3\ s.f.)}$
b) Find the horizontal velocity:
$u = \cos 60° \times 25 = 12.5\ ms^{-1}$
So $s = ut = 12.5 \times 4.413... = \mathbf{55.2\ m\ (to\ 3\ s.f.)}$

Page 107 — Fact Recall Questions
Q1 The only force present in free-fall motion is weight.
Q2 Free-fall motion with an initial velocity is called projectile motion.

10. Drag and Terminal Speed
Page 110 — Application Questions
Q1 a) The ball starts with a large (positive) acceleration as it falls through the air. The acceleration is decreasing slightly (due to air resistance). After it hits the water it experiences a sudden deceleration, which decreases until the ball has reached terminal velocity (3.9 ms⁻¹). It then falls at a constant velocity until it hits the bottom of the cylinder.
b)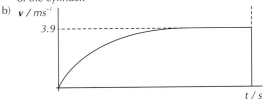

Page 110 — Fact Recall Questions
Q1 Friction acts in the opposite direction to the motion.
Q2 Friction caused by a fluid is called drag or fluid friction.
Q3 When an object reaches terminal velocity, the frictional forces are equal in size to the driving force(s) and in the opposite direction.
Q4 The correct graph is a).
Q5 Skydivers reduce their terminal velocity by using a parachute to increase the drag they experience.

11. Work and Power
Page 113 — Application Questions
Q1 $W = Fd = 203 \times 2.81 = \mathbf{570\ J\ (to\ 3\ s.f.)}$
Q2 $W = Fd\cos\theta = 371 \times 1.39 \times \cos 13.1° = \mathbf{502\ J\ (to\ 3\ s.f.)}$
Q3 $P = Fv \Rightarrow F = \frac{P}{v} = \frac{60\,100}{34.7} = \mathbf{1730\ N\ (to\ 3\ s.f.)}$
Q4 Look at only the horizontal component of the force:
$P = Fv\cos\theta = 83.1 \times 2.99 \times \cos 15.2° = \mathbf{240\ W\ (to\ 3\ s.f.)}$

Page 113 — Fact Recall Questions
Q1 Energy is transferred when work is done.
Q2 Power is the rate of doing work (or transferring energy).

12. Conservation of Energy

Page 117 — Application Questions

Q1 Work is done by the hand to draw back the string, transferring kinetic energy (of the hand) to elastic potential energy (in the catapult), which is transferred to kinetic energy (of the pellet when released).

Q2 efficiency $= \dfrac{\text{useful power output}}{\text{power input}}$

$\Rightarrow$ useful power output = efficiency × power input
$$= 0.2 \times 29\ 000$$
$$= \textbf{5.8 kW}$$

Q3 a) $E_p = mgh = 0.65 \times 9.81 \times 103 = 656.7...$
$$= \textbf{657 J (to 3 s.f.)}$$

b) $\frac{1}{2}mv^2 = 0.95\,mgh \Rightarrow v = \sqrt{\dfrac{2 \times 0.95 \times 656.7...}{0.65}}$
$$= 43.81... = \textbf{43.8 ms}^{-1}\ \textbf{(to 3 s.f.)}$$

c) $mgh = 0.8 \times \frac{1}{2}mv^2 \Rightarrow h = \dfrac{0.4v^2}{g}$
$$= \dfrac{0.4 \times 43.81...^2}{9.81}$$
$$= \textbf{78.3 m (to 3 s.f.)}$$

Even though the falcon has just converted gravitational potential energy into kinetic energy and back again, it's lost some height because some of the energy has been transferred to heat energy, sound, etc.

Page 117 — Fact Recall Questions

Q1 Energy cannot be created or destroyed. Energy can be transferred from one form to another but the total amount of energy in a closed system will not change.

Q2 The efficiency of a machine is defined as the useful power output divided by the power input.

Exam-style Questions — Pages 119-121

1 (a) Vector — e.g. velocity, displacement, acceleration, force, weight *(1 mark)*
   Scalar — e.g. speed, distance, mass, length, height, energy, time, power *(1 mark)*
   (b) (i) $\sin 41° \times F = 3.75 \times 9.81$
   $$F = \dfrac{3.75 \times 9.81}{\sin 41°}$$
   $$= 56.073.... \text{ N} = \textbf{56.1 N (to 3 s.f.)}$$
   (3 marks for correct answer, 1 mark for use of sin 41° × F and 1 mark for correct working if answer is incorrect)
   (ii) $F = ma$
   $$a = \dfrac{\cos 41° \times 56.073....}{3.75} = \textbf{11.3 ms}^{-2}\ \textbf{(to 3 s.f.)}$$
   (2 marks for correct answer, 1 mark for correct working if answer incorrect)
   (c) (i) $E_k = \frac{1}{2}mv^2 = \frac{1}{2} \times 3.75 \times 12.5^2$
   $$= 292.968... \text{ J} = \textbf{293 J (to 3 s.f.)}$$
   (2 marks for correct answer, 1 mark for correct working if answer incorrect)
   (ii) $s = \left(\dfrac{u+v}{2}\right)t = \left(\dfrac{12.5+0}{2}\right) \times 15$
   $$= \textbf{93.8 m (to 3 s.f.)}$$
   (2 marks for correct answer, 1 mark for correct working if answer incorrect)
   (iii) $P = \dfrac{\Delta W}{\Delta t} = \dfrac{292.968...}{15} = \textbf{19.5 W (to 3 s.f.)}$
   (2 marks for correct answer, 1 mark for correct working if answer incorrect)

2 (a) A — The cyclist is decelerating.
   B — The cyclist is moving forwards at a steady speed.
   C — The cyclist isn't moving.
   D — The cyclist is moving back towards the starting point at a steady speed.
   (1 mark for any 2 correct, 2 marks for all 4 correct)
   (b)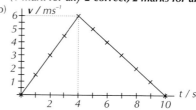
   (1 mark for correct axes with units correctly shown, 1 mark for suitable scales, 1 mark for 8 points plotted correctly, 1 mark for all points plotted correctly, 1 mark for correct shape of graph)
   (c) $E_k = \Delta E_p \Rightarrow \frac{1}{2}mv^2 = mg\Delta h$
   $$\Rightarrow v = \sqrt{2g\Delta h} = \sqrt{2 \times 9.81 \times 22.5}$$
   $$= \textbf{21.0 ms}^{-1}\ \textbf{(to 3 s.f.)}$$
   (3 marks for correct answer, 1 mark for $E_k = \Delta E_p$ if answer is incorrect, 1 mark for correct working if answer is incorrect)
   (d) (i) $v^2 = u^2 + 2as$
   $$\Rightarrow v = -\sqrt{(\sin 29° \times 6.5)^2 + (2 \times -9.81 \times -1.31)}$$
   $$= -5.969... \text{ ms}^{-1} = \textbf{-5.97 ms}^{-1}\ \textbf{(to 3 s.f.)}$$
   (2 marks for correct answer, 1 mark for correct working if answer incorrect)
   ii) $v = u + at \Rightarrow t = \dfrac{v-u}{a} = \dfrac{-5.969... - (\sin 29° \times 6.5)}{-9.81}$
   $$= 0.9297... = \textbf{0.930 s (to 3 s.f.)}$$
   (2 marks for correct answer, 1 mark for correct working if answer incorrect)

Use the negative solution for **v** as it's travelling downwards when it hits the ground.

3 (a) The moment of a force about a point/pivot is equal to the force × the perpendicular distance *(1 mark)* between the line of action of the force and the point/pivot *(1 mark)*.
   (b) (i) The front wheels will feel the most force *(1 mark)* because they're closer to the centre of mass *(1 mark)*.
   (ii) If the front wheels feel no force, the clockwise moments must balance the anticlockwise moments about the pivot (rear wheels).
   anticlockwise moments = clockwise moments
   $\Rightarrow w \times 0.65 = 21\ 000 \times 2.4$
   $\Rightarrow w = \dfrac{21000 \times 2.4}{0.65} = \textbf{78 000 N (to 2 s.f.)}$
   (3 marks for correct answer, 1 mark for anticlockwise moments = clockwise moments and 1 mark for correct working if answer incorrect)

4 (a) The centre of mass is the single point through which all of an object's weight can be considered to act *(1 mark)*.
   (b) If the parrot is balanced the centre of mass must lie vertically in line with the branch *(1 mark)*. As the tail is smaller than the head, it must be made from a heavier material so that the centre of mass is shifted to the right *(1 mark)*.
   (c) Because cranes are tall they have a naturally high centre of mass. The base must therefore be heavy *(1 mark)* and wide *(1 mark)* so that the centre of mass stays within the base and the crane does not topple *(1 mark)*.

Section 2 — Materials

1. Density
Page 122 — Application Questions

Q1 $\rho = \frac{m}{V} = \frac{360}{0.45} = \textbf{800 kg m}^{-3}$

Q2 $\rho = \frac{m}{V}$, so $V = \frac{m}{\rho}$

$V = \frac{91.0}{19.3} = \textbf{4.72 cm}^3$ **(to 3 s.f.)**

Q3 $\rho = \frac{m}{V}$, so $m = \rho \times V$

$m = 2700 \times 9.1 \times 10^{-4} = \textbf{2.5 kg (to 2 s.f.)}$

Q4 4.1×10^{-3} kg = 4.1 g

$\rho = \frac{m}{V}$, so $V = \frac{m}{\rho}$

$V = \frac{4.1}{0.92} = \textbf{4.5 cm}^3$ **(to 2 s.f.)**

Or you could do it by converting 0.92 g cm^{-3} into 920 kg m^{-3}

so $V = \frac{4.1 \times 10^{-3}}{920} = \textbf{4.5} \times \textbf{10}^{-6} \textbf{ m}^3$ **(to 2 s.f.)**

Q5 $V = \frac{4}{3}\pi r^3 = \frac{4}{3}\pi(0.020)^3 = 3.351... \times 10^{-5}$ m^3

$\rho = \frac{m}{V} = \frac{0.80}{3.351... \times 10^{-5}} = \textbf{2.4} \times \textbf{10}^4 \textbf{ kg m}^{-3}$ **(to 2 s.f.)**

2. Hooke's Law
Page 126 — Application Questions

Q1 1.60 cm = 0.0160 m

$F = k\Delta L = 1250 \times 0.0160 = \textbf{20.0 N}$

Q2 0.80 mm = 0.00080 m (= 8.0×10^{-4} m)

Rearrange $F = k\Delta L$ to get $k = \frac{F}{\Delta L}$

$k = \frac{20}{8.0 \times 10^{-4}} = \textbf{25 000 Nm}^{-1}$

Q3 a) extension = new length – original length

= 22.0 – 20.0 = 2.0 cm = **0.020 m**

b) Rearrange $F = k\Delta L$ to get $k = \frac{F}{\Delta L}$

$k = \frac{55.0}{0.020} = \textbf{2800 Nm}^{-1}$ **(to 2 s.f.)**

Q4 a) No, as the first part of the graph isn't a straight line — the force and extension aren't proportional.

b) The band is elastic, because it returns to its original length (i.e. its extension is zero) after all the load has been removed.

Page 126 — Fact Recall Questions

Q1 The extension of a stretched elastic object is proportional to the load or force applied to it.

Q2 $F = k\Delta L$. Where F is the force applied, k is the stiffness constant and ΔL is the extension.

Q3 The force (or load) beyond which a material will be permanently stretched.

Q4 The force beyond which force is no longer proportional to extension.

Q5 A material that is deforming elastically returns to its original shape/length once the forces acting on it are removed.

Q6 A material that is deforming plastically is permanently stretched once the forces acting on it are removed.

3. Stress and Strain
Page 129 — Application Questions

Q1 stress $= \frac{F}{A} = \frac{50}{3.1 \times 10^{-6}}$

$= \textbf{1.6} \times \textbf{10}^7 \textbf{ Pa (or Nm}^{-2}\textbf{) (to 2 s.f)}$

Q2 extension = new length – original length

= 12.3 – 12.0 = 0.3 cm

strain $= \frac{\Delta L}{L} = \frac{0.3}{12.0} = \textbf{0.03 (to 1 s.f.)}$

Remember, there are no units for strain, as it is a ratio. Just make sure when working it out that the extension and original length are in the same units.

Q3 1.2 cm = 0.012 m

$E = \frac{1}{2}F\Delta L = \frac{1}{2} \times 30 \times 0.012 = \textbf{0.18 J}$

Q4 stress $= \frac{F}{A}$

so F = stress $\times A = (3.8 \times 10^8) \times (1.2 \times 10^{-7}) = \textbf{46 N (to 2 s.f.)}$

Page 129 — Fact Recall Questions

Q1 a) The force applied divided by the cross-sectional area.

b) The change in length divided by the original length of a material.

c) The smallest stress that's enough to break a material.

Q2 Work out the area underneath the line/curve of the graph up to the extension required.

Q3 Energy stored = $\frac{1}{2}F\Delta L$

4. The Young Modulus
Page 131 — Application Questions

Q1 a) 1.1 mm = 1.1×10^{-3} m

$A = \pi\left(\frac{\text{diameter}}{2}\right)^2$

$= \pi\left(\frac{1.1 \times 10^{-3}}{2}\right)^2 = 9.503... \times 10^{-7}$

$= \textbf{9.5} \times \textbf{10}^{-7} \textbf{ m}^2$ **(to 2 s.f.)**

b) $\Delta L = 0.20$ mm = 2.0×10^{-4} m

$F = 23$ N, $L = 1.0$ m, $A = 9.503... \times 10^{-7}$ m^2

$E = \frac{FL}{A\Delta L}$

$= \frac{23 \times 1.0}{(9.503... \times 10^{-7}) \times (2.0 \times 10^{-4})}$

$= \textbf{1.2} \times \textbf{10}^{11} \textbf{ Pa (or Nm}^{-2}\textbf{) (to 2 s.f.)}$

Q2 a) stress $= \frac{F}{A} = \frac{100}{8.0 \times 10^{-7}} = 1.25 \times 10^8$

$= \textbf{1.3} \times \textbf{10}^8 \textbf{ Pa (to 2 s.f.)}$

b) $E = \frac{stress}{strain}$ so strain $= \frac{1.25 \times 10^8}{3.5 \times 10^8} = \textbf{0.36 (to 2 s.f.)}$

Page 131 — Fact Recall Questions

Q1 Nm^{-2} or Pa.

Q2 Original length, extension, weights/load, diameter of wire (to find cross-sectional area).

Q3 The Young modulus of the material tested.

Q4 The (strain) energy per unit volume stored in the material.

5. Interpreting Stress-Strain Curves
Page 133 — Application Question

Q1 a) Point B

Point B is the elastic limit — after this point the material will deform plastically and won't return to its original shape when the force is removed.

b) The material is obeying Hooke's law.

c) Point C

d) The Young modulus is the gradient of the graph up to point A, so $150 \times 10^6 \div 0.002 = \textbf{7.5} \times \textbf{10}^{10} \textbf{ Pa}$

Watch out for units — here the graph gives stress in Mpa. You need to be convert this into a value in Pa before you can calculate the Young modulus for the material.

e) Point A is the limit of proportionality. The energy stored per unit volume is given by the area under the graph up to Point A, which is $0.5 \times 0.002 \times 150 = \textbf{0.15 MPa}$.

Page 133 — Fact Recall Questions

Q1 Once beyond the limit of proportionality, a material no longer obeys Hooke's law but will still behave elastically and return to its original shape once the stress is removed. After the elastic limit, a material behaves plastically and will not return to its original shape if the stress is removed.

Q2 The stress at which a large amount of plastic deformation takes place with a constant or reduced load.

6. Brittle Materials

Page 135 — Application Question

Q1 Graph B shows a brittle material as it is just a straight line. Graph A shows a material reaching its elastic limit and undergoing plastic deformation. Brittle materials don't deform plastically.

Page 135 — Fact Recall Questions

Q1 One which doesn't deform plastically, but snaps when the stress on it reaches a certain point.

Q2 Yes. The stress-strain graph for a brittle material is a straight line, which shows it obeys Hooke's law.

Q3 E.g. ceramics, chocolate.

Q4 When a stress applied to a brittle material causes tiny cracks at the material's surface to get bigger and bigger until the material breaks completely.

Exam-style Questions — Pages 136-137

1 (a) The cord returns to its original length/it has no permanent extension *(1 mark)*.

Even though curve B has a different shape to curve A, the graph shows that the cord returns to its original length once all the load has been removed.

(b) The area represents energy stored/work done *(1 mark)*.

(c) $E = \dfrac{FL}{A\Delta L}$

$F = 10$ N, $L = 0.80$ m, $\Delta L = 0.080$ m, $A = 5.0 \times 10^{-6}$ m^2

$E = \dfrac{10 \times 0.80}{5 \times 10^{-6} \times 0.080} = \mathbf{2.0 \times 10^7}$ **Pa**

(3 marks for correct answer, 1 mark for correct working if answer is incorrect, 1 mark for giving correct formula if answer is incorrect)

2 (a) The extension of an object is proportional to the force or load applied to it *(1 mark)*, up to the limit of proportionality *(1 mark)*.

(b) (i) Rearrange $F = k\Delta L$ to get $\Delta L = \dfrac{F}{k}$

$\Delta L = \dfrac{0.90}{600} = 0.0015\,\text{m} = \mathbf{1.5 \times 10^{-3}\,m}$

(2 marks for correct answer, 1 mark for correct working if answer incorrect)

(ii) $F = k\Delta L = 600 \times 0.020 = \mathbf{12\,N}$

(2 marks for correct answer, 1 mark for correct working if answer incorrect)

3 (a) How to grade your answer (pick the description that best matches your answer):

0 marks: There is no relevant information.

1-2 marks: Some of the measurements to be taken are described, but no overall method covered. Several errors with grammar, spelling, punctuation and legibility. Answer has lack of structure, information and backed-up arguments.

3-4 marks: Most of the measurements to be taken are described and a workable method is given. At least one way of making measurements accurately is covered. Only a few errors with grammar, spelling, punctuation and legibility. Answer has some structure, and information and arguments are partially backed up.

5-6 marks: All the measurements to be taken are described and a workable method is given. At least two ways of making measurements accurately are covered. Grammar, spelling and punctuation are used accurately and there is no problem with legibility. Uses an appropriate form and style of writing, and information and arguments are well structured.

Here are some points your answer may include:
- Measure the load/force, original length, extended length (and say how to find extension), diameter.
- Instruments used to make measurements, e.g. ruler, micrometer, travelling microscope.
- Ways of improving accuracy, e.g. repeating readings, measuring wire diameter in several different places, original length of wire should be at least 1 m long.

(b) Young modulus $= \dfrac{\text{stress}}{\text{strain}} = \text{gradient} = \dfrac{\Delta\text{stress}}{\Delta\text{strain}}$

$= \dfrac{5.0 \times 10^8}{3.0 \times 10^{-3}} = \mathbf{1.7 \times 10^{11}\,Pa}$ **(to 2 s.f.)**

(3 marks for correct answer, 1 mark for appropriate unit, 1 mark for correct equation if answer incorrect, 1 mark for correct working if answer incorrect)

You could also give your answer in kPa or GPa.

4 (a) Rearrange $E = \dfrac{FL}{A\Delta L}$ to get $A = \dfrac{FL}{E\Delta L}$

$F = 2.0$ kN $= 2000$ N, $L = 2.0$ m, $E = 2.10 \times 10^{11}$ Pa, $\Delta L = 0.20$ mm $= 2.0 \times 10^{-4}$ m

$A = \dfrac{2000 \times 2.0}{(2.10 \times 10^{11}) \times (2.0 \times 10^{-4})}$

$= \mathbf{9.5 \times 10^{-5}\,m^2}$ **(to 2 s.f.)**

(3 marks for correct answer, 1 mark for correct working if answer is incorrect, 1 mark for giving correct formula if answer is incorrect)

(b) (i) A brittle material is a material that obeys Hooke's law and doesn't deform plastically (it will break instead) *(1 mark)*.

(ii) Material B should be chosen *(1 mark)* because it is brittle and breaks under a lower stress than the other brittle material (material A) *(1 mark)*.

Section 3 — Waves

1. The Nature of Waves

Page 142 — Application Questions

Q1 a) −0.2 m

b) 0.2 m

For displacement the direction matters (it can be negative), but for amplitude you only need a magnitude.

Q2 a) The length of 1.5 oscillations is 0.15 m, so the length of one oscillation is $\dfrac{0.15}{1.5} = 0.1$ m.

So wavelength, $\lambda = 0.1$ m.

b) $c = f\lambda = 30 \times 0.1 = \mathbf{3\,ms^{-1}}$

Q3 $c = f\lambda$, so rearrange for λ. $\lambda = \dfrac{c}{f} = \dfrac{25.0}{2.20} = \mathbf{11.4\,m}$ **(to 3 s.f.)**

Page 142 — Fact Recall Questions

Q1 By causing the particles in the medium to oscillate.

Q2 A change of medium causing the wave to slow down or speed up.

Q3 Displacement (a) can take a negative value.

Q4 A shows the amplitude of the wave.

B shows a crest of the wave.

C shows the wavelength of the wave.

Q5 a) metres (m)

b) metres (m)

c) hertz (Hz)

2. Transverse and Longitudinal Waves

Page 147 — Application Questions

Q1 a) This wave must be transverse because it can be polarised.

b) C represents the transmission axis. It must be the same as the first polarising filter, because all the light that makes it through the first one also gets through the second one.

c) The transmission axis would now be at right angles to the light that made it through from filter 1, so no light would get through the second filter.

Q2 TV signal waves are transmitted by a horizontal transmitter, so they're polarised in that direction. This means they're picked up best by a horizontal aerial — any change in direction and the quality of reception will drop.

Page 147 — Fact Recall Questions

Q1 In transverse waves, the vibrations are at right angles to the direction of travel, whereas in longitudinal waves the vibrations are along the direction of travel.

Q2 Period.

Be careful — this is a displacement-time graph. If it was a displacement-distance graph it would be λ, the wavelength.

Q3 Transverse wave: E.g. electromagnetic waves, water waves, waves on ropes or earthquake shock waves (S-waves).
Longitudinal wave: E.g. sound waves or earthquake shock waves (P-waves).

Q4 No light gets through.

Q5 It is partially polarised — most vibrations of the reflected light are in the same direction.

Q6 Reflected light is partially polarised. Polaroid™ sunglasses block out light in the direction in which the reflected light is partially polarised, but let through light vibrating in other directions. This reduces glare without reducing visibility.

Q7 E.g. Reducing reflections in photography, aligning TV and radio receivers.

3. Refractive Index

Page 150 — Application Questions

Q1 a) $n = \frac{c}{c_s} = \frac{3.00 \times 10^8}{1.94 \times 10^8} = $ **1.55 (to 3 s.f.)**

b) The light will bend towards the normal — air is less optically dense than the material, so light slows down as it crosses the boundary and bends into it, i.e. $n_1 < n_2$, so $\theta_2 < \theta_1$.

Q2 a) When light travelling from the cage meets the water-air boundary, it's refracted (away from the normal). This makes it look like the light is coming from a different point to where the cage actually is.

The light bends away from the normal, so the cage would look like it's in a different place to where it really is.

b) You know: $n_1 = 1.40$, $n_2 = 1.49$, $\theta_1 = 37.2°$, $\theta_2 = ?$
So rearrange the law of refraction to find θ_2:

$n_1 \sin \theta_1 = n_2 \sin \theta_2 \Rightarrow \theta_2 = \sin^{-1}\left(\frac{n_1 \sin \theta_1}{n_2}\right)$

$= \sin^{-1}\left(\frac{1.40 \times \sin 37.2°}{1.49}\right)$

$= $ **34.6° (to 3 s.f.)**

Page 150 — Fact Recall Questions

Q1 It's a measure of the optical density of the material, given by the ratio of the speed of light in a vacuum to the speed of light in the material.

Q2 $n = \frac{c}{c_s}$ where c is the speed of light in a vacuum, n is the refractive index of the material and c_s is the speed of light in the material.

Q3 Use the law of refraction: $n_1 \sin \theta_1 = n_2 \sin \theta_2$

And rearrange to get: $n_2 = \frac{n_1 \sin \theta_1}{\sin \theta_2}$

Q4 It will bend towards the normal.

4. Critical Angle and TIR

Page 153 — Application Questions

Q1 a) $\sin \theta_c = \frac{n_2}{n_1} \Rightarrow \theta_c = \sin^{-1}\left(\frac{n_2}{n_1}\right) = \sin^{-1}\left(\frac{1.40}{1.52}\right)$
$= $ **67.1° (to 3 s.f.)**

b) At least 67.1°.

Q2 The refractive index of material 1 must be higher. Otherwise, light would bend towards the normal ($\theta_1 > \theta_2$ when $n_1 < n_2$).

Q3 If $n_1 > n_2$, using the formula for critical angle (derived from the law of refraction), $\theta_c = \sin^{-1}\left(\frac{n_2}{n_1}\right)$. If $n_1 < n_2$, then $\frac{n_2}{n_1} > 1$. But $\sin^{-1}$ is only defined between −1 and 1, so there is no such θ_c.

Page 153 — Fact Recall Questions

Q1 The critical angle of a boundary is the angle of incidence at which the angle of refraction is 90°.

Q2 Any three from: More information can be carried, almost no energy is lost (e.g. as heat), no electrical interference, cheap to produce, transmits across long distances very quickly.

5. Superposition and Interference

Page 156 — Application Questions

Q1 a)

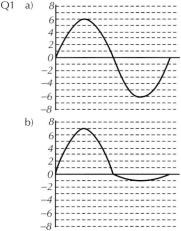

Q2 a) i) Point G
ii) No points.
iii) Point E

b) Two points (C and E).

Page 156 — Fact Recall Questions

Q1 When two or more waves meet, the resultant displacement equals the vector sum of the individual displacements.

Q2 When two waves pass through each other and their displacements combine to make a displacement with greater magnitude.

Q3 When two waves pass through each other and their displacements cancel each other out completely.

Q4 The phase difference of two points on a wave is the difference in their positions in a wave's cycle, measured in degrees of radians.

Q5 When their phase difference is an odd multiple of 180° (or π radians).

Q6 Two waves are in phase if they have a phase difference of 0° (or a multiple of 360°).

6. Stationary Waves
Page 159 — Application Questions
Q1 This wave is at the third harmonic so 1.5 wavelengths fit on the string, so $1.5\lambda = 6$, so $\lambda = $ **4 m**.

Q2 a) The wave is vibrating at the fundamental frequency, so the length of the string is half a wavelength. So $\lambda = 5$ m.
$c = f\lambda = 100 \times 5 = $ **500 ms⁻¹**

b) $c = f\lambda$ so $\lambda = \frac{c}{f} = \frac{500}{200} = 2.5$ m
So one wavelength (or two half wavelengths) would fit on the string at this frequency. This resonant frequency is called the second harmonic (or first overtone).
You could also just look at the frequency — it's twice the fundamental frequency, so 2 × ½ wavelengths fit on the string.

Page 159 — Fact Recall Questions
Q1 When two progressive waves are travelling in opposite directions with the same frequency (or wavelength) and the same amplitude, their superposition creates a stationary wave.

Q2 No.

Q3 A resonant frequency of a string is a frequency at which a stationary wave is formed because an exact number of waves are produced in the time it takes for a wave to get to the end of the string and back again.

Q4 A string is vibrating at its second harmonic if one wavelength fits on the string and there are three nodes and two antinodes.

7. Diffraction
Page 161 — Fact Recall Questions
Q1 All waves.

Q2 A gap whose size is roughly the same as the wavelength of the wave being diffracted.

Q3 Monochromatic light is light made up of only one frequency (and wavelength).

Q4 Laser light is monochromatic, which means all the light has the same frequency (or wavelength). If you used non-monochromatic light, like white light, different wavelengths would diffract different amounts, so the pattern wouldn't be very clear.

Q5 Constructive interference

8. Interference
Page 166 — Application Questions
Q1 a) Laser light is coherent (all waves produced have the same frequency and wavelength and a fixed phase difference), whereas white light is not. Coherent light is needed for a clear interference pattern.
You could also say that laser light is monochromatic.

b) The pattern is formed because of the path difference between waves arriving at the screen from each slit. When the path difference is an integer multiple of λ, a maximum is formed because of constructive interference.
When the path difference is a multiple of $(n + \frac{1}{2})\lambda$ (where n is an integer), a minimum is formed because of total destructive interference.

c) $w = \frac{\lambda D}{s} = \frac{(4.5 \times 10^{-7}) \times 12}{0.00030} = $ **0.018 m**

d) There are 10 maxima with a gap of 0.018 m between each one, so the total width is $9 \times 0.018 = 0.162$ m.
So $x = $ **0.162**.
Even though there are 10 maxima, there are only 9 fringe spacings (the gaps between them).

e) Any two from:
Put up a laser warning sign, wear laser goggles, avoid reflecting the beam, do not point the laser at people, turn off the laser when not in use, do not look directly at the beam.

Q2 Rearrange the double-slit formula: $D = \frac{ws}{\lambda}$
So $D = \frac{(1.29 \times 10^{-2}) \times (0.11 \times 10^{-3})}{615 \times 10^{-9}} = $ **2.3 m (to 2 s.f.)**

Page 166 — Fact Recall Questions
Q1 Two wave sources are coherent if the waves have the same wavelength and frequency and a fixed phase difference between them.

Q2 The amount by which the path travelled by one wave is longer than the path travelled by the other wave.

Q3 At path differences which are an integer multiple of the wavelength ($n\lambda$).

Q4 They must be coherent.

Q5 a) E.g. Have one amplifier attached to two loudspeakers.
b) E.g. Have one coherent light source (e.g. a laser) shining through two slits.

Q6 $w = \frac{\lambda D}{s}$

9. Diffraction Gratings
Page 170 — Application Questions
Q1 Elements B and C are contained in material X.
Element A has lines which are not featured in the spectrum of material X, so element A is not contained in material X.

Q2 a) First work out the slit spacing. It has 4.5×10^5 slits per metre, so the slit spacing $d = \frac{1}{4.5 \times 10^5}$
$= 2.222... \times 10^{-6}$ m
Use the diffraction grating equation, rearranged for θ, and using $n = 3$:
$\theta = \sin^{-1}\left(\frac{n\lambda}{d}\right) = \sin^{-1}\left(\frac{3 \times (5.9 \times 10^{-7})}{2.222... \times 10^{-6}}\right)$
$= $ **52.8° (to 3 s.f.)**

b) No, because $\frac{n\lambda}{d} = \frac{4 \times (5.9 \times 10^{-7})}{2.222... \times 10^{-6}} = 1.1$ (to 2 s.f.).
The sin function is only defined between −1 and 1, so $\sin^{-1} 1.1$ is impossible.

c) The pattern will be more spread out, because the angle is related to n, d and λ. If n and d remain constant, θ with become larger and so each order of maximum will be further from the zero order.

Page 170 — Fact Recall Questions
Q1 A slide or other thin object that contains lots of little equally spaced slits.

Q2 The fringes produced in a diffraction grating experiment are much sharper than those produced with a double-slit set-up.

Q3 The zero order maximum is a line of maximum brightness at the centre of a diffraction pattern. It's in the same direction as the incident beam.

Q4 $d\sin\theta = n\lambda$

Q5 The pattern would spread out.

Q6 White light is made up of a range of different wavelengths. These spread out by different amounts when they pass through the diffraction grating, forming a spectrum.

Q7 E.g. analysing the elements present is stars.

Exam-style Questions — Pages 172-173

1 (a) (i) When the camera is pointed directly at the water, the intense sunlight is reflected directly into the camera causing a glare *(1 mark)*.

(ii) Reflected light is partially polarised. A polarising filter filters out light vibrating in a certain direction. If the polarising filter filters out light vibrating in the main direction of polarisation of reflected light, then glare is reduced while other light that's vibrating at the angle of the filter is transmitted through it. *(1 mark for saying reflected light is partially polarised, 1 mark for mentioning the reduction of light waves vibrating in a certain direction.)*

(b) Longitudinal waves. E.g. Sound; P-waves (earthquake shockwaves). *(1 mark for type of wave, 1 mark for example.)*

(c) $c = f\lambda \Rightarrow f = \frac{c}{\lambda} = \frac{3 \times 10^8}{650 \times 10^{-9}} = $ **4.62 × 10^{14} Hz (to 3 s.f.)** *(2 marks for correct answer, 1 mark for rearranging $c = f\lambda$ if answer incorrect.)*

2 (a) (i) $n = \frac{c}{c_s} = \frac{3.00 \times 10^8}{2.03 \times 10^8} = $ **1.48 (to 3 s.f.)**

(1 mark for substituting the correct values into the correct formula, 1 mark for giving the answer to 3 or 4 significant figures.)

You should always try to give your answer to the lowest number of significant figures given by the numbers in the question. When the question says "give your answer to an appropriate number of significant figures" (or similar) it means you'll get a mark for using the right number.

(ii) Use the law of refraction at the air-core boundary:
$n_1 \sin\theta_1 = n_2 \sin\theta_2$
with $n_1 = 1$, $\theta_1 = 34°$, $\theta_2 = 21°$.

Rearrange: $n_2 = \frac{n_1 \sin\theta_1}{\sin\theta_2} = \frac{1 \times \sin 34°}{\sin 21°} = 1.56...$
$= $ **1.6 (to 2 s.f.)**

(3 marks for correct answer, otherwise 1 mark for substituting into the correct formula and 1 mark for correct rearrangement if answer incorrect.)

(b) (i) $\sin\theta_c = \frac{n_2}{n_1} = \frac{1.48}{1.56} = 0.9487...$
so $\theta_c = \sin^{-1}(0.9487...) = 71.5... = $ **71° (to 2 s.f.)**
(2 marks for correct answer, 1 mark for correct working if answer incorrect.)

(ii) The light ray enters the cladding at an angle of $90° - 21° = 69°$ (the angle has to add to the angle between the cladding and the normal), which is less than the critical angle, so total internal reflection cannot happen and it enters the cladding instead. *(1 mark for $\theta < \theta_c$, 1 mark for mention of total internal reflection.)*

(iii) Ray B has been totally internally reflected because it hits the core-cladding boundary at an angle greater than the critical angle. *(1 mark for total internal reflection, 1 mark for critical angle.)*

If there's a question part that uses values from a previous part of the question, you'll get the marks as long as all your calculations are correct (even if the previous answer was wrong).

(c) Any two from:
They can carry more information, no energy lost as heat, no electrical interference, cheaper to produce, less signal loss over long distances.
(2 marks available — one for each advantage)

3 (a) (i) There are 9 maxima, so 8 fringes.
So fringe spacing $s = \frac{0.24}{8} = 0.03$ m.
To find λ use the double-slit formula:
$w = \frac{\lambda D}{s} \Rightarrow \lambda = \frac{ws}{D} = \frac{0.03 \times 0.15 \times 10^{-3}}{7.5}$
$= 6 \times 10^{-7}$ m $(= 600$ nm$)$
(4 marks for correct answer. Otherwise 1 mark for finding fringe spacing, 1 mark for attempting to use double-slit formula and 1 mark for correct rearrangement of double-slit formula.)

(ii) Lasers are coherent and monochromatic so the diffraction patterns are clearer. *(1 mark for coherent and 1 mark for monochromatic.)*

(b) (i) The maxima would become much clearer / better defined. *(1 mark)*

(ii) Distance between slits $= \frac{1}{2.55 \times 10^5}$
$= 3.921... \times 10^{-6}$ m

$d\sin\theta = n\lambda \Rightarrow \theta = \sin^{-1}\left(\frac{n\lambda}{d}\right)$
$= \sin^{-1}\left(\frac{1 \times (6 \times 10^{-7})}{3.921... \times 10^{-6}}\right)$
$= $ **8.80° (to 3 s.f.)**

(4 marks for correct answer. Otherwise 1 mark for finding the space between slits, 1 mark for rearranging formula to find θ, and 1 mark for correct calculations.)

4 (a) E.g. A progressive wave with a constant frequency is formed by the student who is oscillating the rope. The wave is reflected back down the rope from the fixed end of the rope. The two waves have the same frequency (or wavelength) and the same amplitude. The waves form a superposition and have the correct wavelength to interfere to produce a standing wave. *(3 marks in total — 1 mark for mentioning reflection of wave, 1 mark for same frequency (or wavelength), 1 mark for mentioning superposition.)*

(b) (i) 2.5 Hz *(1 mark)*
The fundamental frequency of a wave is when the standing wave is vibrating at its lowest possible frequency — i.e. when there's only one loop, like in this case.

(ii) $\frac{7.5}{2.5} = 3$, so the rope is vibrating at its 3rd harmonic, so there would be 4 nodes. *(1 mark for finding number of harmonic, 1 mark for number of nodes.)*

There's always one more node than the number of the harmonic.

(iii) The wave is at the 3rd harmonic, so there are 1.5 wavelengths on the rope. So $\lambda = \frac{1.5}{1.5} = 1$ m.
$c = f\lambda = 7.5 \times 1 = 7.5$ ms^{-1}.
(2 marks for correct answer, 1 mark for correct λ if answer incorrect.)

Note that if you calculated the wave speed for the frequency of 2.5 Hz, the wavelength is 3 m so c = 2.4 × 3 = 7.5 ms^{-1} again. For a given length of string, the wave speed is the same in each harmonic.

Glossary

A

Acceleration
The rate of change of velocity.

Accurate result
A result that's really close to the true answer.

Alpha decay
A type of decay in which an unstable nucleus of an atom emits an alpha particle.

Alpha particle
A particle made up of two protons and two neutrons.

Alternating current
A current that changes with time in a regular cycle.

Ammeter
A component used to measure the current flowing through a circuit.

Amplitude
The maximum displacement of a wave, i.e. the distance from the undisturbed position to the crest, or trough.

Angle of incidence
The angle that incoming light makes to the normal of a boundary.

Angle of refraction
The angle that refracted light makes with the normal of a boundary.

Annihilation
The process by which a particle and its antiparticle meet and their mass gets converted to energy in the form of a pair of gamma ray photons.

Anomalous result
A result that doesn't fit in with the pattern of the other results in a set of data.

Antimatter
The name given to all antiparticles.

Antineutrino
The antiparticle of a neutrino.

Antiparticle
A particle with the same rest mass and energy as its corresponding particle, but equal and opposite charge

Atom
A particle made up of protons and neutrons in a central nucleus, and electrons orbiting the nucleus.

Atomic number
The number of protons in an atom of an element.

B

Baryon
A type of hadron made up of three quarks. For example, protons and neutrons.

Baryon number
The number of baryons in a particle.

Beta-minus decay
A type of decay in which an unstable nucleus of an atom emits a beta-minus particle (an electron) and an antineutrino.

Breaking stress
The lowest stress that's big enough to break a material.

Brittle
A brittle material doesn't deform plastically, but snaps when the stress on it reaches a certain point.

Brittle fracture
When a stress applied to a brittle material causes tiny cracks at the material's surface to get bigger until the material breaks completely.

C

Categoric data
Data that can be sorted into categories.

Centre of mass
The point which you can consider all of an object's weight to act through.

Circuit symbol
A pictorial representation of an electrical component.

Coherent
Sources that have the same wavelength and frequency and a fixed phase difference between them are coherent.

Compressive force
A force which squashes something.

Constructive interference
When two waves interfere to make a wave with a larger displacement.

Coulomb (C)
A unit of charge. One coulomb (C) is the amount of charge that passes in 1 second when the current is 1 ampere.

Couple
A pair of forces of equal size which act parallel to each other but in opposite directions.

Critical angle
The angle of incidence at which the angle of refraction is 90°.

Current
The rate of flow of charge in a circuit. Measured in amperes (A).

Continuous data
Data that can have any value on a scale.

D

Density
The mass per unit volume of a material or object.

Dependent variable
The variable that you measure in an experiment.

Destructive interference
When two waves interfere to make a wave with a reduced displacement.

Diffraction
When waves spread out as they pass through a narrow gap or go round obstacles.

Diffraction grating
A slide or other thin object that contains lots of equally spaced slits very close together, used to show diffraction patterns of waves.

Diode
A component designed to allow current flow in one direction only.

Directly proportional
Two variables are directly proportional if one variable = constant × the other variable. This means that a change in one results in a change in the other and that the changes are always related by the same constant.

Discrete data
Data that can only take certain values.

Displacement
How far an object has travelled from its starting point in a given direction. In the case of a wave, it is the distance a point on a wave has moved from its undisturbed position.

Drag
Friction caused by a fluid (gas or liquid).

Efficiency
The ratio of useful energy given out by a machine to the amount of energy put into the machine.

Elastic
An elastic material returns to its original shape/length once the forces acting on it are removed.

Elastic limit
The force beyond which a material will be permanently stretched.

Elastic strain energy
The energy stored in a stretched material.

Electromagnetic force
A fundamental force that causes interactions between charged particles. Virtual photons are the exchange particle.

Electromagnetic spectrum
A continuous spectrum of all the possible frequencies of electromagnetic radiation.

Electromotive force (e.m.f.)
The amount of electrical energy a power supply transfers to each coulomb of charge.

Electron
A lepton with a relative charge of −1 and a relative mass of 0.0005. Sometimes called a β⁻ particle.

Electron capture
The process of a proton-rich nucleus capturing an electron to turn a proton into a neutron, emitting a neutrino.

Electron-proton collision
The process of an electron colliding with a proton and producing a neutron and a neutrino.

Electron volt
The kinetic energy carried by an electron after it has been accelerated through a potential difference of one volt.

Equilibrium
An object is in equilibrium if all the forces acting on it cancel each other out.

Exchange particle
A virtual particle which allows forces to act in a particle interaction.

Excitation
The movement of an electron to a higher energy level in an atom.

Feynman diagram
A diagram used to represent a particle interaction.

First order line
The first line either side of the zero order line in a diffraction grating interference pattern.

First overtone
A resonant frequency of a stationary wave for which the wavelength is the length of the string (also called the second harmonic).

Free fall
The motion of an object undergoing an acceleration of *g*.

Frequency
The number of whole wave cycles (oscillations) per second passing a given point. Or the number of whole wave cycles (oscillations) given out from a source per second.

Friction
A force that opposes motion. It acts in the opposite direction to the motion. It arises when two objects are moving past each other, or an object is moving through a fluid.

Fundamental frequency
A resonant frequency of a stationary wave for which the wavelength is double the length of the string.

Fundamental particle
A particle which cannot be split up into smaller particles.

Gravitational force
A fundamental force which causes attraction between objects with a force proportional to their mass.

Gravitational potential energy
The energy an object gains when lifted up.

Ground state
The lowest energy level of an atom.

Hadron
A particle that is affected by the strong nuclear force.

Hooke's law
The extension of a stretched object is proportional to the load or force applied to it, up to the limit of proportionality.

Hooke's law limit
The point beyond which force is no longer proportional to extension. Also know as the limit of proportionality.

Hypothesis
A specific testable statement, based on a theory, about what will happen in a test situation.

Independent variable
The variable that you change in an experiment.

Interference
The superposition of two or more waves.

Internal resistance
The resistance created in a power source when electrons collide with atoms inside the power source and lose energy.

Ionisation
The process where an electron is removed from (or added to) an atom.

Ionisation energy
The energy required to remove an electron from an atom.

Isotope
An isotope of an element has the same proton number as the element but a different nucleon number.

I-V characteristic
A graph which shows how the current (*I*) flowing through a component changes as the potential difference (*V*) across it is increased.

Kinetic energy
The energy possessed by a moving object.

Lepton
A fundamental particle that is not affected by the strong nuclear force.

Lepton number
The number of leptons in a particle. Lepton number is counted separately for different types of leptons.

Lever
A structure with a rigid object and a pivot, in which an effort force works against a load force.

Light-dependent resistor (LDR)
A resistor with a resistance that depends on the intensity of light falling on it. The resistance decreases with increasing light intensity.

Limit of proportionality
The point beyond which force is no longer proportional to extension. Also known as the Hooke's law limit.

Line spectrum
The pattern of lines produced by photons being emitted or absorbed by electrons moving between energy levels in an atom.

Line absorption spectrum
A light spectrum with dark lines corresponding to different wavelengths of light that have been absorbed.

Line emission spectrum
A spectrum of bright lines on a dark background corresponding to different wavelengths of light that have been emitted from a light source.

Longitudinal wave
A wave in which the vibrations are in the direction of travel of the wave.

Lost volts
The energy wasted per coulomb overcoming the internal resistance of a power source.

Mass
The amount of matter in an object.

Mass number
The number of nucleons in an atom of an element.

Matter
The name given to all particles.

Maximum
The points in an interference pattern where the intensity is brightest (a location of constructive interference).

Meson
A type of hadron made up of a quark and an antiquark. For example, pions or kaons.

Minimum
The points in an interference pattern where the intensity is lowest (a location of destructive interference).

Model
A simplified picture or representation of a real physical situation.

Moment
The turning effect of a force around a turning point.

Monochromatic
A light source that is all of the same wavelength (or frequency).

Nucleon
A particle in the nucleus of an atom.

Nucleon number
The number of nucleons in an atom of an element.

Nucleus
The centre of an atom containing protons and neutrons.

Nuclide notation
A notation, $^A_Z X$, that tells you the nucleon number, A, and proton number, Z, of an element, X.

Neutrino
A lepton with (almost) zero mass and zero charge.

Neutron
A neutral baryon with a relative mass of 1.

Newton's 1st law of motion
The velocity of an object will not change unless a resultant force acts on it.

Newton's 2nd law of motion
The acceleration of an object is proportional to the resultant force acting on it.

Newton's 3rd law of motion
If an object A exerts a force on object B, then object B exerts an equal but opposite force on object A.

Ohm's law
Provided the temperature is constant, the current through an ohmic conductor is directly proportional to the potential difference across it ($I \propto V$).

Ohmic conductor
A component that has a fixed resistance for a particular temperature — it obeys Ohm's law.

Optical density
The property of a medium that describes how fast light travels through it. Light moves slower through a medium with a higher optical density.

Optical fibre
A thin flexible tube of glass or plastic that can carry light signals using total internal reflection.

Ordered / ordinal data
Categoric data where the categories can be put in order.

Pair production
A process of converting energy to mass in which a gamma ray photon has enough energy to produce a particle-antiparticle pair.

Path difference
The amount by which the path travelled by one wave is longer than the path travelled by another wave.

Peer review
The evaluation of a scientific report by other scientists who are experts in the same area (peers). They go through it bit by bit, examining the methods and data, and checking it's all clear and logical.

Period
The time taken for one whole wave cycle to pass a given point.

Phase difference
The amount by which one wave lags behind another, measured as an angle.

Photon
A discrete wave-packet of EM waves.

Photoelectric effect
The emission of electrons from a metal when light of a high enough frequency is shone on it.

Plastic
A plastic material is permanently stretched once the forces acting on it are removed.

Polarising filter
A filter that only transmits vibrations of a wave in one direction or plane, called the plane of transmission.

Polarised wave
A wave in which all the vibrations are in one direction or plane.

Positron
The antiparticle of an electron. Sometimes called a β+ particle.

Potential difference (p.d.)
The work done in moving a unit charge between two points in a circuit.

Potential divider
A circuit containing a voltage source and a pair of resistors. The voltage across one of the resistors is used as an output voltage. If the resistors aren't fixed, the circuit will be capable of producing a variable output voltage.

Power
The rate of transfer of energy or the rate of doing work. It's measured in watts (W), where 1 watt is equivalent to 1 joule per second.

Precise result
A result taken using sensitive instruments that measure in small increments.

Principle of conservation of energy
Energy cannot be created or destroyed. Energy can be transferred from one form to another but the total amount of energy in a closed system will not change.

Progressive wave
A moving wave that carries energy from one place to another without transferring any material.

Proton
A positively charged baryon with a relative mass of 1.

Proton number
The number of protons in an atom of an element.

Q

Quark
A fundamental particle that makes up hadrons.

R

Random error
An error introduced by variables which you cannot control.

Reflection
When a wave bounces back as it hits a boundary.

Refraction
When a wave changes direction and speed as it enters a medium with a different optical density.

Refractive index
The ratio between the speed of light in a vacuum and the speed of light in a material.

Reliable result
A result that can be consistently reproduced in independent experiments.

Resistance
A component has a resistance of 1 Ω if a potential difference of 1 V across it makes a current of 1 A flow through it. Resistance is measured in ohms (Ω).

Resistivity
The resistance of a 1 m length of a material with a 1 m^2 cross-sectional area. It is measured in ohm-metres (Ωm).

Resonant frequency
A frequency at which a stationary wave is formed because an exact number of waves are produced in the time it takes for a wave to get to the end of the vibrating medium and back again.

Resultant vector
The vector that's formed when two or more vectors are added together.

Ripple tank
A shallow tank of water in which water waves are created by a vibrating dipper.

S

Scalar
A quantity with a size but no direction.

Second harmonic
A resonant frequency of a stationary wave for which the wavelength is the length of the string (also called the first overtone).

Semiconductor
A group of materials which conduct electricity (but not as well as metals). When their temperature rises, they can release more charge carriers and their resistance decreases.

Speed
How fast something is moving, regardless of direction.

Stationary wave
A wave created by the superposition of two progressive waves with the same frequency (or wavelength) and amplitude, moving in opposite directions.

Stiffness constant
The force needed to extend an object per unit extension. The units are Nm^{-1}. Each object has its own stiffness constant.

Strain
The change in length divided by the original length of the material.

Strangeness
A property which particles that contain strange quarks have.

Stress
The force applied divided by the cross-sectional area.

Strong nuclear force
A fundamental force with a short range which is repulsive at very small separations and attractive at small separations. Responsible for the stability of nuclei.

Superconductor
A material that has zero resistivity when cooled below a transition temperature.

Superposition
The combination of displacements experienced in the instant that two waves pass each other.

Systematic error
An error introduced by the experimental apparatus or method.

Tensile force
A force which stretches something.

Tensile strain
The change in length divided by the original length of the material.

Tensile stress
The force applied divided by the cross-sectional area.

Terminal speed
The speed at which the driving force(s) match the frictional force(s).

Theory
A possible explanation for something. (Usually something that has been observed.)

Thermistor
A resistor with a resistance that depends on its temperature — it is a type of semiconductor.

Third harmonic
A resonant frequency of a stationary wave for which one and a half wavelengths fit on the string (also called the second overtone).

Threshold frequency
The lowest frequency of light that when shone on a metal will cause electrons to be released from it (the photoelectric effect).

Torque of a couple
The moment caused by two equal forces acting parallel to each other but in opposite directions around a turning point.

Total destructive interference
Destructive interference in which the waves completely cancel each other out.

Total internal reflection
When all light is completely reflected back into a medium at a boundary with another medium, instead of being refracted. It only happens at angles of incidence greater than the critical angle.

Transverse wave
A wave in which the vibrations are at right angles to the direction of travel of the wave.

Turning point
The pivot around which an object rotates when a moment or torque is applied.

Ultimate tensile stress
The maximum stress that a material can withstand.

Valid result
A result which answers the question it was intended to answer.

Validation
The process of repeating an experiment done by someone else, using the theory to make new predictions, and then testing them with new experiments, in order to prove or refute the theory.

Variable
A quantity in an experiment or investigation that can change or be changed.

Vector
A quantity with a size and a direction.

Velocity
The rate of change of displacement.

Virtual particle
A particle that only exists for a short amount of time, e.g. an exchange particle.

Volt (V)
The unit of potential difference. The potential difference across a component is 1 volt when you convert 1 joule of energy moving 1 coulomb of charge through the component.

Voltage
Another name for potential difference. The work done in moving a unit charge between two points in a circuit.

Voltmeter
A component used to measure the potential difference across another component in a circuit.

Watt
The unit of power. A watt is defined as a rate of energy transfer equal to 1 joule per second.

Wavelength
The length of one whole wave oscillation or wave cycle, e.g. the distance between two crests (or troughs) of a wave.

Wave-particle duality
All particles can be shown to have both particle and wave properties. Waves can also show particle properties.

Wave speed
The speed that a wave travels at.

Weak interaction
A fundamental force that has a short range and can change the character of a quark.

Weight
The force experienced by a mass due to a gravitational field.

Work
Work is the amount of energy transferred from one form to another when a force moves an object a distance.

Work function
The minimum amount of energy required for an electron to escape a metal's surface.

Yield point (or yield stress)
The stress at which a large amount of plastic deformation takes place with a constant or reduced load.

Young modulus
The stress divided by strain for a material, up to its limit of proportionality.

Zero order line
The line of maximum brightness at the centre of a diffraction grating interference pattern. It's in the same direction as the incident beam.

Acknowledgements

Photograph acknowledgements

Cover Photo **Adam Hart-Davis**/Science Photo Library, p 1 **Edward Kinsman**/Science Photo Library, p 2 Science Photo Library, p 3 Science Photo Library, p 4 (top) **Steve Allen**/Science Photo Library, p 4 (bottom) **David Parker**/Science Photo Library, p 8 **Klaus Guldbrandsen**/Science Photo Library, p 9 **David Parker & Julian Baum**/Science Photo Library, p 10 **C. Powell, P. Fowler & D. Perkins**/Science Photo Library, p 13 **Carl Anderson**/Science Photo Library, p 14 **Thomas McCauley, Lucas Taylor/CERN**/Science Photo Library, p 15 **Centre Jean Perrin, ISM**/Science Photo Library, p 17 **Goronwy Tudor Jones, University of Birmingham**/Science Photo Library, p 20 **Emilio Segre Visual Archives/American Institute of Physics**/Science Photo Library, p 21 **Michael Gilbert**/Science Photo Library, p 25 **Jean Collombet**/Science Photo Library, p 26 **Physics Today Collection/American Institute of Physics**/Science Photo Library, p 34 **US Library of Congress**/Science Photo Library, p 35 **Pierre Marchal/Look at Sciences**/Science Photo Library, p 38 **Tek Image**/Science Photo Library, p 39 (top) **Dept. of Physics, Imperial College**/Science Photo Library, p 39 (bottom) **GIPhotoStock**/Science Photo Library, p 41 Science Photo Library, p 42 **Andrew Lambert Photography**/Science Photo Library, p 43 **Gustoimages**/Science Photo Library, p 47 **Tek Image**/Science Photo Library, p 48 **Trevor Clifford Photography**/Science Photo Library, p 49 **Trevor Clifford Photography**/Science Photo Library, p 50 **Science Source**/Science Photo Library, p 52 **Trevor Clifford Photography**/Science Photo Library, p 53 **Bildagentur-Online/TH Foto**/Science Photo Library, p 54 **Martyn F. Chillmaid**/Science Photo Library, p 57 **Takeshi Takahara**/Science Photo Library, p 58 **Martyn F. Chillmaid**/Science Photo Library, p 60 **Ton Kinsbergen**/Science Photo Library, p 62 **Health Protection Agency**/Science Photo Library, p 63 **Andrew Lambert Photography**/Science Photo Library, p 65 **Library of Congress**/Science Photo Library, p 66 **Cordelia Molloy**/Science Photo Library, p 68 **Doug Martin**/Science Photo Library, p 71 **Trevor Clifford Photography**/Science Photo Library, p 73 **Andrew Lambert Photography**/Science Photo Library, p 74 **Martyn F. Chillmaid**/Science Photo Library, p 75 **Emmeline Watkins**/Science Photo Library, p 81 **Adam Jones**/Science Photo Library, p 85 **Peter Muller**/Science Photo Library, p 87 **European Space Agency**/Science Photo Library, p 88 **Peter Menzel**/Science Photo Library, p 92 **Mehau Kulyk**/Science Photo Library, p 94 **Ted Kinsman**/Science Photo Library, p 96 **Bjorn Svensson**/Science Photo Library, p 97 **Ken Cavanagh**/Science Photo Library, p 100 **Michael Donne**/Science Photo Library, p 101 **James Cavallini**/Science Photo Library, p 102 **Middle Temple Library**/Science Photo Library, p 103 **P. Hattenberger, Publiphoto Diffusion**/Science Photo Library, p 104 **Dr Jeremy Burgess**/Science Photo Library, p 105 **NASA**/Science Photo Library, p 107 (top) **Ria Novosti**/Science Photo Library, p 107 (bottom) **Edward Kinsman**/Science Photo Library, p 109 **Martyn F. Chillmaid**/Science Photo Library, p 111 **Alan Sirulnikoff**/Science Photo Library, p 112 **David Scharf**/Science Photo Library, p 114 **Photostock-Israel**/Science Photo Library, p 115 **Ian Boddy**/Science Photo Library, p 116 **Charles Angelo**/Science Photo Library, p 117 **Duncan Shaw**/Science Photo Library, p 112 **David Woodfall Images**/Science Photo Library, p 125 **Andrew Lambert Photography**/Science Photo Library, p 128 **Langley Research Center/NASA**/Science Photo Library, p 131 **Alex Bartel**/Science Photo Library, p 132 **Ton Kinsbergen**/Science Photo Library, p 134 **Ted Kinsman**/Science Photo Library, p 138 **Erich Schrempp**/Science Photo Library, p 139 **GIPhotoStock**/Science Photo Library, p 143 **Andrew Lambert Photography**/Science Photo Library, p 144 **Jerome Wexler**/Science Photo Library, p 145 **Carlos Dominguez**/Science Photo Library, p 146 (top) **Lea Paterson**/Science Photo Library, p 146 (bottom) **Alex Bartel**/Science Photo Library, p 148 **Mark Clarke**/Science Photo Library, p 151 **GIPhotoStock**/Science Photo Library, p 152 **GIPhotoStock**/Science Photo Library, p 153 **Omikron**/Science Photo Library, p 155 **Andrew Lambert Photography**/Science Photo Library, p 157 **Andrew Lambert Photography**/Science Photo Library, p 158 **Edward Kinsman**/Science Photo Library, p 159 **Tony McConnell**/Science Photo Library, p 160 **Andrew Lambert Photography**/Science Photo Library, p 161 **Edward Kinsman**/Science Photo Library, p 163 **Berenice Abbott**/Science Photo Library, p 164 (top) **GIPhotoStock**/Science Photo Library, p 164 (bottom) **GIPhotoStock**/Science Photo Library, p 167 (top) **GIPhotoStock**/Science Photo Library, p 167 (bottom) **GIPhotoStock**/Science Photo Library, p 169 **Detlev Van Ravenswaay**/Science Photo Library, p 174 **GIPhotoStock**/Science Photo Library, p 175 **Andrew Lambert Photography**/Science Photo Library, p 179 **Adam Hart-Davis**/Science Photo Library, p 180 **Andrew Lambert Photography**/Science Photo Library, p 183 **Geoff Tompkinson**/Science Photo Library, p 184 Science Photo Library, p 187 **Jon Stokes**/Science Photo Library.

Index

A

acceleration 92-95, 98, 100, 102, 104-105
accuracy 182
adding vectors 80-81
air resistance 104-105, 108-109
alpha decay 10
alpha particles 10
alternating current (a.c.) 73, 75
ammeters 47-48
amplitude (of a wave) 139, 153, 157
angle of incidence 148-149, 151-152
angle of refraction 148-149, 151
annihilation 15
anomalous results 175-176
antibaryons 16, 21
antimatter 13
antineutrinos 10, 13, 17-18
antineutrons 13, 16, 21
antinodes (of stationary waves) 157-159
antiparticles 12-15
antiprotons 13-14, 16, 21
antiquarks 20-21
atomic nuclei 5-8
atomic number 6
atoms 5-8
axial rays 153

B

bar charts 176, 180
baryon number 16, 19-21, 23
baryons 16-17, 19-22
batteries 47, 61-62
beta (minus) decay 10, 17, 22, 27
beta (plus) decay 23, 27
breaking stress 127-128
brittle fractures 134
brittle materials 134

C

categoric data 175-176
causal links 177
cells (electrical) 47, 62

charge
    electrical 48-49, 54, 61, 65
    nuclear 5, 7, 13, 18, 20-23
circuit diagrams 47
circuit symbols 47
cladding 152
coherence 162-164
compressive forces 123-124, 127
conclusions 183
conservation laws for particle interactions 19, 23-24
conservation of (electrical) charge 65
conservation of energy 61, 65, 114-117
constructive interference 154
continuous data 175-176
continuous spectra 39-40
correlation 176-177
coulombs 48-49
couple (of forces) 89
critical angle
    refraction 151-153
    stability 90
current 48, 51, 66
current-voltage (I-V) graphs 51-55

D

data 174-175
de Broglie wavelength 41-43
density 122
dependent variables 174
destructive interference 155, 157, 161-162
diffraction 41-43, 160-161, 164-169
    electron diffraction 42
diffraction gratings 167-169
diodes 47, 54
direct current (d.c.) 73
direct proportion 177
discrete data 174
displacement 94
    of a wave 139, 143, 154
double-slit system 164-166
down quarks 20
drag 108
driving force 108

E

e.m.f. (electromotive force) 61-63
efficiency 114
elastic deformation 125
elastic limit 124, 126
elastic strain energy 128-129
electrical energy 59
electromagnetic force 9, 26
electromagnetic radiation 12, 143
electromotive force (e.m.f.) 61-63
electron-antineutrinos 13
electron capture 28
electron decay 22
electron diffraction 42-43
electron-neutrinos 13
electron-proton collisions 28
electrons 5-6, 10, 18, 35
electron-volt (definition) 37
energy
    conservation 61, 65, 114-117
    efficiency 114
    elastic strain 128-129
    electrical 59
    kinetic 33-35, 115-116
    of a photon 12-15, 37-39
    potential 111, 115-116
energy levels 37-38
equilibrium 84-86
error bars 181-182
ethical considerations 183
evaluating results 182
exam structure 184
exchange particles 25-26
experimental errors 179
experimental uncertainty 179
    error bars 181-182
    percentage uncertainty 181
    reducing uncertainty 180
extension investigations 125
external resistance 61-62

F

Feynman diagrams 26-28
filament lamps 47, 53
first order lines 167-169
first overtone 158
fluorescent tubes 38

force
  compressive 123-124
  electromagnetic 9, 26
  gravitational 9, 26, 87
  strong nuclear 9, 16, 26
  tensile 123-125, 127, 130
force-extension graphs
    124-125, 128
forces in equilibrium 84-86
fourth harmonic 158
free fall 104-105
free-body force diagrams 84
frequency of a wave
    12, 74, 140-141,
    157-158, 162
friction 108
fringe spacing 164-165
fundamental frequency 158
fundamental particles 7
fuses 47

G

glare 145
gradient 177-178
gravitational field strength 87
gravitational force 9, 26, 87
gravitational potential energy 115
ground state 37-38

H

hadrons 16-18
harmonics 158
Hooke's law 123-125
hypotheses 1

I

I-V characteristics 52-55
independent variables 174
inertia 87
intensity 33-35, 145-146
interference 41, 154-157,
    161-169
internal resistance 61-63
isotopes 8

J

joule (definition) 111

K

kaons 17-19
kinetic energy 33-35, 115-116

L

lasers 161, 164-165, 183
  safety 164, 183
law of refraction 148-149
lepton number 18-19, 24
leptons 18
light emitting diodes (LEDs) 47
light-dependent resistors (LDRs)
    47, 55, 71
limit of proportionality 124
line absorption spectra
    39-40, 169
line emission spectra 39-40
line graphs 176-178
load resistance 61-62
longitudinal waves 144
lost volts 61-62

M

magnitude (of vectors) 80
mains electricity supply 75
mass 87
mass number 6
mesons 17-18, 21
metallic conductors 53
models (scientific) 1-2
momentum (of particles) 41
monochromatic light
    161, 164, 167
muons 18

N

neutrinos 18
neutron decay 10, 17, 22, 27
neutrons 5-6,
  quark composition 21
Newton's laws of motion
    102-103, 105
node (of a stationary wave)
    157-158
NTC thermistors 54, 71
nucleon number 6
nucleons 5
nuclide notation 6

O

observations 1, 34-35
Ohm's law 50-51
ohmic conductors 50-51
optical density 148
optical fibres 152-153
  communications 153

ordered (ordinal) data 175
ordinal data 175
oscilloscopes 73-74

P

pair production 14
parallel circuits 66
particle interactions 25-28
particles 5-32
  antiparticles 12-15
  baryons 16-17, 21-22
  electrons 5-6, 10, 18, 35
  hadrons 16-18
  kaons 17-19
  muons 18
  neutrinos 18
  neutrons 5-6, 21
  photons 12-15, 34, 41
  pions 17-18, 21
  protons 5-7, 14, 16, 18, 21
  quarks 20-23
path difference 162-163
peak voltage 74
peak-to-peak voltage 74
peer reviews 2
period (of a wave) 74, 140
phase difference 140,
    155-156, 162
photoelectric effect 33-36
photon energies 12-15, 33-39
photons 12-15, 34, 41
pions 17-18
  quark composition 21
Planck's constant 12, 34, 41
plastic deformation 126
polarisation (of waves) 144-147
polarising filters 144
positron emission 23
positrons 13-15, 23
potential difference 48-49
potential dividers 70-71
potential energy 111, 115-116
  elastic 115
  gravitational 115
potentiometers 71
power 112-113
  electrical 58-60
precision (of results) 182
predictions 1
probability waves 41
progressive waves 138, 157
projectile motion 106-107
proton number 6

proton-proton collisions 14
protons 5-7, 14, 16, 18
    quark composition 21

Q

quality of written communication
    (QWC) 185
quark confinement 22
quarks 20-23

R

radio signals 146
radioactive decay 8, 10, 17,
    22-23
    alpha decay 10
    beta-minus decay
        10, 17, 22, 27
    beta-plus decay 23, 27
random errors 179
refraction 138, 148-152
refractive index
    148-149, 151-152
reliable results 182
repeating measurements 180
resistance 50-51
    I-V graphs 52-55
    internal 61-63
    parallel and series circuits 66-
      67
resistivity 56-57
resistors 47
    variable 47, 52
resolving vectors 82-83, 85-86
resonant frequencies 157-158
resultant force 102-103
resultant vectors 80-81
ripple tanks 160
root mean square (r.m.s.)
    voltage 75

S

safety hazards 183
scalars 80
scale diagrams 80
scatter graphs 176
scientific journals 2
second harmonic 158
second order lines 167-168
second overtone 158
semiconductors 54-55
series
    cells 68

resistors 66
significant figures 186-187
SOH CAH TOA 81
sound waves 144, 159-160, 163
specific charge 7
spectra 39-40, 169
speed 80, 92, 99
    of a wave 141
    speed-time graph 99
    terminal 108-110
spring constant 123-124
stability of objects 90
standard form 187
starter motors 60
stationary waves 157-159
step-index optical fibres 152
stiffness constant 123-124
straight-line graphs 177-178
strain (tensile) 127, 130-131
strange quarks 20
strangeness 20-21, 24
stress (tensile) 127, 130-131
stress-strain graphs 127, 131-132
strong nuclear force 9, 16, 26
superconductors 57
superposition 154, 157
switches 47
systematic errors 179

T

television signals 146, 153
tensile forces 123-125, 127, 130
tensile strain 127, 130-131
tensile stress 127, 130-131
terminal potential difference
    61-62
terminal speed 108-110
theories 1-3
thermistors 47, 54, 71
third harmonic 158
threshold frequency 33-36
time period 74, 140
total destructive interference
    155, 157, 161-162
total internal reflection 152-153
transverse waves 143
    polarisation 145-146
trigonometry 81
two-source interference 162-166

U

ultimate tensile stress 127-128
units 186

unstable nuclei 10
up quarks 20

V

valid results 182
validating theories 2
variable resistors 47, 52
variables 174
vectors 80-86
    adding 80-81
    resolving 82-83, 85-86
velocity 92
    from displacement-time graphs
      95-96
    terminal 108-110
    uniform acceleration
      92-93, 106-107
velocity-time graphs
    98-100, 109-110
virtual particles 26
voltmeters 47, 49
volts 49
volume controls 71

W

W bosons 26-28
watts 58
wave speed 141
wave-particle duality 41-42
wavelength 12, 139
    de Broglie 41-42
    longitudinal and transverse
      waves 143-144
    photons 12, 34, 38
    stationary waves 157-158
waves 138-173
    longitudinal 144
    stationary 157-159
    transverse 143
weak interaction 17-18,
    22-24, 26-28
work 111-112, 128-129

Y

yield point 132
Young modulus 130-131
Young's double-slit 164-165

Z

zero order line 167

Data Tables

This page summarises some of the constants, values and properties that you might need to refer to when answering questions in this book. Everything here will be provided in your exam Data and Formulae Booklet somewhere... so you need to get used to looking them up and using them correctly. If a number isn't given on this sheet — unlucky... you'll need to remember it as it won't be given to you in the exam.

Unit 1 Section 1: Particles and Radiation

Fundamental constants and values

Quantity	Value
electron charge/mass ratio, e/m_e	1.76×10^{11} Ckg^{-1}
electron rest mass, m_e	9.11×10^{-31} kg
magnitude of the charge of electron, e	1.60×10^{-19} C
neutron rest mass, m_n	$1.67(5) \times 10^{-27}$ kg
the Planck constant, h	6.63×10^{-34} Js
proton charge/mass ratio, e/m_p	9.58×10^7 Ckg^{-1}
proton rest mass, m_p	$1.67(3) \times 10^{-27}$ kg
speed of light in vacuo, c	3.00×10^8 ms^{-1}

Particle rest energies

baryon	symbol	rest energy (MeV)
proton	p	938.257
neutron	n	939.551

meson	symbol	rest energy (MeV)
π meson	$\pi^{\pm}$	139.576
	π^0	134.972
K meson	$K^{\pm}$	493.821
	K^0	497.762

lepton	symbol	rest energy (MeV)
neutrino	ν_e	0
	ν_{μ}	0
electron	$e^{\pm}$	0.510999
muon	$\mu^{\pm}$	105.659

Quark properties

All properties are equal and opposite for antiquarks.

type	up	down	strange
symbol	u	d	s
charge	$+\frac{2}{3}e$	$-\frac{1}{3}e$	$-\frac{1}{3}e$
baryon number	$+\frac{1}{3}$	$+\frac{1}{3}$	$+\frac{1}{3}$
strangeness	0	0	-1

Lepton properties

particles with a lepton number of +1	$e^-, \nu_e, \mu^-, \nu_{\mu}$
antiparticles with a lepton number of −1	$e^+, \overline{\nu}_e, \mu^+, \overline{\nu}_{\mu}$

Unit 2 Section 1: Mechanics

Fundamental constants and values

Quantity	Value
acceleration due to gravity, g	9.81 ms^{-2}
gravitational field strength, g	9.81 Nkg^{-1}

PATB51